Youth and the City in the Global South

Tracking Globalization

Robert J. Foster, editor

Editorial advisory board
Mohammed Bamyeh
Lisa Cartwright
Randall Halle

Youth and the City in the Global South

Karen Tranberg Hansen

in collaboration with
Anne Line Dalsgaard,
Katherine V. Gough,
Ulla Ambrosius Madsen,
Karen Valentin, and
Norbert Wildermuth

Indiana University Press
Bloomington and Indianapolis

Published with the support of the Council for Development Research of the
Danish International Development Agency.

This book is a publication of

Indiana University Press
601 North Morton Street
Bloomington, IN 47404-3797 USA

http://iupress.indiana.edu

Telephone orders	800-842-6796
Fax orders	812-855-7931
Orders by e-mail	iuporder@indiana.edu

The paper used in this publication meets the minimum requirements of
American National Standard for Information Sciences—Permanence of Paper
for Printed Library Materials, ANSI Z39.48-1984.

Manufactured in the United States of America

Library of Congress Cataloging-in-Publication Data

Youth and the city in the global south / Karen Tranberg Hansen ; in
collaboration with Anne Line Dalsgaard . . . [et al.].
    p. cm. — (Tracking globalization)
 Includes bibliographical references and index.
 ISBN-13: 978-0-253-35109-8 (cloth : alk. paper)
 ISBN-13: 978-0-253-21969-5 (pbk. : alk. paper) 1. Urban youth—Developing
countries. 2. Urban youth—Cross-cultural studies. I. Hansen, Karen Tranberg.
II. Dalsgaard, Anne Line.
 HQ799.D44Y68 2008
 305.23509173'2091724—dc22

                                                        2007045885

1 2 3 4 5   13 12 11 10 09 08

Contents

List of Figures

Acknowledgments

This book is the outcome of a collaborative, interdisciplinary, four-year research project entitled Youth and the City: Skills, Knowledge, and Social Reproduction, which was conducted between 2001 and 2005 in Recife in Brazil, Hanoi in Vietnam, and Lusaka in Zambia with funding from the Council for Development Research of the Danish International Development Agency (DANIDA). The Institute of Anthropology at the University of Copenhagen hosted the project, which brought together a research team consisting of three anthropologists, Anne Line Dalsgaard, Karen Tranberg Hansen, and Karen Valentin; an education scholar, Ulla Ambrosius Madsen; a human geographer, Katherine V. Gough; and a media studies scholar, Thomas Tufte, who left the project after a few months because of other research obligations and was replaced by Norbert Wildermuth, also a media studies scholar. The team collaborated with colleagues in the three cities: anthropologists Russell Parry Scott and Mónica Franch of the Postgraduate Program of Anthropology, Federal University of Pernambuco, in Recife; demographer Dang Ngyuen Anh of the Institute of Social Studies in Hanoi; and urban planner Chileshe Mulenga at the Institute of Economic and Social Research, University of Zambia, in Lusaka.

A project of this scope would not have been possible without DANIDA's funding, which enabled scholars from several countries and institutions to participate. We are immensely grateful for this assistance and wish in particular to recognize the influence in Copenhagen of Holger Bernt Hansen, Karen Fog Olwig, Michael Whyte, and Jørgen Pedersen in launching, conducting, and completing the project. As individual scholars we also thank our departments, institutes, and home universities in different parts of Denmark and the United States for allowing sufficient flexibility in our academic schedules to enable us to undertake this research.

We were fortunate in that our research project on urban youth attracted the attention of Robert Foster, editor of the Tracking Globalization series at Indiana University Press, and Rebecca Tolen, the Press's anthropology editor. Their keen interests in a publication based on this project stimulated us in innumerable ways.

In particular, Rebecca's cool patience has helped us to smooth out some of the problems that are bound to arise in intercontinental collaborative writing efforts by scholars from different disciplines who do not routinely work in an English-language world. We owe many thanks to the editorial craftsmanship of Shoshanna Green, whose interventions enhance our presentations immeasurably.

The photos that enliven the book were taken by the authors. We thank Kent Pørksen, graphic artist at the Institute of Geography at the University of Copen-hagen, for preparing the maps. Last but not least, DANIDA provided a subvention to ensure the book's distribution at an affordable price in the part of the world that is its focus: the Global South. The research team is grateful for this help, and has waived royalties on the book.

It goes without saying that we could not have completed the research project, which involved wide-ranging travel, or written this book without ongoing support on our home fronts in Denmark and the United States. To our spouses, partners, and children we express our warmest thanks.

Karen Tranberg Hansen and
the Youth and the City team
2007

Part 1. Situating Youth in the City

1

Introduction: Youth and the City

Karen Tranberg Hansen

The world's cities are growing at a tremendous rate, especially in the South, where young people form a huge proportion of the overall population. But in spite of the bearing that youth and the city have on each other, most recent scholarship is trapped in a gulf between youth studies and urban studies that complicates our understanding of ongoing transformations of young people's lives in the era of global capitalism. At issue are demographic and socioeconomic changes that are turning young people in the urban South into lead actors in shaping their countries' futures. For cities are where the action is. Young people make their imprint on them now and will do so in the future, even where life is hard and circumstances are difficult.

Young people in Recife in Brazil, Hanoi in Vietnam, and Lusaka in Zambia share many experiences with youth in the West. Their lives everywhere are associated with both freedom and constraints. The three cities we have studied do not assure their poorest inhabitants, many of whom are young, decent livelihoods. Yet as we demonstrate, the circumstances of the young differ vastly within cities and between countries. Consider 17-year-old Van, a young woman in Hanoi, who feels obligated to fulfill the expectations of her parents before following her own desires. Or Stephen, a 19-year-old carpentry trainee in Lusaka who intends to shelve his marriage plans for five years until he has established himself economically. Unlike Van, Stephen cannot call on support from his parents, but he lives with an older brother, who pays his school fees. There is also Marcelo, a young man, almost 18 years old, of middle-class background in Recife, who failed the university entrance exam and wonders how he will attain the kind of life he wants. Living in an apartment his father has rented, he dreams of becoming independent of his parents and getting married.

Bringing youth and the city together in a way not paralleled elsewhere, this book draws on interdisciplinary and in-depth observations in Recife, Hanoi, and

Lusaka to examine the fluid meanings of youth as a life stage; aspirations for and pathways toward adulthood; class and gender differences among young urban people; and the specificity of urban life. In effect, the combination of youth and the city enables us to analyze the double dynamic of freedom and constraints, inclusion and exclusion, that is at the heart of youths' urban experiences. Such observations have relevance for policy directed to both youth matters and urban development issues, as we discuss in the concluding chapter.

The book makes four arguments that revolve around the importance of the city, comparative youth studies, globalization, and local practices. First, we argue that because cities matter hugely to young people's lives, they compel us to focus our research on youth. Although some recent works feature "urban" or "the city" in their titles (e.g., Chawla 2002; Tienda and Wilson 2002), they do not clarify the significance of "the urban" for young people's experiences: "the city" is taken for granted and serves merely as a setting or backdrop for explorations of a miscellany of youth-related topics. Yet throughout the world today, cities are significant places that will become ever more important in the developing world, not only for demographic reasons but also because cities are the gateways to the global world. We discuss both these issues shortly.

The second argument concerns comparative youth scholarship, in which studies in the West have set the agenda until recently. The transition from youth to adulthood as it has been experienced over the past century in the West is central to the United Nations definition of youth that has been widely accepted worldwide. When the United Nations General Assembly adopted the World Programme of Action for Youth in 1995, youth—defined as the period between ages 15 and 24—became a globally circulating category. Other United Nations agencies, international non-governmental organizations (NGOs), human rights groups, and similar organizations also use this definition. Sue Ruddick has remarked on the irony of exporting this notion to places lacking the socioeconomic resources that helped produce the West's modern ideals of youth (2003, 335). The work we present here from Recife, Hanoi, and Lusaka supports her observation in many ways. We demonstrate that the lives of the young in these three cities do not always replicate past experiences in the West concerning demographic transition, adulthood, and mobility. What is more, we also note that in the West today, the situation of many young people differs from that of their parents' generation. We suggest that in fact the adverse effects of current economic practices on youth employment prospects everywhere may contribute to a convergence of global youth experiences.

The third argument revolves around widespread assumptions about globalization. In popular views, "global" entails uniformity and sameness, influenced by the norms and standards of the West. This deliberately exaggerated characterization of globalization privileges the West as the source of economic dynamism over other local and regional influences, for instance, from Southeast Asia and various parts of Africa. Such a view reduces youth responses to passive imitations, thus promoting the idea that globalization results in homogenization. There is no doubt that flows of popular culture, from music to fashion, are global in their reach and have a leveling effect, yet their consequences are variable. For the meanings of globalization are always filtered through local understandings of gender and power hierarchies. The results of this filtering are particularly marked in urban space, where globalization inspires both local adaptations of, and resistance to, the flows of images and values from across the world (Lewellen 2002).

The fourth argument concerns the role of the local in young people's engagements with global space in a material and physical sense as well as in their imagination. "Global," in this context, refers to increasing interconnections between youth across the world and their awareness of such connections (Schafer 2005, 1035). The media play a powerful role in shaping young people's global engagements. The significance of this role is captured in the notion of youthscapes, which draws attention to how local youth culture is embedded within both national and global contexts (Maira and Soep 2005). Such a perspective signals that global media practices are locally interpreted and their meanings are often reorganized. As actors in their own right in some domains of life (Amit-Talai and Wulff 1995), young people design scripts for new lives through consumption practices and popular culture, and those scripts localize global influences. Indeed, the young urban people we have come to know are well aware of being-in-the world and of what is out there, at the same time as they negotiate their everyday worlds through practices they craft from local resources.

Cities of Youth

With its focus on urban youth in the developing world, this book cuts across social science scholarship that different disciplinary conventions and topical preoccupations have tended to fragment. The recent florescence of studies concerning young people in the West and the developing world presents us with a global research field inhabited by children, adolescents, and youth whose structural positions are not always clarified (Aitken 2001; Ansell 2005; Brown, Larson, and Saraswathi 2002; Jeffrey and McDowell 2004). In fact, there is frequent slippage from one term to another, not only in academic writing, but especially in development policy documents that legitimate specifically targeted programmatic responses, for example to street children and child soldiers. We argue that the difference between these terms matters, and that a focus on youth is particularly compelling.

In more ways than one, Recife, Hanoi, and Lusaka are cities of youth. The combination of youth and the city demands our attention for demographic reasons that have cultural, socioeconomic, and political consequences. Forty-seven percent of the world's total population was urban in 2000. According to recent projections, that proportion will reach 60 percent by 2030. The South will experience the major share of that growth, with Asia and Africa projected to have a higher proportion of urban dwellers than other parts of the world. Already in 2000, Latin America was highly urbanized, with 75 percent of its population living in urban areas (United Nations 2002, 5–7). Three-quarters of the projected population growth will take place, not in great metropolises, but in smaller cities where there is little planning or services (UN-Habitat 2003, 3; 2005).

What these demographic observations reveal are marked shifts in the age composition of urban populations that are important to this book's concerns. While the elderly urban population is increasing in developed countries, it is the young urban population that is growing in developing countries. Young people constitute a growing proportion of the total population almost everywhere in such countries. Of the world's total population of six billion in 1999, young people under the age of 15 constituted one-third of the population in developing countries and nearly half the population in sub-Saharan Africa (Gelbard, Haub, and Kent 1999). Taken together, young people between 15 and 24 years of age comprise almost a quarter of the people in the developing world (World Bank 2005, 1). Most important, in many countries both in the West and in the developing world the interval between the end of childhood and the assumption of adult roles has increased, thus extending the experience of youth.

Scholarship and policy planning that target youth in the South face a problem. Most relevant research focuses either on the urban or on youth. The two concerns are only rarely brought together. While demographers have recently devoted attention to the urban transformation of the developing world, they have not addressed the ramifications of the youth bulge in the urban population (National Research Council 2003).[1] For example, a major commissioned study of the changing transitions from youth to adulthood in developing countries makes no reference to urban settings as the chief stage for youth lives (National Research Council and Institute of Medicine 2005). And a recent overview of young people and development barely engages with the urban dimension of this problematic (Ansell 2005). Conversely, research on the urban South rarely considers youth as important players. Already attracting widespread attention because of his influential work on cities in the United States, Mike Davis recently focused on the Third World's rapidly growing cities. His book *Planet of Slums* (2006) attributes the problems of rapid urbanization to lack of jobs and housing. Linking urban survival to the disproportionate labor efforts of women and children, Davis recognizes the youth bulge only in reference to criminalization. Nowhere does his study support an alternative future, to the creation of which young people in the developing world are actively contributing. As we demonstrate for Recife, Hanoi, and Lusaka, this simple demographic observation has complex implications for resource development, service provision, social organization, and everyday life. But above all, the combination of youth and the city gives rise to salient questions for scholarship and program policy in general about the role of youth in the social reproduction of the cities of tomorrow.

Perspectives on Youth

When does a child become a youth, and when is adolescence succeeded by adulthood? Answers to these questions differ across history and are ultimately cultural. Until the 1970s in much of the West, the notion of youth referred to a distinct stage between childhood and adulthood that emerged as a result of socio-economic shifts and modernity, including the expansion of nuclear families, the development of educational institutions, and the creation of laws regulating the working age. But the circumstances of the post-1970 youth generation differ. A recent comparison of Italy, Sweden, Germany, and the United States reveals that adolescence no longer serves as a life stage in the passage to adulthood (Cook and Furstenberg 2002). In Australia, a large proportion of young people do not experience the transition that the previous generation took for granted when they left school and went straight into full-time jobs (Wyn and White 2000). The transition between home and work in Italy has become discontinuous, with many young people delineating the course of their own lives (Leccardi 2005, 124). What this means is that youth today has become a less clearly demarcated stage than in the past in the institutionalization of the life course. The uncertainty of the process compels young people to draw on diverse resources (economic, social, cultural, and political), depending on where and who they are in gender and class terms, as they negotiate their everyday lives and orient themselves toward the future. As a result, there are not one but many trajectories toward the future (Skelton 2002).

Definitions of youth are contextual and they shift. Regardless of whether our concern is with young people in the West or in a developing country, definitions of youth in terms of biological age are shaped by the cultural politics of their time and place, and by who defines them (Hall and Montgomery 2000). The United Nations Convention on the Rights of the Child, for example, gives the age of 18 as the upper limit of childhood. Biological age has been used to define inclusion and exclusion, in such contexts as obligatory schooling and the right to vote, obtain a driving license, and drink alcohol. National legislation in many countries considers 18 the age of majority even when different age limits may apply in other areas, such as marriage and criminal responsibility. Despite legislation, many young people in both the developed and developing world work for wages, have sexual relations, and bear children before they reach 18 years of age. In both settings, many young people continue to live with relatives after the age of 18. Because of their educational situations or their casual, poorly remunerated jobs, they do not have the means to set up independent households. In other societies, the extended household is an important unit of production, reproduction, and consumption. For example, in urban Vietnam, young people do not necessarily seek to establish independent households either before or after marriage. Much like Van, whom we introduced earlier, they expect to remain with the extended family, not only for economic reasons, but also in order to perform culturally prescribed roles as daughters, sons, and in-laws.

Youth assumes its meanings culturally and relationally rather than chronologically. In cultural terms, children are often distinguished from young people by their dependence. This distinction attaches agency to youth, within the societal constraints under which they operate. Still, many young people are dependent, subject to hierarchical and authoritarian gender- and generation-based relationships with parents, guardians, and the larger society. Thus generation rather than age per se constitutes a major fault line (Cole and Durham 2007; Comaroff and Comaroff 2000). Some scholars have turned to Karl Mannheim's 1952 essay "The Problem of Generations" (Mannheim 1972; Pilcher 1994) to conceptualize such practices relationally with respect to both class and the life cycle. Advocating a sociological and historical approach to generational succession, Mannheim suggested that some young people in urban areas develop new interpretations and perspectives. Viewing such new perspectives as opening "fresh contact," Jennifer Cole argues that the structural liminality of youth, "the fact that they are less embedded than adults in older networks of patronage and exchange," gives them a unique opportunity to take advantage of new social and economic conditions (Cole 2004, 575–76).

When we move the focus from adolescence as a stage of transition to youth as "the here-and-now of young people's experience," we uncover rich insights into the social and cultural practices of young people (Bucholtz 2002, 532). Deborah Durham captures this by considering youth as a social shifter (2000, 116–17). Borrowed from linguistics, this notion brings out the relational, indexical context of everyday youth lives. Showcasing agency, the notion of a shifter highlights the changing position of youth, both in relationship to others and in space. With this analytical turn, Durham invites us to reflect on when and how the idea of youth is mobilized: "Studies of youth must examine not only the[ir] experiences . . . and their reactions to and agency within a larger society but also the political and pragmatic processes through which certain people can make claims to being youth or try to designate others as youth, for the very category itself is also under reconstruction in the context of such processes" (2004, 593).

Regional Youth Constructions

In much of sub-Saharan Africa, the term "youth" is associated with young men from 15 to 30 or even 35 years of age. Many African girls experience youth as a brief interlude between the onset of puberty and marriage and motherhood. But in urban settings, poor women are often considered youth much longer, even if they bear children outside of marriage. Varying culturally, the gender constructions of youth in Latin America and Southeast Asia differ from those of sub-Saharan Africa. In Vietnam, widespread notions of youth are sociopolitical constructions for both sexes between the ages of 15 and 35. Confucian ideology continues to shape social roles and relationships in gender and generational terms, and the institution of the family is ascribed a key role (Drummond and Rydstrøm 2004; Gammeltoft 1999). Combined with a strong emphasis on women's reproductive role, this means that young women are expected to marry and bear children in their early twenties, when they approach adulthood. This expectation in turn conflicts with growing demands for education that motivate some young people to postpone marriage, thus prolonging the period of youth.

In Brazil, the term "youth" refers to people of both sexes from 15 or 18 to 25 years old. This age bracket reflects the influence on Brazilian law of international organizations like the World Health Organisation. It is also shaped by the notion of adolescence that has entered everyday life in Brazil through a discourse on children's rights. *Adolescência* is closely tied to the 12-to-17-year-old age category and is commonly understood as a biological fact, the awakening to sexual life, and a time of psychological turbulence and change. Compared with adolescence, youth is a step toward adult responsibility. A man's responsibility is linked with his ability to be in control and provide for a family, as we noted when describing Marcelo's desire for autonomy. Young men from low-income backgrounds find it more difficult than women of the same age to acquire the attributes of responsibility because of poverty, unemployment, and social marginalization (Scott 1996, 290; Nascimento 1999, 21). Although it is no longer the chief marker of the female adult, childbearing is still part of the cultural construction of responsible womanhood (Scott 1996, 292; Dalsgaard 2004).

Regardless of how youth is defined, limited life opportunities and poor wage-labor prospects are challenging the age and gender ideals that used to guide the social organization of households and families in both the West and the developing world. Recent research in the West has begun to qualify past views of adolescence as a socialization stage leading to adulthood (Bucholtz 2002, 531). When it comes to Africa, such views are flawed. Although young people work hard to reach social adulthood, as we saw in Lusaka in Steven's five-year plan for his future, a large proportion of young men never acquire the experience of culturally defined adulthood that derives from holding positions of headship over spouses and offspring (Masquelier 2005). The spiraling effects of prolonged youth are manifesting themselves in increasing household dependency rates, male frustration and violence, depressed marriage rates, unmarried motherhood, and growing rates of sibling- and child-headed households (Ashforth 1999; Hansen 1997). Bearing evidence of a crisis in urban social reproduction, such practices turn long-held social organizational norms on their heads. Dependency rates in some African urban settings, particularly among people affected by HIV/AIDS, are already high, fueling the increase in numbers of orphans and propelling young people onto the streets. In the process, the meanings of youth change.

Brazil's economy has stabilized somewhat since the economic crisis of the early 1980s, yet a large proportion of its population lives below the poverty line. Young people are demonstrating some economic optimism and growing consumerism at the same time as a huge opportunity gap between low- and high-income groups is making it difficult for many youths to obtain education and work. The result is keen competition, dashed expectations, and hopelessness on the part of some young people, entailing widespread urban violence. The transition from youth to adulthood varies by class: young people from middle-class backgrounds expect to complete university and marry before leaving their parents' home, extending their youth until they are in their late twenties. Low-income youth change this status much earlier, sometimes in their teens. Their transition to adulthood differs by gender, with young women becoming mothers and many young men taking jobs or getting caught up in criminal activities.

Although poverty is widespread in Vietnam, the country has experienced both consistent economic growth and an increase in inequality since the economic reforms, or *doi moi,* were launched in 1986 (Hy V. Long 2003). Many young people in Vietnam are experiencing a time of national economic progress and political stability. Although some of them criticize the political system, young people are growing up with the promise of a better future and more opportunities than their parents' generation had. This has resulted in significant educational pressures that prolong the period of youth in Vietnam's urban areas.

Within the public domain in Recife, Hanoi, and Lusaka, young people tend to be depicted from two angles that leave little scope for agency: from a welfare angle, which views them as dependent and immature, thus in need of "improvement"; and from a problem-oriented angle, which characterizes them as troublesome and therefore prone to problematic behavior that needs controlling and curtailing. It is not surprising that many young people see themselves as excluded by the institutions of the wider society and the deteriorating economic situation (Weiss 2004, 7–10).[2] At the same time, they also view their city as a gateway to a wider world of opportunities that they are keen to tap into. Because the meanings of youth shift contextually, the experiences of many young people are full of contradictions, expressing both agency and dependence. As we noted at the outset, young people experience both freedom and constraints as they negotiate urban life. Rather than being mutually exclusive, these two experiences pertain to different, yet simultaneous, levels of interaction; for instance, the realms of formal employment and of popular culture and electronic media.

The Urban Perspective

One of the most striking aspects of the urban South is the presence of young people. They are everywhere. Their presence invites a range of explorations into the nature and significance of urban space. The comparative urban focus in this book challenges us to qualify widespread approaches to urban research that restrict our understanding of urban livelihoods. Many approaches, for example, introduce unhelpful distinctions between World or Global cities and Third World cities. In the view of some scholars, Global and World cities serve as organizing nodes in the global financial system (Sassen 2001), forming a hierarchical core network and a second tier (Gugler 2004) that excludes vast areas of the urban world from the space of global capitalism (Robinson 2002, 534–35). When they are viewed from this perspective, Third World cities appear to have not yet quite arrived economically. Although Third World cities vary considerably, they have been generally shaped by some common processes: legacies of colonialism, rapid population increase, low levels of economic growth, and expansion of informal settlements. Above all, their relations with global capitalism are unequal and asymmetric (Drakakis-Smith 2000; Robinson 2002, 540). There is an assumption, in this scholarship, that their development path will converge with that of cities in the West.

In contrast to the hierarchical, exclusionary World or Global city approaches and the developmentalism implied in much work on Third World cities, Jennifer Robinson acknowledges the wide range of contemporary cities and the ordinariness of urban life. Rather than privileging specific kinds of cities, she approaches all cities as part of the same field of analysis (2006, 108). Highlighting what these formulaic approaches to World or Global cities and Third World cities hide from view, she considers ordinary cities to be "diverse, creative, modern and distinctive with the possibility to imagine . . . their own futures and distinctive forms of city-ness" (2002, 545–46). In effect, she suggests that all cities are globally interconnected and that urban scholars must recognize such connections.

Such interconnected linkages make cities play important intermediary or brokerage roles (Smart and Smart 2003). The diversity and ordinariness of our research settings invite us to propose an inclusive approach to the city as a space of interaction that brings together people, things, and ideas from around the country and the wider world. In this very inclusive sense, all cities are global, as

Anthony King noted when he claimed that "all cities today are 'world cities'" (1990, 82). Considering globalization as "an integrated phenomenon bringing all the world's cities into a single interconnected life," Ida Susser and Jane Schneider also recognize this (2003, 2). When they propose that we view the enormous social and economic issues facing city-dwellers as urban "wounds," they reckon with the possibility of recuperation in the future. The organic metaphor of wounding implies "a vision of collective well-being that must be negotiated within an identifiable, bounded place" (2003, 1). Many of these wounds arise because the contemporary city is a site of complexity, social inequality, and pressures exerted by the nature and scope of globalization. The suggestion that while urban wounds not only are destructive but also can be healed is provocative. Above all, it challenges us to highlight what is special about the experiences and expectations of young people in Recife, Hanoi, and Lusaka in the first half-decade of this millennium.

With a few recent exceptions (Rogerson 2000; Tomlinson et al. 2003), scholarship on international development cooperation has not been concerned with cities and urban space in the developing world, nor has this work conventionally been part of the literature on globalization. Leading theorists on globalization (Appadurai 2001; Borja and Castells 1997; Castells 1989; Sassen 1998) have been preoccupied with finance and economic circuits, technology, and cultural flows. They have paid little attention to international development cooperation as an important form of globalization or, above all, to how this process reorganizes urban space in the developing world. Yet structural adjustment programs and neoliberal reforms are transforming urban space by reshaping the distribution of economic opportunities throughout specific cities, between cities in specific regions, and globally. In short, globalization as mediated through international development cooperation programs has important implications for urban space. The combination of rapid urban growth and a large proportion of youth turns transformations of urban space into critical matters in the new global economy, not only in Global cities but everywhere. This includes the changing urban economic landscapes of Recife, Hanoi, and Lusaka, with reconfigured land values, property rights, and zoning laws that are promoting private investment. Almost everywhere the poor, including many youth, lose out as formal economies are restructured and housing is relegated to the urban periphery.

None of the three cities in which we conducted research are World or Global cities in the sense described above. But despite their different roles in the global economy, Recife, Hanoi, and Lusaka are connected to and dependent on global arenas in relationships through which local forms of urbanism are produced. In effect, cities like these are the prime sites for local translations of globalization from many different angles. Rather than focusing on their marginal status in the global economy, we approach these three cities as particular types of places for the young. Cities such as these provide a wide range of social and cultural contexts for young people, not only because of their size, density, and built environments, but also because of the people, goods, and information that flow through them. Flows like these help structure space and build social relationships, prompting creativity as well as conflict. As Gill Valentine (2001, 206) argues: "The density and intensity of cities also means that they are above all else sites of *proximity,* the 'place of our meeting with the other' (Barthes 1981), with all the emotions of excitement, frustration or anxiety that this heterogeneity engenders."

Space is an important dimension of the constitution of everyday life, and people and places cannot be studied independently of one another (Aitken 2001; Holloway and Hubbard 2001). Adjusting to their physical environment, young people also adjust to the people around them. "It is socio-spatial practices that define places," explains Linda McDowall, suggesting that such "practices result in overlapping and intersecting places with multiple and changing boundaries, constituted and maintained by social relations of power and exclusion" (1999, 4). But cities are not just built environments of physical structures, they are also products of people's imagination. The meanings urban residents construe of place may change over time as individuals and social groups claim access and territorialize, including some in particular areas and excluding others (Massey 1998). In this way, place and space are bound up with the power relations between different social groups within the city.

Cities are much more than locations—they are ways of life. Providing concrete realities for young people's lives, cities draw our attention to neighborhoods, housing, squares, markets, parks, churches, and streets, among other things. Young people experience their cities as comprising different types of space that may include or exclude them, depending on their background (Beall 2002, 48). Gender and class may structure difference across space, but they are not the only relations to do so. Age or generation may have similar effects, as may religious orientation, which helps shape a particular moral geography, charging some spaces in religious terms and defining others as beyond reach. In short, the built environments of cities are everywhere, but differently, involved in framing urbanism and in creating and managing livelihoods across urban space.

The Comparative Perspective

Anchoring our work in ethnography, we use Recife, Hanoi, and Lusaka as the empirical settings that orient our comparative preoccupation with youth. Although the cities have different histories, they resemble each other in that their major growth has been recent. They all have colonial histories. They are important administrative centers: Recife is the capital of the state of Pernambuco, the poorest region of Brazil, while Hanoi and Lusaka are national capitals. Socioeconomically and culturally heterogeneous, they are characterized by vast inequalities of income and diverse combinations of ethnic, "racial," and religious distinctions. As regional or national hubs, all three cities are experiencing rapid growth, driven by a combination of natural urban population increase and rural-urban migration. Not linked to industrialization to any large degree, their recent rapid growth is a result of a global political conjuncture: the debt crisis of the late 1970s, the IMF-led economic restructuring of the 1980s, and the market liberalization of the 1990s (Davis 2004, 9). Among the consequences in Recife and Lusaka are shrinking opportunities for formal wage employment and education. All three cities have insufficient housing stock, resulting in the rapid growth of informal settlements and inadequate infrastructure for the provision of water, sanitation, electricity, and transportation.

People born today in Vietnam have an average life expectancy of 69, and in Brazil of 68. Zambia, with a life expectancy at birth of just 33 years, offers markedly worse long-term prospects for young people (UNICEF 2005, table 1). While Brazil and Vietnam are on the United Nations Development Programme's list of "medium human development countries," Zambia is near the bottom of the list of "low human development countries."[3] All three cities have undergone economic restructuring—Vietnam only since 1986—most recently the poverty reduction programs set into motion by the neoliberal development agenda of the International Monetary Fund, the World Bank, and donor countries and international agencies that subscribe to the Bank's development priorities. Largely as a result of the development priorities pursued by their governments since the 1970s, young people are growing up in the context of pressures placed on the educational system from grade school through university and an absence of formal employment in many sectors of the economy. Against such backdrops, it is not surprising that governments have difficulty meeting the needs of their growing urban youth populations, and that, everywhere, local and global identities are crucially at stake in young people's negotiation of urban space for the future.

As we approach the end of the twenty-first century's first decade, we cannot consider urban growth from a global perspective without taking into account HIV/AIDS, a disease present in all our research settings, but near its global epicenter in urban Zambia. Even when young people do not talk about AIDS, their fear of the "killer disease" is real. It prompts abstinence as well as sexual predation (LeClerc-Madlala 2003). Because young people constitute such a large population in major cities of societies marked by deep economic and social inequalities, they easily become construed as a problem, being viewed as a risk to society rather than as at risk themselves in many different domains of life. In Brazil, physical violence provoked by hardship, leading to injury and loss of life, is a constant focus in national and global news media, with much attention to street children (Hecht 1998). Southeast Asia is in the news for widespread recruitment of underage workers into homes, fields, industry, and prostitution (Montgomery 2001).

And Africa figures prominently in media descriptions of the "AIDS pandemic," accompanied by the sad figure of the AIDS orphan, while child soldiers are the icons of reports on the continent's many civil wars (Utas 2003; Vigh 2004). Taken together, the media, international organizations, and NGOs tend overwhelmingly to feature the plight of urban children and youth in dramatic terms (Van Zyl Slabbert et al. 1994; UNICEF 2005). This book's inclusive approach to youth and the city tempers such sensationalist media accounts by highlighting young people's everyday experiences not only of marginalization and economic deprivation but also of constructive pursuits of social adulthood.

Organization of the Book

The Youth and the City research team settled on the book's final form after considerable deliberations revolving around the idea of either an edited book with a miscellany of articles from many different angles or what we called a project-book to demonstrate what interdisciplinary, long-term, multi-site research can contribute to our understanding of urban youth in the developing world. Settling on the latter, and showcasing the experiences of young people in three very different cities in the developing world, we believe that *Youth and the City in the Global South* compellingly demonstrates comparative insights into the situation of urban youth in the era of global capitalism. What is more, the book offers insights into the collaborative research process by discussing some of the many challenges the research gave rise to: empirically in terms of access, methodologically in terms of comparison, and theoretically in terms of explanatory frameworks. We trust that the book, with this unique organization and detailed focus on urban youth, will contribute fresh insights into interdisciplinary scholarship both in the West and in the developing world.

The book's three parts knit together the analytical and topical concerns of the overall project. The first part, Situating Youth in the City, consists of this introduction and a chapter on methodology that engages with issues of access, interdisciplinarity, and comparison, and reflects critically on the possibilities and problems of interdisciplinary collaboration. Moving on to the three anthropological case studies, which in different ways deal with the relationship between youth and the city, the second part, Studying Youth in Cities, serves as a contextual framework for the rest of the book. It also raises important questions concerning youth, the urban, and their interrelationships. The third part, Youth Making Meaning, relies on the previous urban chapters for background. Its special concerns are parallel themes and comparisons at a general level that do not presume to be representative or ethnographically detailed. Here, observations drawn from across the three cities are framed within the distinct disciplinary modes of inquiry of a human geographer, an education specialist, and a media scholar.

The methodology chapter, jointly written by Anne Line Dalsgaard and Karen Valentin, takes as its point of departure the framework of the project, itself a response to politically defined interests. Engaging with questions of comparison, interdisciplinarity, and cross-national collaboration, Dalsgaard and Valentin argue that comparison is inherent in all anthropological studies. Individual studies in the project have used a comparative approach with different levels and degrees of explicitness. Such a research strategy may enable or hamper the illumination of specific themes and analytical perspectives. Turning to the issue of interdisciplinarity and cross-national collaboration, they also consider the relationship between different research traditions, positions in academic regimes, what counts as legitimate academic knowledge among whom and where, and current demands for applicability.

Each chapter in the second part of the book sketches recent political and economic changes that are central to young people's opportunities today. The three anthropologists seek to capture what is special about the three cities, each of them bringing their distinct interests and orientations to this work. Anne Line Dalsgaard's approach is primarily phenomenological in its focus on lived experiences and subjective meanings. Situating meaning and motivation in the contested field of social relations, she also engages with socioeconomic and institutional structures beyond young people's immediate lifeworlds. She and her Brazilian colleagues focus on the ways in which youth in Recife orient themselves toward the future in a context marked by social difference and the collapse of employment and other institutions that used to mark the transition to social adulthood. The passage to adulthood is crucial. Competition for vocational training, higher education, and jobs forces many young people, especially those from low-income groups, to find alternative paths, among them early pregnancy and involvement in crime. Drawing on several cases, Dalsgaard, Franch, and Scott argue that normative ideas of a "proper" transition affect young people's evaluation of their actual situations. Highlighting this lack of correspondence between moral discourse and young people's own experiences, they address our responsibility as researchers to develop definitions that capture the complexity and lack of synchrony of many youth transitions.

With a background in educational anthropology and the anthropology of policy, Karen Valentin is concerned with the roles that institutions play in the socialization of young people, structuring and regulating their everyday lives, yet also leaving room for creativity and change. Her chapter on Hanoi focuses on specific urban places, both as contexts for people's actions and as texts that create stories about the wider society. She draws attention to the historical dimension of the city and its narration through material and physical expressions. At the same time, focusing on young people's sociopolitical activities in the Ho Chi Minh Communist Youth Union, she explores youth life as it is shaped by the experience of growing up in an urban environment. A key function of the Youth Union is to provide "meaningful" leisure and to take young people away from supposedly dangerous places in the city by establishing new, morally legitimate places for them. She illustrates how, through their involvement in sociopolitical activities, young people become involved in urban development as part of a wider project of nation-building.

The last decade's development priorities have sharpened long-existing socio-spatial polarizations in Zambia, extending them in new ways that are particularly visible in urban areas. As an urban and economic anthropologist, I am interested in how people create a living under circumstances that are not of their own making. My chapter on Lusaka focuses on urban space, its effects on young people in gender and class terms, and how they in their turn reconfigure it through their actions. Discussing how young women and men from different socioeconomic backgrounds negotiate place, I examine their efforts to gain access across several different urban sites: technical and vocational training, political activity (including NGO involvement), church interaction, and popular music. Although they are constrained by the sluggish economy and circumscribed by society's view of them, many young people in Lusaka contribute to the reshaping and possible changing of dominant meanings of youth from being dependent to taking action.

The book's third part is concerned with cross-cutting, parallel themes, and comparisons across the three cities, rather than with the kind of detailed ethnography provided in the previous chapters. The human geographer Katherine V. Gough adopts a sociospatial perspective in her exploration of the relationship between youth and the home in the different urban contexts of Recife, Hanoi, and Lusaka. Drawing on scholarship about home as a concept, she examines the similarities and differences in young people's living conditions in the home, their experiences of home, and their ability (or inability) to set up their own homes. As a geographer, she is interested in how the relationship between youth and the home varies with culture, class, and gender, working to examine the meanings of home for young people and the nature of the relationship between the concepts of youth and home.

Processes of globalization have complicated scholarship on identity formation among urban youth. This is illustrated in the disciplinary fields of education and media studies. Ulla Ambrosius Madsen analyzes how young people in Recife, Hanoi, and Lusaka shape their sense of self between global ideologies and local productions of the educated person. Her discussion is based on classroom observations and school narratives among secondary school students. Drawing on scholarly work in the field of comparative education and educational anthropology, she argues that schools are channels through which neoliberal ideas of learning, teaching, and being circulate in diverse regional and national contexts. Inscribed into educational policies, institutional organizations, and pedagogical practices, such ideas interact with local constructions of education to provide a framework with which young people practice and construct their own meanings of education.

Norbert Wildermuth takes up mediated forms of communication and the role they play in young people's lives and identity formation. His interest is in how media access, content, and literacy facilitate informal learning processes, and how a globalized media landscape contributes to local understandings. Focusing on different kinds of media in the three cities, he explores the productive relationship between media use, identity work, and knowledge acquisition that urban youth negotiate, with different degrees of success, in the process of shaping their present and future lives. The most important and preferred form of mediated communication technology differs—television in Recife, information technology in Hanoi, and radio in Lusaka—as do the issues these media present when addressing youth.

The conclusions highlight the significance of our findings about youth in rapidly growing cities in parts of the world that often are viewed as if they were set apart, marginal to the West's role as a source of economic dynamism and globalization. The double dynamic of inclusion and exclusion that we have identified poses a challenge with which young people deal in various ways, working with the resources at hand. It is in such efforts, among others, that urban youth from different socioeconomic backgrounds operate, taking steps to transcend the material circumstances that circumscribe their lives. We discuss how and why such interdisciplinary observations matter for policy interventions directed toward youth.

Global Youth?

Cities like Recife, Hanoi, and Lusaka are the prime sites for globalization's translation into local understandings and experiences. Such cities constitute particular types of places for young people, depending on who they are in gender, age, and class terms, as they seek to take charge of their own lives. In order to showcase young people's efforts to push on, this book weaves together four arguments that revolve around the importance of urban life, comparative youth studies, globalization, and its interaction with local practices. We suggest that the significance of urban life in the developing world invites comparative study of young people's exposures to a range of global processes, from economic planning to culture. In their manifestations in distinct urban locations, such exposures resonate in complicated ways with local cultural norms and practices. Taken together, the resources and influences the young draw on in their projects within the household setting, in local institutions, and beyond stem from across the world, rather than the West as the chief source of economic dynamism and globalization.

The convergence this book has noted in youth experiences across the West and the developing world is in part an outcome of a recent global political and economic conjuncture, namely the debt crisis of the 1970s and the IMF-promoted economic restructuring of the 1980s. Fueling recent urban population growth, widespread economic informalization, and illegal housing, these processes have been instrumental in transforming the opportunities of youth across urban space. The recent neoliberal development agenda adds new dynamics to this characterization (Katz 2004; Strickland 2002). Even so, these processes are assuming different shapes in the three cities in which we based our research. While the significance of youth everywhere is shaped by locally specific historical legacies, the decades since the 1970s constitute a crucial time for significant changes in the experience and meaning of youth.

These are new times. Across much of the world today, youth has become a less clearly demarcated stage in the transition toward adulthood than was the case a generation ago. As we demonstrate with reference to the three cities, the category of youth takes on new meanings as young people experience their own biological time through diverse trajectories toward the future. These new meanings are experienced in the double dynamic of simultaneous exclusion and inclusion we delineated earlier. In cities in the Global South today, youth are highly visible in public space but to a large degree left out of mainstream economic and political activity. Compared with the existing constraining definitions that approach youth from a deficit perspective, these new meanings capture experiences of active youth involvement and goal-oriented behavior directed toward social interaction, economic livelihood, and political activity. In these transformed urban settings, young urban people are carving out their own spaces for action that do not always replicate existing forms. These are among the activities that matter to tomorrow's leadership and which society at large and the development industry must come to grips with in order to reckon with the centrality of youth to urban social reproduction.

Acknowledgments

The members of the research team contributed to this introduction in innumerable ways and I thank them for their valuable input. Any shortcomings are my responsibility.

Notes

1. Given the large youth population in urban areas in the developing world, it is remarkable that there is not a separate chapter on youth, and indeed that the term "youth" does not appear in the index, in *Cities Transformed: Demographic Change and Its Implications in the Developing World,* produced by an expert panel on population dynamics of the National Academy of Sciences (National Research Council 2003). There is a section on children in a chapter on

poverty, titled "Diversity and Inequality" (2003, 188–95), and another on urban adolescents in the chapter titled "Fertility and Reproductive Health" (2003, 247–51).

2. Related concerns, pertaining to social exclusion and the "underclass," have been explored by sociologists. See MacDonald 1997.

3. In the UN's *Human Development Report 2004,* the countries of "medium human development" rank from 56 to 141 and "low human development" from 142 to 177. Brazil is ranked 72, Vietnam 112, and Zambia 164. Zambia is the only country on the list whose rank today is lower than it was in 1975 (UNDP 2005).

References

Aitken, Stuart C. 2001. *Geographies of Young People: The Morally Contested Spaces of Identity.* New York: Routledge.

Amit-Talai, Vered, and Helena Wulff, eds. 1995. *Youth Cultures: A Cross-Cultural Perspective.* London: Routledge.

Ansell, Nicola. 2005. *Children, Youth and Development.* New York: Routledge.

Appadurai, Arjun, ed. 2001. *Globalization.* Durham, N.C.: Duke University Press.

Ashforth, Adam. 1999. Weighing Manhood in Soweto. *CODESRIA Bulletin* 3–4:51–58.

Barthes, Roland. 1981. Semiology and the Urban. Cited in Gill Valentine, *Social Geographies: Space and Society* (Harlow: Pearson Education Ltd., 2001).

Beall, Jo. 2002. Globalization and Social Exclusion in Cities: Framing the Debate with Lessons from Africa and Asia. *Environment & Urbanization* 14(1):41–51.

Borja, Jordi, and Manuel Castells, with Mireia Belil and Chris Brenner. 1997. *Local and Global: The Management of Cities in the Information Age.* London: Earthscan.

Brown, B. Bradford, Reed W. Larson, and T. S. Saraswathi, eds. 2002. *The World's Youth: Adolescence in Eight Regions of the Globe.* Cambridge: Cambridge University Press.

Bucholtz, Mary. 2002. Youth and Cultural Practices. *Annual Review of Anthropology* 31:525–52.

Castells, Manuel. 1989. *The Informational City: Information Technology, Economic Restructuring, and the Urban-Regional Process.* Cambridge, Mass.: Blackwell.

Chawla, Louise, ed. 2002. *Growing Up in an Urbanising World.* Paris and London: UNESCO and Earthscan.

Cole, Jennifer. 2004. Fresh Contact in Tamatave, Madagascar: Sex, Money, and Intergenerational Transformation. *American Ethnologist* 31(4):573–88.

Cole, Jennifer, and Deborah Durham. 2007. Age, Regeneration, and the Intimate Politics of Globalization. Introduction to *Generations and Globalization: Youth, Age, and Family in the New World Economy,* 1–28. Bloomington: Indiana University Press.

Comaroff, John, and Jean Comaroff. 2000. Reflexions sur la jeunesse: Du passé a la postcolonie. *Politique Africaine* 80:90–110.

Cook, Thomas D., and Frank F. Furstenberg, Jr. 2002. Explaining Aspects of the Transition to Adulthood in Italy, Sweden, Germany, and the United States: A Cross-Disciplinary, Case Synthesis Approach. *Annals of the American Academy of Political and Social Science,* special issue, Early Adulthood in Cross-National Perspective, March: 257–88.

Dalsgaard, Anne Line. 2004. *Matters of Life and Longing: Female Sterilisation in Northeast Brazil.* Copenhagen: Museum Tusculanum Press.

Davis, Mike. 2004. Planet of Slums: Urban Involution and the Informal Proletariat. *New Left Review* 26:5–34.

———. 2006. *Planet of Slums*. London and New York: Verso.

Drakakis-Smith, David. 2000. *Third World Cities*. 2nd ed. London: Routledge.

Drummond, Lisa, and Helle Rydstrøm. 2004. Introduction to *Gender Practices in Contemporary Vietnam*, 1–25. Singapore: Singapore University Press.

Durham, Deborah. 2000. Youth and the Social Imagination in Africa: Introduction. *Anthropological Quarterly* 73(3):113–20.

———. 2004. Disappearing Youth: Youth as a Social Shifter in Botswana. *American Ethnologist* 31(4):589–605.

Gammeltoft, Tine. 1999. *Women's Bodies, Women's Worries: Health and Family Planning in a Vietnamese Rural Community*. Richmond, England: Curzon.

Gelbard, Alene, Carl Haub, and Mary M. Kent. 1999. World Population beyond Six Billion. *Population Bulletin* 54(1), March. Washington, D.C.: Population Reference Bureau.

Gugler, Josef, ed. 2004. *World Cities beyond the West: Globalization, Development, and Inequality*. Cambridge: Cambridge University Press.

Hall, Tom, and Heather Montgomery. 2000. Home and Away: "Childhood," "Youth" and Young People. *Anthropology Today* 16(3):13–15.

Hansen, Karen Tranberg. 1997. *Keeping House in Lusaka*. New York: Columbia University Press.

Hecht, Tobias. 1998. *At Home in the Street: Street Children of Northeast Brazil*. Cambridge: Cambridge University Press.

Holloway, Lewis, and Phil Hubbard. 2001. *People and Place: The Extraordinary Geographies of Everyday Life*. Harlow, England: Pearson.

Hy V. Luong. 2003. Postwar Vietnamese Society: An Overview of Transformational Dynamics. Introduction to *Postwar Vietnam: Dynamics of a Transforming Society*, 1–26. Singapore: Institute of Southeast Asian Studies; Lanham, Md.: Rowman and Littlefield.

Jeffrey, Craig, and Linda McDowell. 2004. Youth in a Comparative Perspective: Global Change, Local Lives. *Youth & Society* 36(2):131–42.

Katz, Cindy. 2004. *Growing Up Global: Economic Restructuring and Children's Everyday Lives*. Minneapolis: University of Minnesota Press.

King, Anthony. 1990. *Urbanism, Colonialism and the World-Economy: Cultural and Spatial Foundations of the World Urban System*. London: Routledge.

Leccardi, Carmen. 2005. Facing Uncertainty: Temporality and Biographies in the New Century. *Young* 13(2):123–46.

LeClerc-Madlala, Suzanne. 2003. Transactional Sex and the Pursuit of Modernity. *Social Dynamics* 29(2):213–33.

Lewellen, Ted C. 2002. *The Anthropology of Globalization: Cultural Anthropology Enters the 21st Century*. Westport, Conn.: Bergin & Garvey.

MacDonald, Robert, ed. 1997. *Youth, the 'Underclass' and Social Exclusion*. London: Routledge.

Maira, Sunaina, and Elisabeth Soep. 2005. Introduction to *Youthscapes: The Popular, the National, the Global*, xv–xxxv. Philadelphia: University of Pennsylvania Press.

Mannheim, Karl. 1972 [1952]. The Problem of Generations. In *Essays on the Sociology of Knowledge*, 276–322. London: Routledge & Kegan Paul.

Masquelier, Adeline. 2005. The Scorpion's Sting: Youth, Marriage and the Struggle for Social Maturity in Niger. *Journal of the Royal Anthropological Institute* 11:59–83.

Massey, Doreen. 1998. The Spatial Construction of Youth Cultures. In *Cool Places: Geographies of Youth Cultures,* ed. Tracey Skelton and Gill Valentine, 121–29. London: Routledge.

McDowall, Linda. 1999. *Gender, Identity and Place: Understanding Feminist Geographies.* Cambridge: Polity.

Montgomery, Heather. 2001. *Modern Babylon? Prostituting Children in Thailand.* Oxford and New York: Berghahn.

Nascimento, Pedro Francisco Guedes do. 1999. "Ser homem ou nada": Diversidade de experiências e estratégias de atualização do modelo hegemônico da masculinidade em Camaragibe/PE. M.A. thesis, Universidade Federal de Pernambuco.

National Research Council. 2003. *Cities Transformed: Demographic Change and Its Implications in the Developing World.* Washington, D.C.: National Academies Press.

National Research Council and Institute of Medicine. 2005. Executive summary of *Growing Up Global: The Changing Transitions to Adulthood in Developing Countries,* 1–14. Washington, D.C.: National Academies Press.

Pilcher, Jane. 1994. Mannheim's Sociology of Generations: An Undervalued Legacy. *British Journal of Sociology* 45(3):481–95.

Robinson, Jennifer. 2002. Global and World Cities: A View from Off the Map. *International Journal of Urban and Regional Research* 26(3):531–54.

———. 2006. *Ordinary Cities: Between Modernity and Development.* London: Routledge.

Rogerson, Christian M. 2000. Local Economic Development in an Era of Globalization: The Case of South African Cities. *Journal of Economic and Social Geography* 91(4):397–411.

Ruddick, Sue. 2003. The Politics of Aging: Globalization and the Restructuring of Youth and Childhood. *Antipode* 35(2):334–62.

Sassen, Saskia. 1998. *Globalization and Its Discontents: Essays on the New Mobility of People and Money.* New York: New Press.

———. 2001. *The Global City: New York, London, Tokyo.* 2nd ed. Princeton N.J.: Princeton University Press.

Schafer, Wolf. 2005. The Uneven Globality of Children. *Journal of Social History* 38(4):1027–39.

Scott, Russell Parry. 1996. Matrifocal Males: Gender, Perception and Experiences of the Domestic Domain in Brazil. In *Gender, Kinship, Power: A Comparative and Interdisciplinary History,* ed. Mary Jo Maynes et al., 287–301. London: Routledge.

Skelton, Tracey. 2002. Research on Youth Transitions: Some Critical Interventions. In *Young People in Risk Society: The Restructuring of Youth Identities and Transitions in Late Modernity,* ed. Mark Cieslik and Gary Pollock, 100–16. Burlington, Vt.: Ashgate.

Smart, Alan, and Josephine Smart. 2003. Urbanization and the Global Perspective. *Annual Review of Anthropology* 32:263–85.

Strickland, Ronald, ed. 2002. *Growing Up Postmodern: Neoliberalism and the War on the Young.* Lanham, Md.: Rowman and Littlefield.

Susser, Ida, and Jane Schneider. 2003. Wounded Cities: Destruction and Reconstruction in a Globalized World. In *Wounded Cities: Destruction and Reconstruction in a Globalized World,* ed. Jane Schneider and Ida Susser, 1–23. Oxford: Berg.

Tienda, Marta, and William Julius Wilson, eds. 2002. *Youth in Cities: A Cross-National Perspective*. Cambridge: Cambridge University Press.

Tomlinson, Richard, Robert A. Beauregard, Lindsay Brenner, and Xolela Mangcu, eds. 2003. *Emerging Johannesburg: Perspectives on the Postapartheid City*. New York: Routledge.

United Nations. 2002. Department of Economic and Social Affairs, Population Division. *World Urbanization Prospects: The 2001 Revision*. New York: United Nations.

UNDP (United Nations Development Programme). 2005. *Human Development Report 2004*. New York: United Nations Development Programme. Accessed online, March 7, 2005.

UN-Habitat (United Nations Human Settlements Programme). 2003. *The Challenge of the Slums: Global Report on Human Settlements*. London: Earthscan.

———. 2005. *The State of the World's Cities 2004/2005: Globalization and Urban Culture*. UN-Habitat and Earthscan.

UNICEF. 2005. *Childhood under Threat: The State of the World's Children 2005*. http://www .unicef.org/sowc05/english/. Accessed November 10, 2005.

Utas, Mats. 2003. Sweet Battlefields: Youth and the Liberian Civil War. Ph.D. dissertation, Uppsala University.

Valentine, Gill. 2001. *Social Geographies: Space and Society*. Harlow, England: Pearson Education.

Van Zyl Slabbert, F., Charles Malan, Hendrik Marais, Johan Olivier, and Rory Riordan, eds. 1994. *Youth in the New South Africa: Towards Policy Formation; Main Report of the Co-operative Research Program: South African Youth*. Pretoria: HSRC.

Vigh, Henrik. 2004. Navigating Terrains of War: Youth and Soldiering in Guinea Bissau. Ph.D. dissertation, University of Copenhagen.

Weiss, Brad. 2004. Contentious Futures: Past and Present. Introduction to *Producing African Futures: Ritual and Reproduction in a Neoliberal Age*, 1–20. Leiden: Brill.

World Bank. 2005. Introduction to *The Provisional Outline of the 2007 World Development Report: Development and the Next Generation*, i–ii. Washington, D.C.: World Bank. http:// econ.worldbank.org/. Accessed January 24, 2006.

Wyn, Johanna, and Rob White. 2000. Negotiating Social Change: The Paradox of Youth. *Youth & Society* 32(2):165–83.

2

Youth across the Globe: Comparison, Interdisciplinarity, and Cross-National Collaboration

Anne Line Dalsgaard and Karen Valentin

What are the challenges in interdisciplinary research? How can three such different cities as Recife, Hanoi, and Lusaka be compared? And why insist on local collaboration? Starting by discussing the methodological framework of the project, this chapter explores questions of comparison, interdisciplinarity, and cross-national collaboration. The research project, Youth and the City, was designed with explicit comparison in mind. On the basis of anthropological discussions of comparison, we examine the levels and degrees of explicitness in our comparative approach, the ways in which the different studies in the project have dealt with this approach, and consequently the themes and analytical perspectives that such a research strategy makes possible. In discussing the issues of interdisciplinarity and cross-national collaboration, we also aim to shed light on the relationship between different research traditions, the conditions in which critical and socially engaged research may be conducted, and the current demands for applicability and relevance in different societies.

The Background of the Project

This book is one outcome of a collaborative research project conducted over the four-year period from 2001 to 2005. The project was funded by the Council for Development Research of DANIDA (the Danish International Development Agency of the Danish Ministry of Foreign Affairs). As part of the wider poverty-reduction strategy that forms the basis of Denmark's development aid policy, the Council for Development Research supports research and research capacity–building in developing countries, advising the Ministry of Foreign Affairs.

Acknowledging the scale of urban growth in the contemporary developing world and its demographic, economic, political, and social implications, the Council for Development Research explicitly made the theme of urbanization in developing countries its priority in its annual call for research proposals in 2000, though the specific research approach of particular proposals was left open. Given the centrality of youth to urban social reproduction, the research team decided to approach the city by focusing on young people as active participants and agents of change in urban development (see Hansen, introduction, this volume). From a political point of view, studies of young people were indeed timely, and a project on urban youth fed into the ongoing debate about the status of children and young people in Danish development aid, as demonstrated recently in a set of guidelines based on the UN Convention on the Rights of the Child (Denmark, Ministry of Foreign Affairs 2005). The project was therefore conditioned by politically defined demands, which meant that certain premises were present right from the outset. This was the case not only thematically, in the focus on cities in the developing world, but also in the requirement for institutional collaboration, both nationally and internationally, as well as in the project's interdisciplinarity, long-term nature, and use of multi-sited locations.

The methodological framework on which the project is based integrates in-depth anthropological research in each city with three topically oriented, cross-cutting studies. A multi-sited research methodology (Marcus 1995) is particularly compelling for the interdisciplinary field of youth studies, which by its very nature cuts across different sites, not only regionally but also institutionally. This methodological approach acknowledges the interconnections of young people's lives and their movements between different sites and captures the fluidity that characterizes their everyday practices. It also sheds light on the growing impact of globalization and the institutionalization of policy in international governance (Shore and Wright 1997), which, through various conventions and regulations, contributes to defining "youth" as a universal category and to setting standards for young people's lives (see Hansen, conclusion, this volume).

The project was endorsed by Michael Whyte, who at that time was department head of the Institute of Anthropology, Copenhagen University. He brought together the three anthropologists, Anne Line Dalsgaard, Karen Tranberg Hansen, and Karen Valentin, as the core of the project, and on the basis of their initial discussions scholars from relevant research fields (geography, media studies, and education studies) were included in the team. Initially we chose Recife, Lusaka, and Kathmandu as our research sites, as all three anthropologists had long-term acquaintances with these cities. We deemed that the project could profit from their prior knowledge and local contacts. However, the political conflict in Nepal escalated drastically in the aftermath of the royal massacre in 2001, which resulted in an intensification of armed confrontations between government forces and Maoist insurgents. We were concerned both about our team's personal safety and about the sustainability of a four-year project. At fairly short notice we therefore decided to change research location from Kathmandu to Hanoi, where colleagues from the Institute of Anthropology were already engaged in DANIDA-funded collaborative research.

The three cities—Recife, Lusaka, and Hanoi—are interesting not only in their own right, but also in comparison with one another, because they all, from a developmentalist perspective, are located on the periphery of the world economy. We assumed that this location might throw light on some common conditions for growing up urban in the South in an era of intensified globalization and, by implication, on shared experiences of youth as a specific phase in the life course, not least in situations of vulnerability, poverty, and social exclusion. But we also found significant variations between the cities both in their structural conditions, visible in different forms of social stratification and state-subject relations, and in dominant social and cultural constructions of youth and other generational and age-related categories. As this volume demonstrates, these contextually defined circumstances have tremendous impact on the way in which youth as a category is dealt with in different societies, and how young people as living subjects make sense of and shape their lives, today and in future.

Research Methodology

The three urban case studies carried out by the anthropologists on the project were constructed as parallel studies, but the timing of the research in the field differed. We started working in both Recife and Lusaka in 2001, but did not begin in Hanoi until 2003. The late beginning in Hanoi was partly related to the change of research site from Kathmandu to Hanoi. Because of the different professional and personal obligations of the members of the research team, organization of the stints of fieldwork was also different. Hansen spent two months in Lusaka every summer for four years, whereas Dalsgaard and Valentin each carried out five months of field research over a two-year period. Although the timing and length of our periods of field research differed, we developed a common methodology for the three urban case studies in an attempt to generate ethnographic observations of the same order.

The research methodology we developed aimed to capture the activities, views, and aspirations of young people between the ages of 12 and 25, whom we sampled using a brief household survey in residential areas characterized by different socioeconomic standards: low income, middle income, and high income. This categorization was based on average income level and gave a sense of the sociospatial organization of each city, but it also tended to conceal social

Figure 2.1. The initial steps of the project: a workshop in Lusaka, 2001.
Photo: Karen Valentin

and economic heterogeneity within specific areas. This was not just a practical problem; as we discuss later in this chapter, it related to fundamental questions about the categories used for comparative analysis. Because of time constraints, the Hanoi team ended up concentrating on only two residential areas.

The aim of the household survey was to assess the nature and scope of the economic and social resources available to young people of both sexes within their households and immediate neighborhoods. The survey also elicited local views, from both young people and members of the parental generation, about meanings of youth. For various logistical reasons affecting the scope and nature of our field research, we adjusted the specificity of questions and topics in the household survey to the situation on the ground. For example, questions about access to a car were only relevant in Recife, whereas the Hanoi survey asked about possession of motorbikes and karaoke sets to assess what young people themselves considered important markers for urban youth life. In Lusaka, the majority of the young people were born in the city, yet many had lived intermittently with relatives or guardians or attended school elsewhere. Tracing these movements became a specific concern of the survey.

As we did not have the same opportunities to interact with young people in the three cities, it became difficult to follow the same methodological framework and develop comparable sets of categories. Like other research projects conducted in Vietnam, ours was subject to bureaucratic and political controls on our research procedures (Gammeltoft 1999, 38–44; Marr 1996, 2–3). The project had to be approved by the local authorities, the People's Committee, in each ward. As the youth branch of the Communist Party of Vietnam, and considered to be the auxiliary of the People's Committee, the Youth Union is involved in all youth-related policy issues. In order to obtain the necessary permissions, we repeatedly had to consult the local Youth Union leaders, who were therefore assigned a central role as both facilitators and gatekeepers throughout the period of field research. The Danish research team was mainly introduced to politically conforming young people, including students and workers with fairly stable jobs who were active in the Youth Union (see Valentin, this volume), and access to secondary schools was restricted (see Madsen, this volume). Both socioeconomic and political factors were important in these selection processes and meant that we contacted neither the poorest segments of society, nor potential politically critical voices.

In contrast to Hanoi, where access was largely determined by politically informed interests and an effort to emphasize the "good examples," in Recife positions based on social class were important criteria for access. In Brazilian middle-income areas, homes are generally protected by private guards. Because of the difficulty of gaining entry to these homes, we contacted economically better-off young people through two private schools, a university, and our personal networks. Consequently, the Brazilian observations offer more evidence of violence, economic scarcity, and social marginalization in the lives of poor youth than they do about the circumstances of economically privileged young people who live in fenced-in homes in residential areas to which strangers do not have immediate access. This was, at times, the case in Lusaka too. When conducting the household survey, we were occasionally refused permission to interview in the high-income area of Kabulonga, where most residents live in walled or fenced houses, many with round-the-clock security guards. Because bypassing authority by talking directly with young people might be seen as intruding, we aimed the Lusaka survey toward households, interviewing both an adult member and a young person. This adult household member was not always a parent, as several young people stayed with guardians, and some had moved a lot.

The different degrees of access proved to be a challenge for the methodological framework of the project, which we continuously readjusted, either finding other ways of arriving at the issues or, in some cases, not pursuing certain groups of youth at all. "Rebellious" and socially marginalized young people in Hanoi continued to be a category that was more or less out of reach for the Danish research team, whereas upper-class young people in Brazil had to be identified through schools rather than their residential areas.

Our degree of contact with the families and friends of the young persons we interviewed, and the amount of insight we gained into their everyday life, varied considerably across the cities as a result of several factors. In Recife Dalsgaard worked with Mónica Franch, a young scholar from the Federal University of Pernambuco. They conducted field research in two low-income residential areas, with which they were familiar from previous research (Dalsgaard 2004; Franch 2000). Dalsgaard's part-time accommodation in Santa Barbara and Franch's long-term acquaintance with families in Vietnã lent themselves readily to participant observation. Their close contact with families in these areas was, however, quite unlike their more formal visits to middle-class homes. In Hanoi, the control of the neighborhood by the People's Committee made it difficult to establish more informal contacts, and following young people to school, work, or leisure activities was only possible if the necessary official paperwork had been completed. Through her long research experience with life in Lusaka, Hansen had extensive contacts that facilitated her access to schools and many public domains of young people's lives. Yet her senior status as an adult of European background also distanced her from the more intimate details of young people's everyday experiences. As a result, she has drawn on extensive collaboration with young assistants. These were among some of the many practical challenges that we had to find ways of dealing with.

In all three cities, the case study methodology focused on places where young people get together, including work settings, markets, streets, and private homes. We conducted interviews and made informal and topically focused observations in schools, vocational training centers, churches, and places where young people hang out for leisure and pleasure, among them shopping malls, bars, and parks. In effect, we explored the construction of their urban social and cultural maps as products of their activities and interactions with persons of different genders, generations, and classes, and across many different institutions and situations. In addition, students or young scholars from the local research institutions with which we collaborated carried out mini-ethnographies on selected sites. In Recife, Russell Parry Scott led the work with three mini-ethnographies carried out by his students: Márcia Reis Longhi studied two computer courses of very different standards, Jonnhy Cantarelli focused on youth involvement in church, and Madiana Rodrigues carried out a brief survey of vocational training. In Hanoi, Dang Nguyen Anh organized two studies of a similar kind: one was a study on youth employment carried out by Phi Hai Nam and Nghiem Thi Thuy, and the other was on marriage strategies and was conducted by Nguyen Duc Chien. In Lusaka, Maurice Pengele, one of Hansen's assistants, carried out a snap survey of newspaper, fruit, and vegetable vendors who hawk their goods to drivers at some of the city's major traffic junctions.

The core design of the project is the integration of the anthropological case studies with the cross-cutting, thematic studies. The thematic research was conducted by three scholars with disciplinary backgrounds in human geography (Katherine V. Gough), education studies (Ulla Ambrosius Madsen), and media research (Norbert Wildermuth). Conducting field research for one month in each city, they used parallel approaches in examining aspects of housing, education, and media appropriation that were relevant to young people in the three cities. Tracing how ideas of and practices related to these three themes were expressed and interpreted in different ways by young people in the three cities, the thematic studies employed a multi-sited approach in the most literal sense. In each city, they drew on contacts established by the local collaborators and the anthropologist. Likewise, in each case data already collected by the anthropologist served as background information for the thematic optics. The strength of the cross-cutting studies, thus, lies in their efforts to focus narrowly on the particular topics and to develop them within theoretical frameworks informed by the scholars' respective research traditions.

Throughout the project, it was difficult to follow a common methodology based on parallel studies in and across the three cities. As we discuss below, this challenge compelled us to rethink and critically question key methodological principles in comparative and interdisciplinary work.

The Comparative Challenge

The Youth and the City project was designed with cross-class and cross-regional comparison in mind. It engaged with comparison from different perspectives: as implicit, in-built comparison, inherent in any social science research, and as explicit comparison, most clearly exemplified by the three thematic studies. This approach has raised fundamental methodological questions about the units of comparison and ultimately about the nature of the knowledge produced. In other words, what are we comparing, and what is the epistemological value of a comparative approach?

Sally Falk Moore recently made a plea for a comparative anthropology that does not, unlike much comparative work in the twentieth century, insist on synchronic societal ethnographies that merely describe details of variation and difference in an effort to develop a typology (2005, 2). Instead she argues for a time-conscious, processual approach to comparison in order to bring both context and cross-cutting themes into focus. Her strategy calls for a redefinition of the object of study, as well as attention to the passage of time (2005, 10). In a similar vein, Marit Melhuus reminds us of the importance of contexts rather than entities in cross-cultural comparison: "We are not comparing objects, names of things or essences, but meanings, ways of constructing relationships between objects, persons, situations, events. Because similarities or differences are not given in the things themselves but in the ways they are contextualized, i.e. in the relations of which they form a part, we must compare frameworks, processes of meaning construction, structures of discourses" (2002, 82). This observation implies that the comparative axis is a set of open analytical questions that are posed differently in each place, rather than predefined entities which may overshadow contextually significant variables. In other words, we were not just portraying the lives of young people in Brazil, Vietnam, and Zambia, but also comparing the structural conditions and processes of agency that contribute to shaping notions of youth and youth life in different parts of the world.

Comparison is inherent in any kind of cultural translation, but its levels and degrees of explicitness vary. Richard Fox and André Gingrich (2002) distinguish between three different dimensions of comparison. First, there is a basic dimension that is fundamental to human cognition and therefore relevant to scholars in all fields. Secondly, there is implicit comparison, which is particularly relevant to anthropologists and scholars in related fields who engage in cultural translation and therefore are constantly confronted with constructions of Otherness. This dimension is present in all kinds of fieldwork, including the single-sited, where particularities of certain places, phenomena, situations, and relations stand out in contrast to previous experiences, which we always carry with us in the field. Finally, the explicit, or epistemological, dimension of comparison is the specific interest in developing comparative inventories and in openly producing knowledge as a result of the comparative analysis (Fox and Gingrich 2002, 20–21). In engaging all three aspects of comparison, the Youth and the City project was particularly remarkable for its efforts to strengthen the dimension of epistemological comparison by making the implicit explicit. This was most obvious in the three thematic studies, in which the researchers crossed regional and national boundaries in person to pursue the same set of questions structured around the themes of housing, education, and media. The urban case studies, conducted independently by three different researchers, were concerned with explicit comparison in the search for comparable aspects for further analysis, such as the meaning of generation in a life-course perspective and as a structural category; the role of institutions in young people's lives and in the construction of youth; and processes of inclusion and exclusion in relation to urban youth (see Hansen, conclusion, this volume). To strengthen the comparative approach, we developed a methodology to help us reveal differences and similarities between the lives of young people in different parts of the world. Explicit cross-cultural comparison involves a fundamental problem in defining the units of comparison and, consequently, a need to stay critical and reflective throughout the study (Kuper 2002, 146). Acknowledging the centrality of context, each study had to be adjusted according to the political, economic, ethical, and practical circumstances framing the investigations in each of the three cities. In the following we briefly discuss how we dealt with the question of comparison in the different studies.

A key challenge in the three anthropological case studies was to develop a comparative framework across cities that did not tie us to rigid categories. The first step was to agree upon a definition of youth which was methodologically operational in all three places, but flexible enough to include the widely different nature of youth around the world. One option was to enter the field with a completely open mind and search for local definitions of youth as constructed in relation to class, gender, ethnicity, and other culturally variable factors. Well aware that this approach might prove too time-consuming and diffuse, we decided as a starting point to define youth as the age range from 12 to 25. This was partly for pragmatic reasons, and partly because this range covers what many policy documents term adolescence and youth. Even then, our aim was not to restrict youth to this age category, but rather to question its boundaries, which often become real when translated into policy terms, with consequences for young people's rights and restrictions. All our studies clearly show that notions of youth stretch far beyond these age limits, especially at the upper end, and that there is a range of simultaneously negotiated and contradictory definitions of youth.

Another challenge was to establish comparable categories for a cross-class analysis of urban youth within cities and across countries. We decided to identify three residential areas of different socioeconomic status in each city and use these as a basis for our household survey. This decision gave rise to a number of questions related to the comparative challenge. Firstly, what criteria could be used to link particular areas to particular social classes and subsequently to use them as a basis for cross-class comparison? Such selection criteria presuppose that there is an identifiable correspondence between geographically delimited urban areas and socioeconomic status. This was not necessarily the case everywhere, and we were therefore compelled to consider and analyze how systems of social stratification were contextually constructed and became visible in urban landscapes. Secondly, was it methodologically meaningful to make cross-cultural comparisons of residential areas if we took into account the highly different structural conditions, economic systems, and historical contexts of the three countries? Social class affiliation was differently expressed in the three cities and was based not on socioeconomic status alone, but also, for example, on political position, ethnicity, race, religious status, or educational achievement. Rather than treating class as an essentialized social category, it was constructive to think of it in terms of symbolic forms (Lawler 2005) and as a social construction bound to both economic resources and cultural practices (Liechty 2003, 4). With Melhuus's (2002) argument in mind, we conceptualized the residential areas as contexts within which class-based identities were produced. Thus, we compared residential areas not as isolated entities, but with regard to how they were imagined and realized as places of social interaction through social relations in different contexts (Amit

Figure 2.2. The research team visiting a low-income area in Recife, 2002.
Photo: Karen Tranberg Hansen

2002, 18). We brought into focus the subjective dimension by asking what mean-ing people, especially young people, attributed to specific neighborhoods, and how, through social actions and relations, they contributed to the production of these meanings (Appadurai 1995).

A focus on globalization calls for a comparative perspective because global connections provide a frame of comparable conditions to which people relate and react, sometimes in converging ways, at other times in diverging ones (Fox and Gingrich 2002, 6–7). Illustrating how global processes become localized through social practice (Shore and Wright 1997, 13), the multi-sited approach of the three thematic studies provided a unique way of exploring how young people interpret and respond to various global flows. This was particularly pro-nounced in the studies of education by Ulla Ambrosius Madsen and of young people's media appropriation by Norbert Wildermuth. Madsen's contribution represents a critical corrective to the field of comparative education and its con-cern for comparing national education systems. In line with the work of Kathryn Anderson-Levitt (2003), Madsen demonstrates how global standardizations within the field of education are leading to a similarity of educational structures, systems, and curricula. Shifting the focus from systems to culturally and socially located classrooms inhabited by students, she also sheds light on young people's own experiences of education as these are influenced by globalizing forces, national ideologies, and local practices. In contrast to formal education, which provides a highly institutionalized arena for the circulation of global ideologies and discourses, media represents an area that is often associated with a global, media-driven youth culture. It is less institutionalized and centers around music, movie and sports stars, particular consumer goods and lifestyles, and specific new media technologies. In Wildermuth's study, these prevailing assumptions about a global, media-driven youth culture provide the axis for the comparison he makes between young people's different forms of media appropriation in the three cities. Katherine V. Gough's study of the meaning of home diverges from that of Madsen and Wildermuth because global connections between local practices of "home-making" are much less visible than in the cases of education and media. Although housing strategies are undoubtedly affected by certain global trends, such as increasing privatization and marketization, the home stands out as a place of local anchoring and belonging that make such connections less discernible. A key question arising from this was how young people construct and attribute different meanings to home in a globalized world.

The Interdisciplinary Aspect:
Working and Writing across Disciplines

The Youth and the City project was interdisciplinary, but also strongly informed by the approaches of each participating discipline. As individual researchers, we are positioned in different academic professions, which all have research histories of their own. However, since the academic fields of youth studies and urban studies are both characterized by a high degree of interdisciplinarity, we have specifically sought the mutual inspiration that can come from interdisciplinary collaboration. But what do we mean by interdisciplinarity? For a definition, we propose that an effective interdisciplinary approach involves not only a common thematic framework, but also a theoretical and methodological sharing across disciplines. This makes it distinct from a multi-disciplinary approach. Whereas multi-disciplinarity refers to research in which each discipline works in a self-contained manner, interdisciplinarity implies the integration of disciplines, so that issues are approached from a range of disciplinary perspectives (Bruce et al. 2004). However, only those parts of the theoretical models of the disciplines involved that are compatible with one another are integrated (Ramadier 2004). Interdisciplinarity is therefore not an effort to reach beyond disciplines (trans-disciplinarity), but to identify and develop discussions between disciplines, each of which has its distinct tradition, concepts, and values. These are, of course, all somewhat artificial distinctions. We probably all know moments of synthesis in thought across disciplines, which are subject to the same paradigmatic waves.

It is therefore hard to think of any discipline which has not been inspired by or entered into dialogue with other research traditions. Nonetheless, in the present discussion of questions of collaboration and its results, it may be fruitful to keep the distinction between types of teamwork in mind.

Coming from four different, yet related, disciplines, we have approached the two central themes of the project differently, identified different objects of study, raised different questions, and applied different concepts. Urban studies in anthropology and geography frequently have the city as their focus, while in education and media the city is generally perceived as the context or backdrop for young people's cultural practices and learning processes. In education and media studies youth is a privileged subject, especially in the latter, where many discussions of youth culture have developed as part of, or at least in relation to, cultural studies. In anthropology the study of "youth culture" has been marginalized and has somehow never really gained status (Amit 2001), though studies of young people's position and agency in the wider society are manifold. This is partly due to the overlapping but growing body of childhood studies, which focus on children's agency and the socially and culturally constructed character of childhood (Stephens 1995; James, Jenks, and Prout 1998). Geography has contributed to the field of youth studies through its increasing interest in the relationship between youth, spatiality, and place-making (Skelton and Valentine 1998). Given the considerable overlap between the disciplines, no single discipline can colonize either youth or the city. Indeed, our disciplinary approaches and understandings of the subjects do differ. When we look more closely into these differences, they seem to relate not only to choice of object, but also to differences in epistemology.

In general, all our research is inspired by ethnographic methods. We have all conducted qualitative interviews and, to various degrees, participant observation. But we have used our data differently according to our different epistemological concerns. The role of the researcher in data collection and the validity of data are issues that gradually showed themselves to be, if not contested, then differently perceived. This became evident, for instance, when Wildermuth and Dalsgaard co-authored an article on youth and media use in Recife (2006). Where Dalsgaard sought validity in the contextualization and interpretation of informants' words, Wildermuth found evidence in the identification of recurring patterns of explanation and justification in young people's speech. Likewise, a discussion about the use of theory recurred several times in the research period, and again in the process of writing this book. During the research period, the three anthropologists worked with a more implicit theoretical outline than did Madsen and Wildermuth, who both advocated a strong, explicit theoretical framework. In the writing process, we had to reckon with these differences in epistemology and writing style, and while in co-authored articles we found compromises, we have chosen to let the differences remain in the individual texts of the present volume.

Academic disciplines have sometimes been characterized as "tribes" or "territories" (Becher and Trowler 2001), that is, bounded entities with essentialized characteristics or natures. Against such a view it can be argued, first, that rather than being essentially different, academic disciplines are the results of specific historical productions of knowledge (Messer-Davidow 1992, 679) and, on the local level, of institutional tradition and boundary setting. Secondly, it may be right, as Arabella Lyon suggests, that other metaphors than "tribes" or "territories" are more appropriate for the history of academia and more helpful to present-day practice. Lyon proposes that we look at disciplines as rivers or currents, thus giving up the emphasis on definite boundaries and focusing more on the "potentially oceanic outcome" (Lyon 1992, 682). The Youth and the City project demonstrates the relevance of both perspectives, as we have had to acknowledge our distinct disciplinary profiles, as well as the benefit we all gain by allowing them to meet.

How do we measure the success of our endeavor? In their contribution to an online discussion on interdisciplinarity, Veronica Boix Mansilla and Howard Gardener (2003) address the lack of available criteria with which to assess interdisciplinary work on its own terms. In interviews with sixty researchers working in interdisciplinary institutes within the natural sciences, they found that researchers relied more on indirect quality indicators (e.g., number of patents and publications, or type of journals and funding agencies associated with the work) than on the epistemic dimensions of interdisciplinary work (e.g., explanatory power, aesthetic appeal, comprehensiveness). These epistemic dimensions, they argue, are difficult to measure, as they are often indiscernible in the final research results. In a recent article, Marilyn Strathern argues that the same is true of information-sharing. The quality of "information-sharing is invisible precisely because it is part of the ordinary nexus of interactions among collaborators, instrumental to their purposes, not expressive of them" (Strathern 2005, 84). The only evidence of integration of viewpoints and information-sharing lies in the testimony of those involved. Readers need to be told how, when, and to what degree such sharing has taken place (2005, 85).

Interdisciplinarity may have become a sort of buzzword in academic circles (Quayson 1998), and perhaps also a word with too many meanings to mean anything specific. Despite the contested status of this term, and the fact that the results of our endeavors might just as well be called multi-disciplinary, we insist on describing the Youth and the City project as an interdisciplinary research enterprise. In doing so, we emphasize the process and the striving toward a shared methodology, a common vocabulary, and linkages between the understandings of different aspects of young people's lives. The fact that this striving has not led to coherence and synthesis is not a failure, but a potential result of any interdisciplinary project. We find that in engaging with others a process of objectification (of one's own approach) and reflection is speeded up, which may very well lead to a strengthening of the disciplinary perspective. The immeasurable but nevertheless real gain in interdisciplinarity may thus occur both on the empirical level (information-sharing) and on the epistemological level (the objectification of perspectives).

Cross-National Collaboration

The Youth and the City project was designed to provide feedback in response to the political demands of DANIDA, which—as part of its development strategy, Partnership 2000—is calling for cross-national collaboration in knowledge production and local capacity-building as an instrument of poverty reduction (Denmark, Ministry of Foreign Affairs 2000, 26). In practical terms, this implies that all research projects should be linked with local research institutions, and that they should contribute to research capacity–building by including scholars from the partner countries. In all three cities, we worked within local institutional frameworks and were to different degrees and in different ways dependent on them. The forms of collaboration varied, depending upon the specific history and profile of local research traditions, local expectations of the role of academia, and the demands for applicability and relevance in the different countries.

In Recife, our institutional contact was the Federal University of Pernambuco. In Brazil intellectuals have played a significant role in the development of the present democratic society. Neither of our two principal colleagues in Recife, Russell Parry Scott and Mónica Franch, are Brazilian nationals, but they have lived in Brazil for many years and have been raised within an academic system imbued by feelings of social engagement and responsibility to Brazilian society. In our discussions with Scott and Franch, we experienced this backdrop as an urge to be constructive in analytical conclusions and "not leave people without hope," as Franch expressed it.

In Hanoi, we collaborated with the Institute of Sociology in the National Centre for Humanities and Social Sciences under the guidance of a senior collaborator, Dang Nguyen Anh, a sociologist educated in the United States. Institutionally, however, academia in Vietnam has been shaped by the strong influence of the former Eastern Bloc. This is reflected in the organization of the educational system and in the fact that many older and middle-aged researchers were trained in former Eastern Bloc countries. The research assistants, who were primarily trained in quantitative research methodologies, felt confident in developing surveys and conducting structured interviews, but they remained skeptical of the ethnographic quest to become part of everyday life through participant observation.

Our institutional counterpart in Lusaka was the Institute for Economic and Social Research (INESOR), a multi-disciplinary research wing of the University of Zambia. Our local counterpart was Chileshe L. Mulenga, a geographer and urban planner who undertook his postgraduate training in the United Kingdom. INE-SOR is the successor of the Rhodes-Livingstone Institute, one of the preeminent research institutions for the promotion of urban research by anthropologists in Africa. Social research in Zambia focuses on Zambian society, but local priorities have for years been subordinate to priorities set by the agendas of international funding organizations.

In all three cities, we sought to contribute to research capacity–building by involving young scholars as assistants. In Lusaka we were assisted by several young women and men, some of whom were recent graduates of the University of Zambia while others were completing their first degree. In Recife and Hanoi we supported, in total, six masters' students, who were invited to conduct "mini-ethnographies" on specific themes. The involvement of the young assistants and students differed in the three cities. For some it was an opportunity to develop their skills, especially in relation to research methodologies, while for others the most attractive aspect of the work was the opportunity to become part of a wider network of scholars. The project as a whole benefited from the involvement of its young research assistants, partly because they could easily establish a rapport with other young people, but also because in many ways their own experiences embodied some of the youth dilemmas we identify in this book.

Cross-national collaboration was also embodied in a series of four research seminars, the first in Lusaka in July 2001, the second in Recife in March 2002, the third in Hanoi in March 2004, and the final, concluding one in Copenhagen in March 2005. The entire research team, including senior and some junior collaborators from each country, participated in the seminars. The aim of these was to strengthen team members' dialogue across national and institutional boundaries; to provide a forum for disseminating preliminary research findings to national-level scholars and policy-makers; and, finally, to "open the field" for each other in order to develop the comparative dimension of the project.

The demand for cross-national collaboration is closely related to the institutional foundation of the project, that is, its source of funding and its politically motivated interest in contributing to social change in a world of profound structural inequalities. It represents a laudable effort to retrieve and counter the historically grounded imbalances that characterize development work and research, although this is not an easy task. The danger of just masking such inequalities and reproducing imperialist discourses about a Southern "other" through a rhetoric of "participation" and "collaboration" still persists. The quest to engage local expertise in development-related research indirectly responds to and parallels two major academic debates: first, the postcolonial critique of

Figure 2.3. Research seminar in Hanoi, 2004. *Photo: Karen Valentin*

the "othering" of research subjects; and second, the demand for a participatory approach, which has both analytical and methodological implications. In the remaining part of the chapter, we elaborate on these debates with specific reference to our project.

The postcolonial critique has shed light on the inherent power relations in and challenges of interchanges between the Western researcher and the "native." In an era in which increasing numbers of people from countries outside Europe and North America are entering academia, and anthropology in particular, this critique is even more relevant, as it concerns not only relationships with research subjects but also the way in which "we," as Euro-American researchers, encounter and interact with our academic colleagues from the South (Gupta and Ferguson 1997, 16). In many ways, this project has contributed to making the unequal relationship visible, but in doing so it has also forced us to question our own positions and consequently to rethink the potential of cross-national collaboration.

The project has raised important questions about the presumed legitimacy of a "native voice" as a guarantee of better local knowledge. After all, who is the native (Narayan 1993)? The composition of the entire research team, including both Danish and non-Danish collaborators, ironically illustrates the difficulties involved in maintaining a dichotomy between "insiders" and "outsiders,"

Figure 2.4. Dr. Chileshe Mulenga, from Zambia, with research assistant
Mr. Phi Hai Nam and interpreter Ms. Nguyen Chung Thuy. Hanoi, 2004.
Photo: Karen Tranberg Hansen

because the boundaries of the field are fluid. As graduates of universities in,
respectively, the United States and the United Kingdom, our Vietnamese and
Zambian counterparts were trained within a Euro-American tradition. Our
"Brazilian" collaborators are citizens of the United States and Spain. Similarly, the
"Danish" research team includes a Briton, a German, and a Danish American.
We are differently linked to the people and places we study, not least through
differing colonial pasts and contemporary political and economic relations. As
Kirin Narayan (1993, 678) has pointed out, rather than trying to define who is
native and who is not, it is more productive to look at ways in which different
scholars are situated in relation to the people they study.

The demand to include local expertise is also closely related to the increased
attention being paid to participatory approaches and to the demand that scientific
work be applicable and relevant. This is partly a way of countering the Western
bias and the colonization of knowledge, which the postcolonial critique has reminded us of, but it is also a way of taking seriously the fact that the social and
economic inequalities of today's world call for social action. The participatory

approach is largely derived from the field of planned development, and represents an attempt to counter the power imbalances inherent in the top-down models that have tended to dominate development programs. As a development approach, participation is thought of as an empowering process, which ideally enables local people to take control of the development process through self-help and self-sufficiency (Chambers 1995). Participatory approaches, thus, have been developed as a way to give voice to marginalized, socially muted groups. The methodological implication of this is the use of a wide range of participatory techniques, which implies in its turn that the "local people" are actively involved in, and throughout, all phases of development projects. The participatory approach has also had an impact on academically informed development research, reflected in the quest for knowledge-sharing and joint partnership in the research process. This in itself is a praiseworthy ambition, but, as has been observed in many development programs, institutional procedures may work counter to this (Nelson and Wright 1995). One crucial aspect which can easily conflict with the ideal of participation is the "project economy," that is, the forms of capital, investments, and competing agendas that are at stake for the differently positioned social actors in any particular project.

Funding is the most obvious prerequisite for the implementation and completion of a comprehensive research project like Youth and the City. Money was a central asset to the economy of this particular project. On the one hand, the fact that it was the Danish research team who provided the money and was responsible for its use gave us, the Danish research team, a privileged position in relation to our collaborators. On the other hand, these privileges were also contested, for example in the case of Hanoi, where using political power to deny us access to certain institutions and groups of young people turned out to be an effective way of questioning our positions. Similarly, in Recife, our privileged economic position was outweighed by a strong academic self-consciousness among our colleagues. This raised fundamental questions in all three places about the assumed "expert role": who is the expert on whom and on what?

It is inevitable that the conditions for conducting research in a European welfare state like Denmark differ from those in all three countries represented in this project. In Vietnam and Zambia especially, state-sector salaries are extremely low and force many academics to take contract work in private, and possibly foreign-funded, consultancies in order to earn a supplementary income. We linked up with public research institutions, but we sought to balance the salaries we paid our collaborators between the low rates of pay in the state sector and the often extraordinarily high salaries of the foreign-funded consultancies. To varying degrees, our collaborators were engaged in other research and consultancy work during the project period and could not invest all their time in this project.

Especially for our Vietnamese and Zambian colleagues, this limited the time they could spend collecting and writing up project data. This also explains why the chapter on youth in Recife (see Dalsgaard, Franch, and Scott, this volume) is the only co-authored city case study in the book.

Standards for scientifically valid and politically acceptable research are determined far away from the encounter between Northern and Southern members of the research team, that is, in government circles, funding organizations, and academic journals and auditoriums. Involvement in joint research will always be conditioned by these standards and will therefore restrict the outcome of that research. The basic conditions of our project, including the overall theme of urbanization, were set from the beginning, and that a good part of the project had already been formulated when we encountered our colleagues from Brazil, Vietnam, and Zambia was a precondition for, but also a constant challenge to, the collaboration.

Conclusion

This book is the outcome of a comprehensive, and in many ways ambitious, research project. We have dealt with three methodological core issues here—comparison, interdisciplinarity, and cross-national collaboration—in our efforts to present and discuss some of the challenges we have faced as the project has progressed. Although we have discussed the three themes separately, analytically they are closely interrelated. The methodological framework of the project links the comparative and the cross-national dimensions through our focus on the notion of global youth and through our comparison of young lives across national boundaries. Given the institutional foundation and the development-related agenda of the project, cross-national collaboration is an implication of the multi-sited research methodology inherent in the comparative approach. Similarly, interdisciplinarity also implies a comparative dimension in the concern for sharing and discussing data and results across disciplines, compelling the individual researcher to develop a sense of his or her own disciplinary self and consequently the selves of the disciplinary Others. In other words, although genuine interdisciplinary work strives toward the dissolution of disciplinary boundaries, it demands that we confront constructions of disciplinary Otherness. Finally, questions about disciplinarity and interdisciplinarity are further challenged in a context of cross-national collaboration and shed light both on the relationship between different research traditions and on the historical and national contexts in which they are produced.

Beginning with the same set of methodological and analytical premises, we have gone in different directions in our attempts to elucidate how the lives of young people in Recife, Hanoi, and Lusaka are shaped by and respond to the urban experience in an era of increasing globalization. The chapters presented here are the outcomes of varying political and economic circumstances and practical possibilities, as well as of our individual epistemological and disciplinary approaches. They teach us about young people in three cities and about the structural conditions under which contemporary youth grow up. The broad methodological framework has opened up an array of possible ways to approach urban youth: by unraveling the research process and key methodological questions, as we have done here, we are also reminded that knowledge is always situated. As Richard Shweder states, "we can never be everywhere at once (even in a global mind), any more than we can be nowhere in particular" (1991, 18–19). It is by joining our partial views that we may arrive at a larger vision, and it is in comparing differing social research environments that we are forced to acknowledge the social conditions of knowledge production.

Reminded by the work of our collaborators in Brazil, Vietnam, and Zambia that social research belongs to society and that it has implications for our perception of and action in the world, we find our research design particularly helpful. Without the frustrating moments of partial views that could never become a whole, we might have forgotten that holism is not an ontological aspect of the world but an instrument of social analysis. Facts are consequences of scientific work rather than its causes (Rapport and Overing 2000, 330), and the search for holisms in social science has allowed the production of a wealth of impersonal social facts, one of which is certainly "youth." Political and scientific notions of youth influence the way young people perceive themselves and their opportunities in life (see Dalsgaard, Franch, and Scott, this volume). It is therefore important to bear in mind the plurality of perspectives and the multiple truths about youth (and other issues with potential public-policy implications) when we, as scholars and academics, are confronted with the growing demand for usable social analysis. It may help us to remember the inherent provisionality of understanding (Mansilla and Gardner 2003), as well as keep us alert to the tenacity of established academic and political doctrines.

Acknowledgments

This chapter has been inspired by the numerous methodological discussions which the research team has conducted throughout the project period. We are grateful to the team members for their valuable contributions. We also thank Lotte Meinert for constructive comments. Any shortcomings are ours.

References

Amit, Vered. 2001. The Study of Youth Culture: Why It's Marginal but Doesn't Need to Be So. *EUROPAEA: Journal of the Europeanists* 7(1–2):145–54.

———. 2002. Reconceptualizing Community. In *Realizing Community: Concepts, Social Relationships and Sentiments,* ed. Vered Amit, 1–20. London and New York: Routledge.

Anderson-Levitt, Kathryn M. 2003. A World Culture of Schooling? In *Local Meanings, Global Schooling: Anthropology and World Culture Theory,* ed. Kathryn M. Anderson-Levitt, 1–26. New York: Palgrave Macmillan.

Appadurai, Arjun. 1995. The Production of Locality. In *Counterworks: Managing the Diversity of Knowledge,* ed. Richard Fardon, 204–25. London and New York: Routledge.

Becher, Tony, and Paul R. Trowler. 2001 [1989]. *Academic Tribes and Territories: Intellectual Enquiry and the Cultures of Disciplines.* Buckingham, England: Society for Research into Higher Education and Open University Press.

Bruce, Ann, Catherine Lyall, Joyce Tait, and Robin Williams. 2004. Interdisciplinary Integration in Europe: The Case of the Fifth Framework Programme. *Futures* 36(4):423–39.

Chambers, Richard. 1995. Paradigm Shifts and the Practice of Participatory Research and Development. In *Power and Participatory Development: Theory and Practice,* ed. Nici Nelson and Susan Wright, 30–42. London: Intermediate Technology Publications.

Dalsgaard, Anne Line. 2004. *Matters of Life and Longing: Female Sterilisation in Northeast Brazil.* Copenhagen: Museum Tusculanum Press.

Denmark. Ministry of Foreign Affairs. 2000. *Danmarks udviklingspolitik: Partnerskab 2000.* Danish International Development Agency.

———. 2005. *Children and Young People in Danish Development Cooperation: Guidelines.* Danish International Development Agency.

Fox, Richard, and André Gingrich. 2002. Introduction to *Anthropology, by Comparison,* by André Gingrich and Richard Fox, 1–24. London and New York: Routledge.

Franch, Mónica. 2000. Tardes ao léu: Um ensaio etnográfico sobre o tempo livre entre jovens de periferia. Master's thesis, Universidade Federal de Pernambuco, Recife.

Gammeltoft, Tine. 1999. *Women's Bodies, Women's Worries: Health and Family Planning in a Vietnamese Rural Community.* Richmond, England: Curzon.

Gupta, Akhil, and James Ferguson. 1997. Discipline and Practice: "The Field" as Site, Method, and Location in Anthropology. In *Anthropological Locations: Boundaries and Grounds of a Field Science,* ed. Akhil Gupta and James Ferguson, 1–46. Berkeley: University of California Press.

James, Allison, Chris Jenks, and Alan Prout. 1998. *Theorizing Childhood.* Cambridge: Polity.

Kuper, Adam. 2002. Comparison and Contextualization: Reflections on South Africa. In *Anthropology, by Comparison,* ed. André Gingrich and Richard Fox, 143–66. London and New York: Routledge.

Lawler, Stephanie. 2005. Introduction: Class, Culture and Identity. *Sociology* 39(5):797–806.

Liechty, Mark. 2003. *Suitably Modern: Making Middle-Class Culture in a New Consumer Society.* Princeton, N.J.: Princeton University Press.

Lyon, Arabella. 1992. Interdisciplinarity: Giving Up Territory. *College English* 54(6):681–93.

Mansilla, Veronica Boix, and Howard Gardener. 2003. Assessing Interdisciplinary Work at the Frontier: An Empirical Exploration of "Symptoms of Quality." http://www.interdisciplines .org/interdisciplinarity/papers/6. Accessed February 23, 2006.

Marcus, George E. 1995. Ethnography in/of the World System: The Emergence of Multi-sited Ethnography. *Annual Review of Anthropology* 24:95–117.

Marr, David G. 1996. Vietnamese Youth in the 1990s. Australian-Vietnam Research Project, Working Paper no. 3. Sydney, Australia: School of Economic and Financial Studies, Macquarie University.

Melhuus, Marit. 2002. Issues of Relevance: Anthropology and the Challenges of Cross-Cultural Comparison. In *Anthropology, by Comparison,* ed. André Gingrich and Richard Fox, 70–91. London and New York: Routledge.

Messer-Davidow, Ellen. 1992. Review of *Academic Tribes and Territories: Intellectual Enquiry and the Cultures of Disciplines,* by Tony Becher and Paul R. Trowler. *Signs* 17(3):676–88.

Moore, Sally Falk. 2005. Comparisons: Possible and Impossible. *Annual Review of Anthropology* 34:1–11.

Narayan, Kirin. 1993. How Native Is a "Native" Anthropologist? *American Anthropologist* 95:671–86.

Nelson, Nici, and Susan Wright. 1995. Participation and Power. In *Power and Participatory Development: Theory and Practice,* ed. Nici Nelson and Susan Wright, 1–18. London: Intermediate Technology Publications.

Quayson, Ato. 1998. Means and Meanings: Methodological Issues in Africanist Interdisciplinary Research. *History in Africa* 25:307–18.

Ramadier, Thierry. 2004. Transdisciplinarity and Its Challenges: The Case of Urban Studies. *Futures* 36(4):423–39.

Rapport, Nigel, and Joanna Overing. 2000. *Social and Cultural Anthropology: The Key Concepts.* London: Routledge.

Shore, Cris, and Susan Wright. 1997. Policy: A New Field of Anthropology. In *Anthropology of Policy: Critical Perspectives on Governance and Power,* ed. Cris Shore and Susan Wright, 3–39. London and New York: Routledge.

Shweder, Richard A. 1991. *Thinking through Cultures: Expeditions in Cultural Psychology.* Cambridge, Mass.: Harvard University Press.

Skelton, Tracey, and Gill Valentine, eds. 1998. *Cool Places: Geographies of Youth Cultures.* London and New York: Routledge.

Stephens, Sharon. 1995. Children and the Politics of Culture in "Late Capitalism." Introduction to *Children and the Politics of Culture,* 3–48. Princeton, N.J.: Princeton University Press.

Strathern, Marilyn. 2005. Experiments in Interdisciplinarity. *Social Anthropology* 13(1):75–90.

Wildermuth, Norbert, and Anne Line Dalsgaard. 2006. Imagined Futures, Present Lives: Youth, Media and Modernity in the Changing Economy of Northeast Brazil. *Young: Nordic Journal of Youth Research* 14(1):9–31.

Part 2. Studying Youth in Cities

3

Dominant Ideas, Uncertain Lives: The Meaning of Youth in Recife

*Anne Line Dalsgaard, Mónica Franch, and
Russell Parry Scott*

Recife is a city with many faces. Like other Brazilian cities, it is often described as a junction of opposite worlds, a focus for social tension and suffering.[1] The city is known for its urban "wounds" (Susser and Schneider 2003), which arise from the huge developments in Brazilian society since the 1960s: social inequality, unemployment, and one of the highest rates of violent death among young men in Brazil. The contrast between skyscrapers and *favela* shacks draws the eye. The presence of street children next to billboards advertising expensive health insurance and elite private schools tells of huge differences in living conditions, and shopping centers full of well-dressed consumers offer visual signs of economic exclusion. Recurring campaigns in public space for condoms tell observers that Recife, like the rest of Brazil, is both subject to the AIDS pandemic and a pioneer in prevention,[2] at the same time as prostitutes frequent particular streets waiting for clients, many of them tourists in search of sun, sea, and sex. Yet the emphasis on contrasts hides central aspects of life in Recife: the many families who are neither rich nor miserable; the mixing of skyscrapers, old apartment blocks, villas, and *favelas* in the same residential areas; and a general struggle to conform to social norms and values informed by global policies and a consumer market much larger than the national. Segregation and integration both characterize life in Recife, and in their wishes for the future, people draw on differing social experiences as well as shared ideas.

This chapter focuses on the ways in which young people in Recife steer toward the future in a context of uncertainty, marked by social differences and the collapse of employment and other institutions that used to be landmarks on the way to social adulthood. Poor and rich alike perceive youth as a period of transition, but their resources and chances in life differ, as does their path toward that

49

Figure 3.1. The beach is for all. Recife, 2005. *Photo: Norbert Wildermuth*

which they identify as adulthood. Using ethnographic examples, we discuss the consequences of the lack of correspondence between dominant understandings of what is considered to be a "proper" transition and young people's own experiences. Arguing that ideas about life and individuality are embedded in specific social and material environments and hence are influenced by them, we combine data on young people's choices and trajectories with descriptions of the relevant material and social structures of the places in which they occur.

Initially, we describe the city, its history, and the places where we worked. Then we unfold local perceptions of youth, giving special attention to the importance of transition, and we explain why becoming an adult is not at all easy in modern Recife. Through brief portraits of three of our informants we argue that many young people from low-income neighborhoods do not move neatly from youth to adulthood, but instead often experience a frustrating "non-synchrony of roles" (Johnson-Hanks 2002). This lack of synchrony contrasts with a generic cultural script for middle-class youth's passage to adulthood. This contrast between non-synchrony and script is paralleled in the material and social environments in which young people live, but this does not imply that they simply conform to their situation without friction. As we demonstrate, some low-income young people expect more than what is possible for them, while those who are better off have to struggle hard to fit into the script. The idea of a "proper" transition dominates both groups' evaluations of their actual situations. We conclude that in Recife the dominant notion of youth as a clearly marked transitional stage is influenced by a middle-class lifestyle, and leaves little room for the uncertainty that encompasses young people's lives nowadays. This is true for youth of all social groups, but especially for young people from low-income groups who cannot achieve the expected transition and therefore are often cast by parents, authorities, and the media as problematic and at risk.

In our focus on transition as a notion belonging to the field (i.e., to young people themselves, their parents, and society in general) and not as an analytical term, we call for reflection upon the way we as youth researchers describe and analyze young people's lives. Taking into account the fact that both analytic and local categories of youth have consequences, we propose a plural and "non-synchronic" understanding of youth (following Johnson-Hanks), which accords much better with the actual practices of most young people in Recife.

Recife: A City between Past and Future

Recife is the capital of the state of Pernambuco, located in the Nordeste, one of Brazil's poorest regions. As in the rest of Brazil, everyday life in the Nordeste has changed over the last four decades. Structural changes in agricultural production have forced small farmers and rural workers to move to urban areas. Almost thirty million Brazilians (more than one-third of the population in 1970) migrated to the cities between 1960 and 1980 (Martine, Das Gupta, and Chen 1998, 198). These changes mean that an immense number of families have come to live in slum-like conditions in the cities. Industrialization and the service sector provided urban work opportunities not just for adult men but also for young people and women, who entered the labor market in huge numbers. These processes had effects on the consumption market. If the 1940s and 1950s were responsible for the formation of a consumer society in Brazil, the 1960s and 1970s were devoted to its consolidation. Credit policies designed to expand markets for the growing national industry further integrated the lower economic strata of the population into consumption patterns. Television spread rapidly after 1964, when the military regime invested in the telecommunications system; in 1979 Brazil had the fifth largest television audience in the world, and it continues to grow (Mattos 2000). In all this, the young became more significant actors in the market economy, as consumers but also as producers of many goods for the so-called "teenage market" (Ortiz 1988).

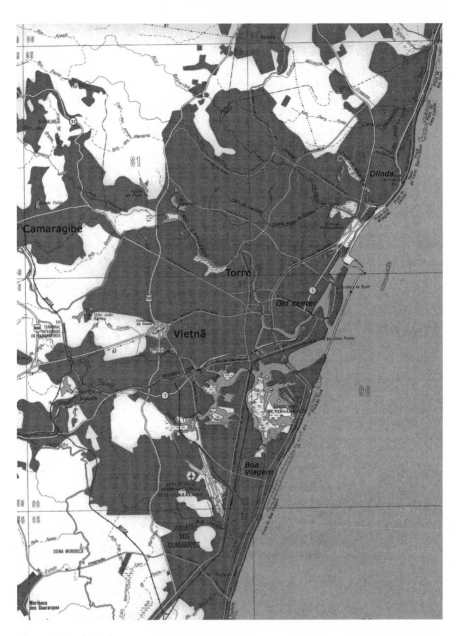

Map 1. Map of Recife

Brazil's foreign debt ranked as the largest in the developing world at the end of the military dictatorship in 1985 and throughout the 1980s, the so-called "lost decade," with its galloping inflation, economic stagnation, and, consequently, persistent growth in the number of families below the poverty line. In 1989, just one year after the promulgation of a new constitution that was intended to consolidate the welfare state in Brazil, structural adjustment programs (SAPs) and neoliberal reforms were implemented. As in other Latin American countries, these policies included liberalization of the economy, the privatization of national industries, and cuts in social expenditure in order to pay for servicing the debt (Franch, Camurça, and Batista 2003; Soares 1999). SAPs and neoliberal reforms, together with the high rate of inflation, led to a growth in social inequality in Brazil and a stratified citizenship despite promises of equal rights: on one level the new law gave all Brazilians the right to public education, health assistance, and other social benefits; on another level, however, because of a lack of public investment, these services were very precarious, and those who could afford to provided themselves with private health insurance and private schooling. Not before 1994 was the inflation rate brought under control with a successful financial plan (Plano Real) that introduced some optimism to the country. But even so, the poor performance of the Brazilian economy during the 1990s and the lack of public policies create distressing scenarios for those who intend to find a job and form a family in the 2000s, namely young people. As one of Brazil's poorest regions, economically stagnant and with a low degree of industrialization, the Nordeste suffers seriously from this development.

After many years of economic decline, Recife is now struggling to be a modern, global metropolis. Emblems of modernity are sought and embellished: the city proudly displays what is said to be the largest shopping mall in Brazil, boasts about its highly developed information technology (IT) and medical know-how, and shows off its new, ultra-modern international airport. Over a few years the landscape of the city has changed significantly, as has the geographic distribution of the different socioeconomic groups (Scott 1996). The old center of the city has lost its leading position as a place for the elite to live and it is today a business and commercial center mainly for low-income citizens. Better-off families inhabit new residential areas with high apartment blocks along the beach or on the banks of the Capibaribe River. Some live in lower-quality apartment blocks in less affluent areas, while others still occupy old villas (Gough and Franch 2005). Low-income areas in Recife, the so-called *bairros populares,* consist of houses of very mixed standards built on lots distributed by public or private owners, and although over the years some houses have reached a higher standard, others are still lagging behind. However, as a result of failing public housing policies, large sections of Recife have grown up without any formal planning, and 46.32 percent of the population are estimated to live in squatter settlements.[3] These *favelas* are spread all over the city, even in wealthier areas, and are often located either on reclaimed swampland or on steep hillsides, making them susceptible to flooding or landslides after heavy rains.

The Importance of Place

The choice of research sites for the present study embraced these differences in housing standards. We have worked in two low-income areas, Vietnã and Santa Barbara, and two areas with more expensive housing, Torre and Graças, located near the Capibaribe River. Vietnã is an old *favela* that was occupied in the late 1960s by rural migrants and families from other areas of Recife who had been displaced by urban planning. It is located seven kilometers from the center of Recife and is quite close to public services, such as a municipal market, schools, and hospitals. The other low-income research site, Santa Barbara, is situated in the municipality of Camaragibe, which, neighboring Recife, forms part of the so-called metropolitan area of the city. Santa Barbara is a *bairro popular* that was intended to receive the many newcomers to the capital during the intense flow of rural-urban migration in the 1970s. Included in the *bairro* is also a large and still growing *favela*, in which some of the young people we met lived.

The social contacts of better-off young people are not determined by their place of residence, and it is difficult to gain entry into middle-class homes. We therefore contacted better-off youth through two private schools in Torre and Graças. Most of the students whom we interviewed live in the high apartment blocks in these areas.

Everywhere we went, social life was influenced by the material environment. The structure of the street system influenced the routes people took from place to place, and distances between houses shaped distances between people. In Vietnã and Santa Barbara it is easy to shout from one house to another. Piles of rubbish, networks of muddy lanes between houses, houses that do not keep sounds and smells in or out, a fleeting sense of time (meaning that days have few fixed points), the movement of family members in and out: all these are manifestations of a fluidity in time and space that dominates life in Recife's low-income *bairros*. The young people we met here often moved between homes, living with grandparents, uncles, aunts, nephews and nieces, and other relatives in constant interaction. Most young people did not have their own room, but slept with other family members. Space and the social relationships thus established gave rise to a particular use of the streets.[4] Houses here are usually small and streets too narrow for cars, so the latter become an extension of the former: children play in the streets, while young people hang out, talking with friends and doing their work in home-based stores, repair shops, and other relatively informal economic

Figure 3.2. Urban crowding. Recife, 2002. *Photo: Katherine V. Gough*

undertakings. Their lives are embedded in "high-density social networks" (Bott 1968), in which they make friends, encounter relatives, and spend much of their working and leisure time.

The fluidity and density of life in Vietnã and Santa Barbara distinguish these neighborhoods from the structured, safely guarded, and socially divided environments of the better-off areas in which we worked. The young people we met here live in small families. They usually have a room of their own, and the family normally employs a maid on a regular basis. For middle-class residents, the street is a space of threatening social contacts. Servants, workers, and those who try to make a living in the public space (mainly sellers and beggars) walk the unkempt sidewalks, while members of wealthy families prefer to go about by car. Better-off young people rarely hang out in the streets. On the one hand, they are afraid of violence and prefer their comfortable houses, which offer Internet access and all kinds of facilities; on the other hand, the street does not offer significant opportunities for them to accumulate social capital. Streets are made for cars, and little room is left for people. In wealthier areas, the increase in apartment buildings means that the streets are bordered by high walls and security fences, with fewer and fewer small shops, bars, or other businesses—the neighborhood becomes a "city of walls" like São Paulo (Caldeira 2000). Here the social relations of the young form "low-density social networks" (Bott 1968), through which they usually meet their friends at school and in other formal settings, such as language schools and, later, universities. Friends and relatives live all over the city, and where one lives has little effect on the creation of social contacts.

The Multiple Meanings of Juventude

The different environments and possibilities for young people in Recife resonated with the different meanings of youth that we found, but so also did a dominant reference framework constituted by the law. Youth is a popular subject nowadays in Brazil, including in Recife. Local journals publish news about youth topics almost every week. Academic debates are held, cultural events celebrated, networks and institutions created, and, last but not least, policies on youth implemented. When we asked directly for a definition of *juventude,* young people and parents from all groups defined it as an age category, from around 15 or 18 to 25 years of age. The lower and upper limits were not always precise and changed from person to person, yet they were close to the chronological definitions employed by international organizations such as UNESCO and WHO. The Brazilian National Policy of Youth, implemented in 2005, defines the period of youth as from 15 to 25. This new policy exemplifies what has been evident throughout history: the significance of age as a landmark is a result of the establishment of modern states and their need to identify target groups and different spheres of action (Ariès 1965; Debert 1999). In Brazil this need has become increasingly vital in relation to youth, as the demographic statistics are showing a "youth bulge" (*onda jovem*). In 2000 there were 34.1 million Brazilians between 15 and 24 years of age, which is 20.1 percent of the total population, one of the highest proportions in Brazilian demographic history. The "youth bulge" has social, economic, and cultural significance, and has turned political and judicial attention toward this age group.

Legally, youth have obtained certain rights as responsible actors before the law. While the former civil code defined the age of legal majority as 21, anyone who is 18 years of age or above is an adult according to the new civil code, implemented in 2002, and is legally responsible for his or her own actions. Brazilian citizens can vote when they are 16, and voting becomes compulsory at the age of 18. Simultaneously, people under 19 are protected by a specific law, created in 1989 as a result of the mobilization of civil society and international agencies: the Statute of Children and Adolescents (ECA). The ECA declares that all children (0–11)

Figure 3.3. Street scene. Recife, 2002. *Photo: Katherine V. Gough*

and adolescents (12–18) have full rights and deserve special protection because they are still developing, and that those under 16 are not allowed to work without special permission. The new, stricter distinction between youth as productive and responsible and children as vulnerable and belonging to the sphere of re-production (home and school) is not an isolated Brazilian phenomenon. Global discourses on children's rights as promulgated by UNICEF, ILO, and especially the United Nations Convention on the Rights of the Child (UNCRC) (1989), which Brazil has ratified, have influenced policies regarding children and young people almost everywhere in the developing world.

People's ideas about youth are informed by these legal definitions, as well as by the growing participation of the young in public spheres in Brazilian society, especially in consumption. When we asked young people and their parents more specifically about what it means to be *jovem* (young), it became clear that youth is not just a matter of age—the term *juventude* was repeatedly used to identify a specific set of attitudes and behavior. A playful, open, and unworried attitude to life seemed to be a crucial attribute for a person to be classified as *jovem*. But while *responsabilidade* (responsibility) is related to adulthood, *juventude* in itself is also seen as a step toward *responsabilidade*. The nature of responsibility changes according to the social position of the person concerned: being responsible is different when you are single or married, with or without children, going to school or to university. Among the middle classes, young people have *responsabilidade* when studying, which is the main expectation that adults have of them. Entering university is often a milestone in the transition between adolescence and youth, as university education (unlike compulsory schooling) is perceived as involving a commitment to an individual, self-chosen future. This idea of an individual project is very clear in the words of Carol, a journalism student in a private university in Recife: "The school is based on the idea that you have to study in order to pass—your parents expect it of you—but you just want to live, to enjoy life, play, whatever your age may be. But here [at the university] you are aware of it being for you, you do it for your own life . . . for your parents, too, but it is more . . . first of all it is investment." Middle-class youth use the word "independence" very often to define adulthood, which they imagine to be totally autonomous: adults are free to make their own decisions, work and earn their own money, and have their own place to live. Family is important, and some say that getting married and having children are landmarks of adulthood. But it is not enough to have a family. As Pedro, a middle-class boy living in a two-floor apartment in the neighborhood of Torre, said to us, "There are fifteen-year-old girls who have children, but that does not mean that they are adults. It is one child caring for another."

For low-income young people, *responsabilidade* also includes studying or, as many drop out of school very early, other activities that may help in the future: traineeships, vocational training courses, jobs. Nevertheless, the relationship between responsibility, family (especially parenthood), and adulthood is stronger for them than for economically better off young people. Being an adult means having *responsabilidade* for a family, either taking care of it (a girl's responsibility) or providing for it (a boy's responsibility)—or at least trying to. Although most young people want some degree of autonomy in their lives, independence is not considered a condition of adulthood. Thus Tomás, 25, considered himself an adult because he took care of his son and wife, despite the fact that he was unemployed and lived on his brother's earnings. Rubem, Tomas's brother, was single and 24 years old when we talked to him and he considered himself a young person with "an adult side": the fact that he supported his brother's family did not, in itself, turn him into an adult. Having time for leisure activities is one of the most important attributes of young people in this context. This is especially the case for young men, who do not have any family restrictions on going out and thus often stay in the streets playing cards or dominoes or just "doing nothing."

Becoming an adult is expected to unfold in chronological stages, from adolescence through youth to adulthood, but these stages may not unfold properly. For instance, a mother of seven children in Santa Barbara could say, "We have that thing now that *jovens* at the age of 30–31 just want to be *boyzinhos* [little playboys]. There are others who at the age of 19–20 have the mentality of an adult. [. . .] Very few. There are more of the others. Nobody takes responsibility for anything." The existence of people "out of categories," like *boyzinhos,* indicates that something has gone wrong in the passage to adulthood. People would speak of the deviation in terms of taking or not taking responsibility, but a closer look into the structural conditions that youth had to respond to indicates that traditional attributes of adulthood, like education, work, and economic independence, are restricted capital in Recife.

Education, Work, and the Fear of Being Left Behind

Youth in Brazil are living in a period of social crises (Singer 2005) that primarily affects their entry into the labor market. The economy has not grown quickly enough to create work opportunities for those who are part of the "youth bulge" of the 1990s and 2000s. Besides, the entry of the Brazilian economy into the global market and the application of SAPs and neoliberal reforms have caused changes in the labor market that especially affect those trying to obtain their first job. As Silva and Kassouf (2002) have noted, age, more than sex or race, is the single most decisive disadvantageous factor in finding a job. Young people have the highest rates of unemployment (18 percent in 2001 compared to 9.4 percent for the total population[5]), and those from low-income families are particularly disadvantaged. It is difficult for them to find a job, and when they do succeed, the work they find is often extremely badly paid. Young women may work in private homes, where they are expected to work every day until late and sleep there overnight, often without having a room of their own. Young men usually obtain only physically demanding jobs or temporary employment in the construction industry, as office boys, or in private shops. As Oliveira (2000, 9) writes, young poor people enter the labor market to be "strong arms" and "agile legs."

The investment in social and cultural capital represented by ongoing schooling diminishes the rate of unemployment for middle-class young people, even though they too are anxious to find employment. Their parents' economic investment in their education and the longer time they spend as dependents living with their parents also ease their difficulties, yet their fear of competition from other young people and their desire for consumer products leads many to enter the disadvantageous labor market. Several program agencies organize traineeships particularly for young people, which provide experience and a temporary income. In her research on traineeships in Recife, Madiana Rodrigues (2002) found that, rather than being a real step toward future employment, vocational training courses attract young people because of the decline of jobs in the formal labor market. In several cases she found that trainees did routine work, serving mainly as cheap labor without rights legally guaranteed to workers. But as prospects for proper employment are few, traineeships are generally in demand.

Formal education is considered to be crucial for future employment, but only 42 percent of Brazilians between 15 and 24 years of age reach middle school (IBGE 2005). Still, there is no doubt that there has been an increase in schooling, in terms of both numbers of students and years of school attendance, and a change in attitudes toward formal education over the last twenty years. All social groups have positive attitudes toward education at the same time as there are official discourses stressing the importance of education for social mobility. Most families have only two or three children, all of whom are expected to go to school. But expectations vary: middle-class young people are expected to go to university, but in general the goal of those of low-income backgrounds is merely to finish secondary school. These attitudes are reflected in practice: in the age group from 15 to 17, 70.6 percent of the poorest and 93.3 percent of the richest section of Recife's population go to school (IBGE 2005). This difference in school attendance between social classes increases with age. Better-off families send their children to good private schools, where they are prepared to enter university. Poorer families' children study at public schools, which are often not good enough to keep up the students' interest. Teachers are inadequately educated and poorly paid, and many pupils repeat classes several times and eventually drop out, as Ulla Ambrosius Madsen shows in her chapter in this volume.

In addition to wanting a basic education, Brazilians increasingly want to be qualified for the competitive labor market. Some demands are common to all social groups, such as for courses in IT and foreign languages, especially English. Other demands are more differentiated. Middle- and upper-class young people concentrate on university education and courses which prepare them for the vestibular, the university entrance exams. Poorer and lower-middle-class young people prefer vocational training courses. One factor bringing prestige to residential areas in Recife is the number of private schools and universities, language schools, and other educational facilities for middle-class consumers. In an attempt to relieve their worries about the daily exposure of their offspring to violence, many families prefer living near these services, so that their young sons and daughters can concentrate their activities nearer home. Something similar occurs in poorer areas, some of which have a concentration of official and alternative vocational courses offered by foundations, churches, and other organizations (Scott and Cantarelli 2005; see also Cantarelli 2002).

Educational facilities such as these somewhat lessen the effects of social exclusion on the poorer young, but simultaneously they indirectly create a kind of

Figure 3.4. Advertisement for an English-language course. Recife, 2002.
Photo: Anne Line Dalsgaard

hierarchy, since some residential areas have several such facilities, while others have none at all (Novaes 2003). As a result, some young people get more chances to acquire skills than others. This hierarchical distribution was noticeable in our fieldwork observations. In Vietnã the young have several possibilities, as they say, "to make a curriculum," which they do not have in Santa Barbara. The *bairro* is near a large hydroelectric power station, which, encouraged by local community leaders, offers special courses in music and computer use. The Presbyterian Church runs an elementary school and a training center, which offers courses in woodworking, hairdressing, cooking, decorative tapestry painting, and recently computers. The Salesian Order of the Catholic Church also has a large vocational training center fifteen minutes' walk from the *bairro*.

The proliferation of courses, projects, and programs for low-income young people does not necessarily lead to their social inclusion: it may simply create more ways to keep the young off the streets, as the rhetoric of many institutions suggests (Franch 2000). Many courses have been criticized for offering only low-quality training that will, at best, reproduce young people's existing class conditions. Sometimes the young themselves complain, because they enroll in courses with high expectations and finish them without having learned what they need. As part of the present study, we followed a three-month baking course, publicly financed and organized by a community leader. Young people attending the course received a small monthly wage, but besides this immediate economic gain and the creation of social networks, they felt they had learned very little. In fact, none of them learned to make bread. Market logic also creates a hierarchy of skills that tends to disadvantage low-income young people. In her study of youth and the market for computer courses in Recife, Márcia Longhi (2002) shows that, despite the expansion of courses and the official rhetoric against digital exclusion, the market is still organized to exclude young people from the poorest sectors of society. One way in which this occurs is through the rapid succession of new certificates and specialized courses related to new technologies that make courses taken by young people from marginal areas obsolete before they can use them to find jobs.

The lack of employment is a recurring theme in everyday conversations among the young and adults at all levels of Brazilian society, but especially in low-income groups. Among parents at this level of society, "juvenile idleness" is often seen as potentially dangerous and as a symptom of a generation that has experienced very little child labor, but which in compensation (or perhaps even as a result) is constantly exposed to risks unknown to former generations, like drugs, early sexual experience, AIDS, and criminal activities. But among young people themselves, the lack of employment is, rather, translated into what Regina Novaes (2005) has very fittingly called "the fear of being left behind," a fear that seems to cast its shadow over the future and to complicate the present for the majority of the young in Recife.

Trajectories Marked by Class and Gender

In their search for education, a profession, or just an income, the young people we met simultaneously positioned themselves in the here and now and also strove for results in the future. For instance, when telling us that she wanted to become a nurse, one young woman, Evinha, presented herself as a young, responsible person who saw for herself a future with room for agency and an improvement in her living conditions. But identifying a future for oneself is not the same as attaining it. Life trajectories are marked by vital conjunctures, that is, "moments when seemingly established futures are called into question and when actors are called on to manage durations of radical uncertainty" (Johnson-Hanks 2002, 878). They can only be known in retrospect. At present the subject steers toward an imagined horizon, hoped or feared as it may be, often uncertain about the consequences of actions once they have been taken. In our project we found not only a variety of subjective identifications with potential futures, but also different trajectories, indicating that transition to adulthood is neither a linear process nor something that happens in a single, distinct step (Galland 2004).

Figure 3.5. Young people in a *favela* with plenty of time in the afternoon. Recife, 2003.
Photo: Anne Line Dalsgaard

As the experiences of Evinha and Roberto will demonstrate, any idea of life stages must fail when confronted with the many different roles that young people occupy. At the same time, transition was vital in young people's experience and associated with real dangers, as the story of Luis shows. This was also the case for middle-class young people, for whom it was critical to follow a generic cultural script for a proper transition. Uncertainty, reflections on their own situations, and fear of becoming stuck are common to these stories. However, there are differences too. The young are positioned in different fields of possibilities, meaning that their properties (class, gender, and race, among others) offer different, and unequal, opportunities for them to build their life trajectories.

Youth, Motherhood, and Uncertain Futures

When we first met Evinha, she was 18 years old and had completed secondary school. She later said, "I thought my future would be easy, that I would get an education, a job, and have my income guaranteed." Evinha had imagined a future for herself as a nurse, and she had saved money for the nursing school entrance fee. She wanted to become a "realized" person, someone who could act and do as she pleased, including buying the things she needed. But she soon got pregnant by her boyfriend Beto, and postponed her plans. She went to live in a little shack that Beto had built next to his mother's house, and, with their newborn son, they had a kind of family life for a while. When Beto lost his job, he started drinking heavily and began to mistreat Evinha, not coming home until late, arriving drunk with no food for her or the baby, being violent and wanting sex, which she did not feel any pleasure in giving him. Soon Evinha returned to her parents' house, where, living with her son, she had no income at all and was totally dependent on her parents. She helped in the household as much as she could, washing clothes, cleaning, and caring for her youngest sister, but she felt she was always in debt.

Evinha was caught between categories. She was considered a woman, as she had had sex and even lived with a man. She was also considered an adult, as she had to care for a child. Her days were full of worries about money. As her younger brother Jefferson said, "Evinha is an adult. I do everything I like, Evinha doesn't. Evinha has to work in order to provide for her child." However, Evinha could not find a job. In the eyes of others and in her own, she would have been better off had she entered nursing school, which would have been considered a responsible act leading toward future employment. Now she was dependent on her mother again, without knowing how to leave her dependence. Her mother did not consider her an adult. She said, "Evinha does not have the head of an adult, no, she has a child, but she is not an adult. Despite the fact that she has a child, I think Evinha is *jovem*." Evinha herself put it like this:

> I am 23 years old, I became a woman [had sex] at the age of 19, had my child at 20 and I consider myself a *garotinha* [girl] because till now I have done nothing, never worked. I finished secondary school and pronto, the age is not enough, you are still a child, you have no independence, you are only a woman when you are independent; when you are dependent on others, you are still a child.

In low-income families, young women are generally expected to become mothers earlier than among the middle classes. Skills related to childcare and housework are part of their habitus (Bourdieu 1977), as they learn very early in life how to take care of their younger siblings and "play dolls" with other women's babies. While no longer the only marker of the female adult, having children is still part of the cultural construction of responsible womanhood (Scott 1990; Scott and Franch 2005; see also Dalsgaard 2004). However, the expectation of motherhood competes with ideals of women's independence and autonomy, which are increasingly entering into everyday discourse. In the schools, on television programs, and also at home, young women hear about the importance of having a profession, since, as it is commonly said, "today marriage guarantees a woman no future."

Teenage pregnancy (between ages 12 and 20, according to WHO) is often presented in Brazil and many other countries as one of the most significant "social problems" hampering the development of young people and their insertion into the adult world. Adolescents today in Brazil are the only age group that is maintaining and even increasing its birth rate, which is decreasing in other age groups. In 2003, 20 percent of newborn babies in Brazil were born to adolescents of 15 to 19 years of age (IBGE 2005). However, teenage pregnancy in Brazil today may equally be seen as a strategy for gaining adulthood in a society in which it is much easier to become pregnant than to get a job.

Evinha said that she became pregnant in order to get away from home, her authoritarian parents, and the large amount of housework expected of her. Some young mothers we met did not have any professional plans for the future; they were either happy in their new role, or somewhat disillusioned. Others, like Evinha, were frustrated and felt they had made a wrong choice on the way to the identity they had envisioned. One day, Evinha said, "This is a hole—nothing is happening!" She had to face the uncertainty of not knowing how to proceed and the fear of not being able to provide for her son. Although motherhood is not necessarily the end of a girl's youth, Evinha was in serious trouble.

Young Men Walking a Tightrope

Roberto and Luis were born in almost the same year and almost the same street of a poor neighborhood. Their childhoods were very similar: they played in the same streets, studied at the same school, and had some of the same friends. But their paths separated in adolescence, when Roberto "followed the right way" while Luis "chose the wrong way."

We met Roberto in 1999. He was a jovial and carefree young man, who played in a local samba band and enjoyed going out with his friends. His father was still alive and working, so he could keep some of the money he earned to spend in bars, on music, and with girlfriends, as young men are expected to do. Three years later, when we met him again, he looked more serious. Music and going out with friends had been left behind: "When I started to work in [the supermarket], I began to like being at home." After his father's death, he had become the only provider in the family. He considered himself "practically an adult" because of the responsibilities he had: he was supporting his mother, three children of a brother who was in prison, another of his brothers, and this brother's wife, who was pregnant.

Like many other young men we met, Roberto started to work when he was 10 years old, as a trash scavenger. The 1980s were a period of working-class impoverishment, and global (and also local) ideas of children's rights had as yet had little effect, so children's work was often an uncriticized resource for impoverished families. In Roberto's narrative, work is a crucial element in his commitment to his family and in the building of his own identity. It is work that provides the basis for masculine identity, which is complementary to women's. Ideally, men work and thus provide, while women take care of the house, although they can "help" with expenses. And it is work, not consumption, that makes a meaningful distinction in the neighborhood: workers are defined in contrast to the so-called "marginals," who make a living from robbery, drug trafficking, and other illegal activities (Sarti 1996; Zaluar 1985; see also French 2000). The importance of work as an identity marker became clear when Roberto proudly remembered his first experiences as a trash scavenger: "People in the streets were surprised to see a child pushing a cart. . . . I've always been *esforçado* [tried hard]."

Roberto was often described to us as *um bom rapaz*, a good guy. In contrast, Luis was labeled *doido*, crazy, when we met him in 1999, and he was starting to become known as a "wrong person" two years later, when we met him again. Luis began doing "wrong things" after he left school because of a fight with a classmate. The fight was probably just the motive (or maybe the justification) for Luis to end a frustrating school career, full of low grades, repeated classes, and changes from one school to another. He soon became involved in illegal activities, such as counterfeiting money and checks and dealing in stolen mobile phones. He also started to carry a gun and became involved in fights with other young men in Vietnã and surrounding *bairros*. Trying to protect him from bad influences, his stepfather found him a job as a security guard in a small supermarket, but he had some problems with a local gang and had to quit. Luis did not have much patience with the job anyway, as he could obtain much more money dealing in stolen mobile phones.

Working was not a key element in Luis's identity. Unlike Roberto, he just wanted to enjoy life as a young person, not thinking about his future or caring about his family's needs. Eventually he was killed in the *bairro* where he was born. His relatives, friends, and neighbors went to his burial in a hired bus. Many girls were crying, although nobody was really surprised by his fate, which had become increasingly common in places like Vietnã. UNESCO calculates that there are 54.5 homicides for every 100,000 young men in Recife, which is more than twice the rate in the population as a whole (Waiselfisz 2002). Most of these homicides are concentrated in poor *bairros* like Santa Barbara and Vietnã, the victims usually being young black men like Luis.

If young men are expected to be "strong arms" and "agile legs" in the labor market (Oliveira 2000), neither Roberto nor Luis liked this prospect. Roberto tried to transcend it by studying, as he had always heard that this was the only way for poor people to achieve social mobility. He finished secondary education, the last step before the university entrance exam, but soon realized that he would not have a better life than his parents. One day, thinking about his own life, he said to us, "I finished my second degree. I have work experience. But where's my opportunity?" Luis's opportunities were even fewer, as he never finished his basic education. Under these circumstances, criminal activities appeared as a possible "career," although they involved high risks and breaking with some of the moral principles of his relatives and friends. The immediate motives for young Brazilians to get involved in criminal activities have been described as acceptance of risk based on cultural male expectations, drug addiction, desire for revenge, and desire for power and consumption (Oliveira 2000; Zaluar 1985; see also Franch 2003). Luis was just one of many.

Keeping Up Middle-Class Standards

Young people from middle-class families in Recife are first of all students. For them there seems to be no route to adulthood other than through education. As schooling has become compulsory in Brazil and the level of literacy has increased dramatically, a sharp distinction has arisen between public and private schooling. People at all levels of Brazilian society are very conscious of this. When she was asked if private schooling had made a difference in her chances in life, one middle-class university student answered, "Yes, it makes a difference, because the situation at the public schools is not good. Our parents studied at public schools, and at that time they were good, . . . but today they are all messed up." This distinction is clearly related to what Bourdieu points out in his analysis of the French school system, namely that when the privilege of schooling is no longer a symbol of class but becomes available to the many, it is devalued and new distinctions are needed (Bourdieu and Passeron 2000).

The middle-class young people we met lived at home, relatively free from economic and practical responsibilities. Having at least one domestic worker in the house is a mark of status and prestige for the middle and upper classes (see also Goldstein 2003, 68), and the young from these families are very aware of this. A young medical student, the daughter of a well-known medical doctor in Recife, mentioned the presence of domestic workers in the house after having listed the number of bedrooms, bathrooms, televisions, and computers it had. Another young woman, Elizabeth, whose parents were separated, with the mother still trying to keep up standards without help in the house, clearly positioned herself when she told us that she did not intend to do any housework in her own future. As her mother said, "She wants to work, to become a lawyer and work in an office, so she will not have much time for housework." Young people from middle-class families mark their class and employment ambitions by refusing to learn to perform the most basic chores, such as cleaning and cooking. Even making oneself a cup of coffee was a mystery to some of our informants. This "cultivated incompetence" (Goldstein 2003, 68) is an important sign of class.

However, among the better-off young people, lack of economic and practical responsibilities contrasted to a strong sense of responsibility for their studies. As Donna Goldstein writes, a "middle-class child knows that he or she must do well enough in school and master the vestibular examination in order to advance educationally and occupy a middle-class position" (2003, 203). One young man, Marcelo, nearly 18, was therefore in a serious situation, as he had failed the vestibular for the university and thus was a year behind his classmates. Middle-class young people are expected to know what they want to do in the future, since they take a vestibular for a specific subject, in Marcelo's case computer science. "But I do not know if that is what I want to do. What I want is to get through as soon as possible in order to gain my independence. My dream is to leave my parents, my home, create autonomy, get married." Marcelo had a girlfriend, with whom he wanted to live and have children, but he had to wait for his financial independence and, as he said, psychological maturity: "Because it is difficult, like … you have always lived with your parents. But the most difficult is the economy, and I still have to pass the vestibular, do the course, and maybe do a traineeship in the middle, and, when I finish, I will be around 24 years old." Marcelo had an apartment that his father had bought for him. But even so, as an adult he would have to pay for all his daily necessities, including health insurance and probably a weekly domestic worker. He could not escape the university, and in order to get him through the exam, his father had helped him study.

In our meetings with middle-class young people, we became increasingly aware of the script that seemed to dominate their orientations toward the future. They expected to study in private schools, pass the vestibular, go to university, have their first work experiences as trainees while studying, find a good job, and then marry, move away from home, and have children. Even when something didn't work as it should, for instance when a teenage pregnancy occurred, the essence of the script was maintained: families helped the young parents to finish their education (see also Brandão 2003). On the way to adulthood, parents' celebrations of their daughters' fifteenth birthdays (performed as small weddings without a groom, accentuating both virginity and future fertility[6]) and young men's acquisition of a driving license (accentuating masculine mobility) were crucial steps. Also important was the cultural capital implied in the ability to speak foreign languages (primarily English), use a computer and other hi-tech consumer goods, and travel abroad. Thus, Elizabeth's mother was worried because her daughter could not study English at a private school, and they did not have a computer in the house. She knew that these lacks would be crucial later on, when Elizabeth would have to compete with others for a job.

Both Elizabeth and Marcelo knew they had to compete. They had to follow the script, take their exams, and become successful. While gender roles are complementary among the young in low-income areas of Recife, young men and women from the city's wealthier families had very similar professional and personal expectations of themselves. But nothing was certain in Marcelo's and Elizabeth's lives: at the moment in life when we met them, they both had to work hard in order not to fall below middle-class standards. For them, becoming parents would not, in itself, constitute social adulthood.

Facing Different Horizons in the Same City

Youth in Recife has many meanings, as diverse as the ways in which young people experience it and become adults. Class and gender distinctions are responsible for differences in social expectations and in access to resources. Class differences, for instance, shape the timing of the social recognition of adulthood, so that young people are recognized as adults earlier in poorer families than in middle-class ones, even though they have fewer means to fulfill all the traditional expectations of an adult role. Another important difference is that, among middle-class young people, gender does not play as strong a differentiating role as among their low-income age counterparts. While middle-class young people try to follow a cultural script for the passage to adulthood, in the lower classes they take a variety of paths to adulthood, and the plurality of roles may be the most important characteristic of this period of their lives. Evinha and Roberto on the one hand and Marcelo and Elisabeth on the other are examples of both patterns. To some extent, this contrast between non-synchrony and script is mirrored in the contrast between the types of residence in which the young grow up: the flexibility and fluidity of the poorer *bairros* versus the order and stability of middle-class apartment blocks, the large household with its membership constantly in flux and people sharing living spaces and even beds versus the private room of the middle-class teenager. And yet there are similarities: the risk of "dropping below" the class standards that dominate the lives of middle-class young people parallels the fear of becoming "marginalized" in the poorer *bairros*.

Whereas anthropological and sociological studies of socialization and transition traditionally have focused on mechanisms for the integration of the young into adult society, in this chapter we have examined the way in which local notions of transition dominate young people's trajectories. At the point in life when we met them, they had not reached what they themselves, or those around them, considered adulthood, and sometimes they found themselves frustrated and uncertain about the steps they had to take. While taking on family responsibilities constituted both a burden and a partial passage to adulthood for Evinha and Roberto, Marcelo had to postpone marriage and children in order to maintain his middle-class identity. In his social environment, gender differences are less accentuated, and both young men and women see youth the same way: as a period for individualization and study for a profession. Evinha and Roberto were not unaffected by the ideas of professionalization and personal success implicit in the middle-class script: Evinha wished to have a profession and to work at one of the big hospitals in Recife, while Roberto felt that he deserved more than a supermarket job.

The script that defines youth as a transition to an independent and autonomous adulthood influenced Evinha's and Roberto's evaluations of their own lives. But more than that, it influences the society's definitions of "proper" and "improper" transitions, which lie behind the cultural construction of "social problems" like early school leaving, teenage pregnancy, child labor, and juvenile delinquency. From a different perspective, these could all be seen as steps toward imagined horizons of adulthood, responsibility, personal agency, and recognition (maybe even love). As social researchers we may want on a theoretical level to apply a definition of youth that includes this perspective; for the young people we met, the meaning of youth was lived and negotiated in practice. The fluid and flexible lifeworld of the *bairro* allows certain futures and hinders others; so also does the more structured life of the middle class. But young people in both contexts may have to bear the burden of norms and expectations that they either cannot or do not wish to fulfill. They all have to take into account dominant ideas about what it means to become an adult in Recife—a city of frustrating contrasts, to be sure, but also of shared dilemmas and uncertainties.

Acknowledgments

The Federal University of Pernambuco (UFPE), Recife, has supported our research in several ways, not least during the project workshop and by providing Parry Scott with time to participate. The Ford Foundation also financially supported Brazilian participation, for which we are equally grateful. When conducting our research we received the always engaged and careful help of Madiana Rodrigues, an anthropologist from UFPE. We wish to thank her warmly for that. In addition, Madiana, Márcia Longhi, and Jonnhy Cantarelli each added substantially to the project by conducting a mini-ethnographic study. In Vietnã and Santa Barbara we have received help from friends in countless ways. Susanne Højlund and Tine Gammeltoft have been critical and constructive readers. We are grateful for it all.

Notes

1. In his book *Brésil, terre des contrastes* (1957), Roger Bastide defined Brazil as a "country of contrasts," a characterization that has persisted also in the discussion of Brazilian cities.

2. The AIDS epidemic in Brazil is stabilizing, with a rate of 18.2 cases per 100,000. In 2005 around six hundred thousand Brazilians were estimated to be HIV-infected. Intensive

campaigns directed toward young people appear to have had an effect, as the incidence rate among men age 13 to 29 has decreased. Among women between the ages of 13 and 24, incidence has decreased slightly, while for women in general it has increased (*Boletim Epidemiológico* 2005).

3. For details, see Prefeitura do Recife 2007.

4. Descriptions of this use of the street in low-income *bairros* in Brazil can be found in the Brazilian literature on urban anthropology (see for instance Magnani 1998). See also Gough and Franch 2005, Franch 2003, and Scott and Franch 2005, all publications of the Youth and the City project.

5. Data on instruction and employment are from the 2001 Pesquisa nacional por amostra de domicílos (national household sample), Instituto Cidadania 2004.

6. Girls in the poorer *bairros* also celebrate their fifteenth birthday, although most families do not have the resources for a large party. And today, girls from better-off families may prefer other ways of celebrating: with a trip abroad or perhaps a computer.

References

Ariès, Philippe. 1965. *Centuries of Childhood: A Social History of Family Life.* Trans. Robert Baldick. New York: Vintage.

Bastide, Roger. 1957. *Brésil, terre des contrastes.* Paris: L'Harmattan.

Boletim Epidemiológico. 2005. http://www.aids.gov.br/data/Pages/LUMIS9A49113DPTBRIE.htm.

Bott, Elizabeth. 1968. *Family and Social Network: Roles, Norms, and External Relations in Ordinary Urban Families.* London: Tavistock.

Bourdieu, Pierre. 1977. *Outline of a Theory of Practice.* Cambridge: Cambridge University Press.

Bourdieu, Pierre, and Jean-Claude Passeron. 2000 [1977]. *Reproduction in Education, Society and Culture.* Trans. Richard Nice. London: Sage.

Brandão, Elaine Reis. 2003. Individualização e vínculo familiar em camadas médias: Um olhar através da gravidez na adolescência. Master's thesis, Instituto de Medicina Social, Universidade do Estado do Rio de Janeiro.

Caldeira, Teresa P. R. 2000. *City of Walls: Crime, Segregation, and Citizenship in São Paulo.* Berkeley: University of California Press.

Cantarelli, Jonnhy. 2002. Os jovens e a cidade: Jovens de igreja. Research report from the Youth and the City: Skills, Knowledge, and Social Reproduction.

Dalsgaard, Anne Line. 2004. *Matters of Life and Longing: Female Sterilisation in Northeast Brazil.* Copenhagen: Museum Tusculanum Press.

Debert, Guita Grin. 1999. *A reinvenção da velhice: Socialização e processos de reprivatização do envelhecimento.* São Paulo: Editora da Universidade de São Paulo.

Franch, Mónica. 2000. Tardes ao léu: Um ensaio etnográfico sobre o tempo livre entre jovens de periferia. Master's thesis, Universidade Federal de Pernambuco, Recife.

―――. 2003. A Toast to Life: Thoughts on Violence, Youth and Harm Reduction in Brazil. In *Alcohol and Harm Reduction: An Innovative Approach for Countries in Transition,* ed.

Ernst Buning et al., 47–72. Amsterdam: International Coalition on Alcohol and Harm Reduction.

Franch, Mónica, Silvia Camurça, and Carla Batista. 2003. *Ajuste estrutural, pobreza e desigualdade de gênero.* 2nd ed. Recife: Iniciativa de Gênero/SOS Corpo, Gênero e Cidadania.

Galland, Olivier. 2004. *Sociologie de la jeunesse.* Paris: Armand Collin.

Goldstein, Donna M. 2003. *Laughter out of Place: Race, Class, Violence, and Sexuality in a Rio Shantytown.* Berkeley: University of California Press.

Gough, Katherine V., and Mónica Franch. 2005. Spaces of the Street: Socio-spatial Mobility and Exclusion of Youth in Recife. *Children's Geographies* 3(2):149–66.

IBGE (Instituto Brasileiro de Geografia e Estatistica). 2005. *Síntese de indicadores sociais.* Rio de Janeiro: Instituto Brasileiro de Geografia e Estatistica.

Instituto Cidadania. 2004. *Projeto juventude: Documento de conclusão; Versão inicial para discussado, complementação e ajustes.* Sao Paolo: Instituto Cidadania.

Johnson-Hanks, Jennifer. 2002. On the Limits of Life Stages in Ethnography: Toward a Theory of Vital Conjunctures. *American Anthropologist* 104(3):865–80.

Longhi, Márcia Reis. 2002. Os jovens e a cidade: A informática e os jovens. Research report from the Youth and the City: Skills, Knowledge, and Social Reproduction.

Magnani, José Guilherme Cantor. 1998. *Festa no pedaço: Lazer e cultura popular na cidade.* 2nd ed. São Paulo: Hucitec.

Martine, George, Monica Das Gupta, and Lincoln C. Chen, eds. 1998. *Reproductive Change in India and Brazil.* Delhi: Oxford University Press.

Mattos, Sérgio. 2000. *A televisão no Brasil: 50 anos de historia (1950–2000).* Salvador: Editora PAS-Edições Ianamá.

Novaes, Regina. 2003. Juventude, exclusão e inclusão social: Aspectos e controvérsias de um debate em curso. In *Políticas públicas: Juventude em Pauta,* ed. Maria Virgínia de Freitas and Fernanda de Carvalho Papa, 46–69. São Paulo: Cortez, Ação Educativa, Assessoria, Pesquisa e Informação.

———. 2005. Juventude, percepções e comportamentos. In *Retratos da juventude brasileira: Análises de uma pesquisa nacional,* ed. Helena W. E Abramo and Pedro Paulo Martoni Branco, 263–90. São Paulo: Instituto Cidadania, Editora Fundação Perseu Abramo.

Oliveira, Jane Souto de. 2000. Barreiras, transgressões e invenções de mercado: a inserção econômica de jovens pobres. *Anais do XII encontro nacional de estudos populacionais.* http://www.abep.nepo.unicamp.br/docs/anais/pdf/2000/Todos/trat19_2.pdf.

Ortiz, Renato. 1988. *A moderna tradição brasileira: Cultura brasileira e indústria cultural.* São Paulo: Brasiliense.

Prefeitura do Recife. 2007. Plano Diretor do Recife, http://www.recife.pe.gov.br/secplanejamento/planodiretor/diagnostico. Accessed January 21, 2007.

Rodrigues, Madiana. 2002. Os jovens e a cidade: Estágios no Recife. Research report from the Youth and the City: Skills, Knowledge, and Social Reproduction.

Sarti, Cynthia Andersen. 1996. *A família como espelho: Um estudo sobre a moral dos pobres.* Campinas, SP: Autores Associados.

Scott, Russell Parry. 1990. O homem na matrifocalidade: Gênero, percepção e experiências do domínio doméstico. *Cadernos de pesquisa* 73:38–47.

————. 1996. Remoção populacional e projetos de desenvolvimento urbano. *Anais do X Encontro de Estudos Populacionais* 2:813–34.

Scott, Russell Parry, and Jonnhy Cantarelli. 2005. Jovens, religiosidade e aquisição de conhecimentos e habilidades entre camadas populares. *Cadernos CRH* 17(42):375–88.

Scott, Russell Parry, and Mónica Franch. 2005 [2001]. Jovens, moradia e reprodução social: Processos domésticos e espaciais na aquisição de habilidades e conhecimentos. *Estudos de Sociologia: Revista do Programa de Pós-Graduação em Sociologia da UFPE* 7(1–2):95–125.

Silva, Nancy de Deus Vieira, and Ana Lúcia Kassouf. 2002. A exclusão social dos jovens no mercado de trabalho brasileiro. *Revista Brasileira de Estudos Populacionais* 19(2):99–115.

Singer, Paulo. 2005. A juventude como coorte: Uma geração em tempos de crise social. In *Retratos da Juventude Brasileira; Análises de uma pesquisa nacional,* ed. Helena W. E Abramo and Pedro Paulo Martoni Branco, 27–35. São Paulo: Instituto Cidadania, Editora Fundação Perseu Abramo.

Soares, Laura Tavares Riveiro. 1999. *Ajuste neoliberal e desajuste social na América Latina.* Rio de Janeiro: Editoria de Escola de Enfermagem Ana Nery, Universidade Federal do Rio de Janeiro.

Susser, Ida, and Jane Schneider. 2003. Wounded Cities: Destruction and Reconstruction in a Globalized World. In *Wounded Cities: Destruction and Reconstruction in a Globalized World,* ed. Jane Schneider and Ida Susser, 1–23. Oxford and New York: Berg.

Waiselfisz, Julio Jacobo. 2002. *Mapa da violência III.* Brasília: UNESCO, Instituto Ayrton Senna, Ministério da Justiça/SEDH.

Zaluar, Alba. 1985. *A máquina e a revolta: As organizações populares e o significado da pobreza.* São Paulo: Editora Brasiliense.

4

Politicized Leisure in the Wake of *Doi Moi:* A Study of Youth in Hanoi

Karen Valentin

A walk along Hoan Kiem Lake is a walk through history, from the ancient Jade Temple in the north to the new department store, Trang Tien Plaza, in the south. Hoan Kiem Lake is located in the center of Hanoi, Vietnam's capital and second largest city, with a population of three million. Separating the ancient part of the city in the north from the French quarter in the south, the lake area is a green, lush spot with blossoming trees and narrow paths. On benches around the lake, young couples sit closely together in search of intimacy, which is difficult to find in the small, crowded homes of many Hanoians. Elderly people practice *tai chi,* alone or in groups, and at the weekends the lakeside is a popular place for families to stroll. Approaching the many tourists who enjoy the peaceful atmosphere around the lake, shoeshine boys, postcard sellers, and fruit vendors try to earn their meager daily incomes. On the one-way street encircling the lake, there is a constant flow of motorbikes carrying smartly dressed young men and women, who chat and talk on their mobile phones as they roam around the city. Expensive cafés and supermarkets selling imported foreign goods at sky-rocketing prices lie side by side and attract the expanding middle and upper classes, not least their young people, a generation that is expected to bring Vietnam well into the twenty-first century. Young people aged 14–25 are currently the largest demographic segment, constituting 24.5 percent of the total population of Vietnam (Ministry of Health 2005, 14). Of these, nearly one in four live in urban areas (Dang Nguyen Anh, Le Bach Duong, and Nguyen Hai Van 2005).

Social life around Hoan Kiem Lake gives us a picture of a society in rapid transition from a state-controlled planned economy to a socialist market economy, characterized by economic growth and technological progress, but also by increasing social and economic inequalities. The built environment around the lake also teaches us about changing political and ideological systems and the influence of foreign powers in the political history of Vietnam.

The Jade Temple, Den Ngoc Son, is situated on a small island at the northern end of Hoan Kiem Lake. It builds on a blend of Confucian, Buddhist, and Taoist principles, its location in the lake representing a traditional Vietnamese architectural practice combined with a classical Chinese design (Logan 2000, 48). Like the ancient part of Hanoi, it is evidence of the massive Chinese influence in Vietnam, including the spread of Confucianism, following about a thousand years of Chinese dominance in the period from 111 BC to AD 939 (Jamieson 1993). Today the temple is a popular tourist attraction and a perfect background for taking photographs of newly wed couples. On the eastern side of the lake coming from the north one first encounters an icon of the Soviet period—a white, massive, squared block, which houses the Hanoi People's Committee—and a few minutes' walk further south, the former Hanoi post office, built by the French around 1905 (Logan 2000, 83). In the 1960s a new, modernist block was built for the post office just next to the old building, which fell into decay until it was restored in 2004. At the southeast end of the lake, on the corner of Trang Tien and Hang Bai Streets, is a new, posh department store, Trang Tien Plaza, which sells everything from gold watches and Western designer clothes to imported wines and cosmetics.

The recent transformations that characterize the political history of Vietnam—Chinese-inspired Confucianism, French colonialism, Soviet-supported communism, and present-day market socialism—are all salient features in the built environment of Hanoi (Valentin 2005). They not only remind us of the radical shifts in official ideology, they are also evidence of historically anchored processes of globalization that, over time, have integrated Vietnam into changing political and economic interdependencies with other nations. While different political systems have introduced different buildings, public spaces, and monuments into the urban landscape (Thomas 2002, 1613), transformations in the political economy and structural conditions of the society also have a strong influence on its social organization and human use (Nguyen Quang and Kammeier 2002).

Specific urban places are contexts for people's actions, but they are also texts that produce their own stories. Approaching the place called Hanoi from this double perspective, I draw attention to the historical dimension of the city and the way in which it is narrated through the city's material and physical expressions, partly as a chronological series of events that have taken place in the past, but partly as a temporally specific narrative about the wider society and its people. In other words, by reading the physical structures of buildings, streets, and plazas we learn one version of history, that is, the one reflecting dominant politico-ideological regimes. But the human use of specific urban places—at different historical

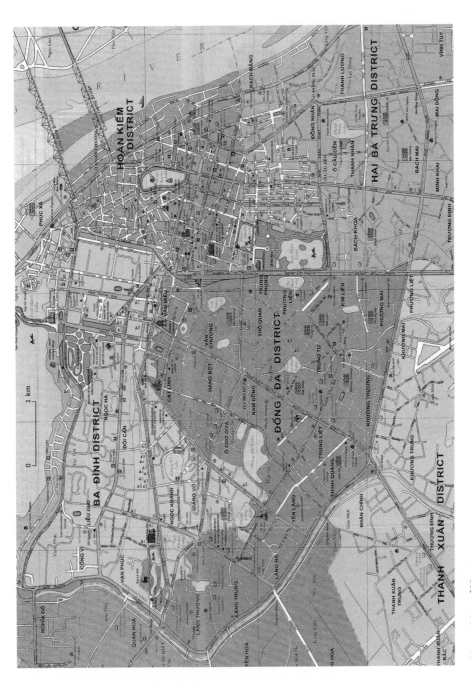

Map 2. Map of Hanoi

moments and as conditioned by political and economic structures—teaches us different and simultaneously produced stories about the city, which all depend upon the perspective of different social actors.

This book examines cities as particular types of places for young people and as spaces of interaction that bring together people, things, and ideas from the wider world (Hansen, introduction, this volume). Cities form intersections among rural connections and networks, urban lives, and national ideologies and structures, as well as global political and economic interests. We explore how young people experience and produce localized understandings of such complex relationships, which are inscribed into the social and material life of concrete urban places. The Hanoi City study was shaped by the sociopolitical conditions that determined the framework for conducting fieldwork and working with youth through formal channels in Vietnam (see Dalsgaard and Valentin, this volume). Hence, with a particular focus on young people's sociopolitical activities in the Ho Chi Minh Communist Youth Union, the youth branch of the Communist Party, this chapter focuses on politicized aspects of contemporary Hanoian youth life as it is shaped by urban experience in an era of competing leisure activities and consumerism driven by the global market. These are omnipresent in Hanoi in the form of, for instance, Western-style discos and bars, shops selling imported goods from all over the world, and the popular South Korean movies. As has been observed in other authoritarian, centralized societies, one of the functions of state-organized youth associations is to provide "meaningful" and politically correct leisure for young people.[1] The Ho Chi Minh Communist Youth Union (henceforward the Youth Union) not only occupies young people's spare time, it also takes them away from supposedly dangerous places and activities in the city and establishes new, morally legitimate places for them.

In addressing the relationship between the categories of youth and the city analytically, I am influenced by the work on children's places by Karen Fog Olwig and Eva Gulløv (2003), which, with its focus on generational relations, can be equally well applied to young people. Inspired by the geographer Yi-Fu Tuan, Olwig and Gulløv conceptualize "place" as referring to both physical locations and social positions within generational hierarchies. These two meanings of the concept of place are interrelated, as placements in and on concrete physical locations are determined to a great extent by social placements in generational hierarchies (Olwig and Gulløv 2003, 1–2). This perspective compels us to look at the dynamic interplay between the city as a concrete physical location in which young people live, and youth as a structural category that both emplaces and displaces young people in specific urban sites. In other words, certain places in the city, though mostly defined by adult moral values, are allocated to young people because they are considered proper and safe for them. Other places are seen as being physically or morally destructive for young people, who are therefore denied access, either indirectly through moral condemnation or directly through legal sanctions. Controlling young people's access to particular places implies a politicization of space in which both guardians and the state are central actors.

While examining the relationship between young Hanoians and their city, and the role of the Youth Union in the politicization of urban space, it is important to keep in mind two aspects of the physical and social organization of contemporary Hanoi. First, conceptualizations of the divide between public and private space have changed following the economic liberalizations of the "renovation policy" or *doi moi,* launched in 1986 (Drummond 2000). This has, among other things, resulted in a revitalization and commercialization of public spaces, and consequently changed the conditions for the trade, consumption, and leisure activities that take place on streets, pavements, and plazas. Secondly, state power is symbolically displayed not only in the numerous monumental buildings of different epochs, such as the President's Palace (built by the French in 1900–1908) and the Ho Chi Minh Mausoleum (constructed in 1973–75), but also in the physical presence of state institutions, for example, the People's Committees, whose buildings are found in every ward and district. Specific sites in the city function as national symbols, as rallying grounds for nationalistic sentiments, and are important in the nation-building process, in which young people in Vietnam are ascribed a key role.

In the first part of the chapter I examine local constructions of youth, which in the context of Vietnam are influenced by Confucian values. I then move on to a discussion of the two wards where fieldwork was conducted and the way in which these specific places contributed to shaping young people's experience of the urban. In the third and last part of the chapter I explore young people's engagement in community development programs run by the local branches of the Youth Union and how this relates to the wider nation-building project.

Defining "Urban Youth" in Contemporary Vietnam

Youth is a socially constructed category that assumes meaning relationally (Hansen, introduction, this volume). A relational approach to the study of youth requires that we examine young people with reference to their positions in generational hierarchies as they experience and negotiate them. But it also compels us to analyze how youth as a generational category is reconstructed over time as the political and economic foundations of society change. Ultimately we need to ask what youth means in specific cultural and historical contexts and how concepts of youth are defined cross-culturally.

The Vietnamese term for youth, *thanh nien,* originally designated only young men, but today it encompasses both genders (Marr 1996, 3). A related concept, *vi thanh nien,* is occasionally translated as "adolescent" and refers to the empirical

Figure 4.1. City scene from Hoan Kiem District. Hanoi, 2003. *Photo: Karen Valentin*

category of the "younger youth." Seeking to gain an understanding of the meaning of youth in Vietnam, we asked young people to define the term *thanh nien*
in terms of age and to describe the responsibilities, duties, and rights associated
with this particular period of life. They generally agreed that the period of youth
begins somewhere between the ages of 15 and 18 and ends around 30–35. They
explained that it is a period characterized by increasing responsibilities: preparing oneself for a professional career, getting married, supporting one's parents
financially, observing the law, and, as citizens, contributing to the development
of the nation. This age-based definition of youth corresponds more or less with
the age limits set for membership in the Youth Union (15–28 years) and the
Youth Federation (15–35 years),[2] but few explicitly acknowledged this. It was
striking that one young woman in a focus-group discussion about the life course
suggested an alternative concept for this period, that of "union member" (*doan*

vien), explicitly referring to Youth Union membership. In the English translations of my Vietnamese assistants, I often noticed a confusing, but remarkable overlap between the English terms "Youth [Union] members" and "youth." Although this was partly due to inconsistencies in the translations, which made it difficult to know whether we were speaking about the same group of people, it nonetheless revealed an interesting slippage from one conceptual category to another.

While notions of youth defined by the young people themselves are informed by sociopolitical constructions, romantic love and marriage are also crucial in defining the period of youth. The young people we spoke to generally agreed that youth is a period characterized by increasing independence, when young people start developing romantic relationships. Such relationships are highly visible in public urban spaces, where intimate encounters between young men and women are everyday occurrences (Gammeltoft 2002). Several of the young people we interviewed identified marriage as marking the end of the period of youth because of the responsibility for and devotion to the family associated with married life. Dao, a 25-year-old unmarried man, expressed it so:

> I still feel young. I think I will finish my youth the moment I get married. When I won't be free to do what I want to because of my responsibility for family matters. In my opinion, youth is associated with freedom, so getting married is the same as finishing youth.[3]

The young people generally agreed that the early to mid-twenties were the ideal age for marriage, though both women and men maintained that it was important to have a stable job first in order to be able to feed a family.[4] Another term mentioned now and then in conversations with young people was *day thi* (puberty), a reference to the physical development of the body. According to some, the period of youth starts around the age of 12–13. The way in which young people spoke about the category of youth in their attempt to define it often revealed contradictions depending upon the criteria they used. Still, although they drew on a mixture of biological, sociopolitical, and cultural constructions, it was nonetheless obvious that youth (*thanh nien*) is a culturally meaningful category, though contextually defined and subject to much debate (Bucholtz 2002).

Youth, like other age and generational categories, must be studied relationally (Wyn and White 1997, 11). In the context of Vietnam, this means paying attention to the marked generational hierarchies and inherent power relations shaped by Confucianism. The Confucian doctrine builds on a set of moral relations, which are fundamentally hierarchical and thus imply a superior and an inferior position: father-children, elder brother-younger brother, husband-wife, king-subjects, friend-friend. The positions of superior and inferior are established on the basis of parentage, age, and social position (Tran Dinh Huou 1991, 27). The father-child relation is characterized by, among other things, the notion of filial duty

Figure 4.2. Group of young people gathering after a Youth Union meeting. Hanoi, 2003.
Photo: Karen Valentin

(*hieu*), implying that children are expected to obey, pay respect to, and take care of their parents. As Tine Gammeltoft and Karen Fog Olwig have pointed out, the expectation of filial duty has a strong influence on ways of thinking and acting in relation to children in many contexts of life in Vietnam, and on the way in which children are defined and acted upon as a social category of people (2005, 18–19). This view of children is, as Rachel Burr reminds us in her ethnographic study of working children in Hanoi (2006), also reflected in the Law on Child Protection, Care, and Education, passed by the national assembly in 1991. It is remarkable that this law includes a paragraph on the expectation that Vietnamese children will show love, respect, and piety to their grandparents and parents.

Although they cannot be categorized as children, similar expectations are held of young people, who remain structurally inferior to their parents and are therefore expected to live up to the ideals of filial devotion. Irrespective of social class and gender identity, most young people we talked to maintained that they had a responsibility to their parents, which continued after their own marriages. They explained that they should feel gratitude for being born and raised, and be able to support their parents and remain economically independent in order to relieve the latter's financial burdens. Van, a 17-year-old woman from Mai Ninh who was her parents' only child, added a gender perspective to these responsibilities by pointing out that males and females are not equally able to live up to such expectations:

> They [children] should make them [their parents] happy for what they have done. Besides, they shouldn't forget who gave birth to them, who brought them up, who took care of them, so that they will become more responsible in taking care of their parents in their old age. However, daughters have greater difficulties in fulfilling their parents' expectations because, after they get married, they traditionally move to their husband's house. My mother wants me to live with my parents together with my husband, which cannot be decided beforehand because it depends on the willingness of my parents-in-law once I become a daughter-in-law. Anyway, I will try my best to carry out my duties perfectly.

Pinpointing the fact that daughters have to repay their parents in different ways than sons because of predominating marriage arrangements and the practice of patrilocal residence, Van's statement supports the idea that filial duty might be expressed in very different ways, depending upon different life circumstances (Gammeltoft and Olwig 2005, 19). Notions of filial duty in contemporary Vietnam must also be understood within the context of state-controlled family-planning programs, especially the launching of the two-child policy in 1988. In her study of Chinese teenagers who grew up as the first single-child generation after China's promulgation of its one-child policy in 1979, Vanessa Fong (2004) has shown how this policy led to heavy parental investments in, among other things, education, and consequently to increasing expectations of children, not only within individual families but also nationally. Although population control has not been as rigidly enforced in Vietnam, similar trends were evident among the young people in this study, who, as dedicated students and Youth Union members, expressed strong commitments to and feelings of obligation toward their families and the nation. If we are to comprehend how family-planning policy in Vietnam is appropriated by young people and their families, it is crucial to explore how policy interplays with and potentially reinforces cultural practices related to Confucian values that are still central to the shaping of social relations across gender and generation.

"Placing" Youth: Mai Ninh and Truc Tuyet

Human beings are not only *in* places, but also *of* places, and therefore human experience is always emplaced (Casey 1996, 19). The young people who are the focus of this chapter come from two different wards, Mai Ninh and Truc Tuyet, urban administrative units corresponding to what are termed "communes" in rural Vietnam. They are also residential areas and constitute what Arjun Appadurai has termed "neighborhoods," in the sense that they are historically produced as recognizable, social, human, and situated lifeworlds. They are contexts within which meaningful social action can be generated and interpreted, but they also require and produce contexts (Appadurai 1995, 208–209). The two selected areas date back to and appear as prototypes of different historical epochs, Mai Ninh of the period of the Soviet-supported planned economy, and Truc Tuyet of the precolonial, Chinese-inspired Confucian era. They are legacies of different po-litico-ideological systems and foreign powers that have contributed to shaping the city. As a result of the economic liberalizations following *doi moi,* including the increasing privatization of housing and changes in production systems, both areas have undergone profound changes (see Gough, this volume). These changes are expressed in different ways. The two areas do not look especially socioeconomically different, but the average income is about ten times higher in Truc Tuyet than in Mai Ninh. Although Vietnam has witnessed significant economic growth in recent years, poverty is still widespread, and social and economic disparities have increased since the introduction of *doi moi* (Hy V. Luong 2003, 16). However, "urban wounds" in the form of poverty, criminality, and segregation (Susser and Schneider 2003) are not as visible in the landscape of Hanoi as they are in Recife and Lusaka. As Chae (2003, 228) writes, on the basis of a study of Ho Chi Minh City, the reform policy can be interpreted as an attempt to heal the "wounds" of the previous periods of the American War and Soviet-supported communism. The healing of wounds implies restoration, but it does not necessarily prevent new injuries. While some of the critical economic and political problems of the past may have been reduced following *doi moi,* new problems have appeared, leaving their marks on the city.

Mai Ninh ward, located in the southeast of Hanoi, consists of a large number of apartment buildings with a population of about thirteen thousand, many of whom are migrants from suburbs and neighboring districts. The area stands out physically, with yellow five-story buildings symmetrically lined up, one after another. Intended to provide housing for the workers in a nearby factory, Mai Ninh was constructed in two phases, in the 1960s and 1970s, during the period of the planned economy. A small proportion of the apartments were allocated to ex-soldiers. Mai Ninh shares traits with other apartment blocks in Hanoi built during the planned economy under Soviet architectural influence, when the ideal was to provide mass housing in close proximity to industrial production sites, and with easy access to education, health, and commercial services (Logan 2000, 202–208; Nguyen Quang and Kammeier 2002, 379). Housing was state-subsidized, but in the wake of the economic reforms and increasing privatization, many apartments have been sold (Trinh Duy Luan and Nguyen Quang Vinh 2001). Despite the uniformity in the physical layout of Mai Ninh, the buildings are distinctive because of illegal extensions. Some have been extended on the ground floor with space for small shops, while second-, third-, and fourth-floor apartments have grown extensions like small birdcages plastered onto the wall. Because of the humid climate and a lack of maintenance, the buildings are in a very dilapidated state. Many apartments are crowded, and not all have separate kitchens and bathrooms. Because of privatization and rising apartment prices, the population of the area has become more mixed and socially stratified, as people who are not engaged in industrial production are now allowed to buy apartments in the area. There are still many manual workers in Mai Ninh, as some of the blocks are still owned by nearby government-owned factories that provide inexpensive housing to their workers.

We met several parents, 45–55 years old, who had retired at an early age (35–45) because of reductions in the state sector following *doi moi.* In addition to a nominal pension from the state, they depended upon the income they could make from small-scale enterprises, such as running food stalls, selling in the market, or looking after parked motorbikes. Although most of our key informants were students or employees of state companies, it was obvious from observations in the public areas that a large number of young people were also engaged in small-scale private businesses, for example, motorbike repairs, beauty parlors, and small restaurants. A recurrent theme in conversations with young people from Mai Ninh was the issue of "social evils," a term they commonly used to describe supposedly immoral habits and behavior such as drug use, prostitution, and gambling. Drug use in particular was mentioned as a problem in Mai Ninh, which made the place less attractive for young people and was a reason to move somewhere else in the future. Young people did recognize that the local authorities had been relatively successful in combating the problem through, among other things, advocacy among youth and increased control and rehabilitation of drug addicts. In effect, the problem had been transferred to the neighboring ward, where drugs were easily available.

The other ward, Truc Tuyet, is located in the ancient part of Hanoi, also known as the "area of thirty-six commercial streets." This name refers to the area's history as the commercial center of Hanoi after it was established as a capital city in the eleventh century, under the name of Thang Long (Hoang Huu Pee and Nishimura 2000, 14). The Confucian administration organized the area into thirty-six administrative units, which functioned as guilds. Each area was named after the kind of merchandise that was originally sold in the area's main street. Truc Tuyet covers little more than half a square kilometer and has a population of about twelve thousand. In contrast to the inhabitants of Mai Ninh, many people in Truc Tuyet consider themselves to be Hanoian, meaning that they have lived in the city for several generations. The area was severely damaged during the American War, but has since then been restored and upgraded. Because it is considered an attractive place to live, house prices have increased dramatically in recent years. With their four or five stories, narrow façades, and unusual depth,

Figure 4.3. Scene from Mai
Ninh. Hanoi, 2003.
Photo: Karen Valentin

the houses are characteristic of old Hanoi. Some of them are owned by wealthy families, with only four or five people inhabiting the entire house, but others have been split up into smaller apartments and rooms and may accommodate up to twenty or thirty families.

Like other areas in the old part of Hanoi, Truc Tuyet is known for its traditional handicrafts, including brass molding. Although production has largely moved out of the city, some families are still engaged in handicraft production and trade, including for export. In contrast to the workers of Mai Ninh, many people in Truc Tuyet were in high-prestige white-collar jobs. A large number of the people we spoke to were employed in either private companies or government offices. This was also true of the young people who had already finished higher education. More than their contemporaries in Mai Ninh, they were exposed to and oriented themselves toward a world outside Vietnam; this orientation was reflected in, among other things, ideas of going abroad for further studies or work, which were kept alive through connections with friends and relatives living in Australia and Europe. The young people generally spoke of Truc Tuyet as a safe environment to grow up in and appreciated its central location in the area around Hoan Kiem Lake, which, with all its cafés, shops, and places of entertainment, offered them a place in the cultural space of a consuming middle-class youth. It was therefore closely associated with the emergence of the new economic middle class in Vietnam, which, through various networks, has greater access to the world outside the country.

Although many families in both areas have given up the occupations that previously characterized the neighborhood—industrial work and handicraft production—the two areas represent different periods in Hanoi's history. This is evident not only in the built environment, but also in the structural conditions of the inhabitants and consequently in young people's experiences of their immediate environment. Dao, the 25-year-old man quoted above, summarized contemporary life in Mai Ninh in the following way:

> Living conditions have become better. The fact that most of the residents are pensioners from the [. . .] factory can explain why the living conditions are better but not high enough. Workers' wages are relatively low, hence their low pensions. Some of them have small businesses at home selling groceries. Life is still tough.

Describing life in Truc Tuyet, 23-year-old Thien made the following comment:

> This is the place we've got used to. We've been living here since we were born, and that's maybe the reason we find it good in terms of living conditions and security. Moreover, it is close to Hanoi's old business center, the thirty-six old streets, and also an area with many places to entertain or relax, like Ho Tay.

These two statements capture the overall impression I gained from observing and speaking with young people in the two areas, namely that they were conscious of, and to a great extent identified with, their particular wards. Many young people growing up in Mai Ninh remained in a more marginal position than their contemporaries in Truc Tuyet, both economically and spatially, in relation to the urban center. Still, they had in common a shared identity as Youth Union members, which provided them with a position in the sociopolitical hierarchy that cut across economic and spatial boundaries.

Youth, Community Development, and Nation-Building: The Role of the Youth Union

Social practices relating to sociopolitical activities involving leisure become visible in the urban landscape. These activities are connected to the wider project of nation-building, an inherent part of the Youth Union's rationale and legitimacy. Through its structure and its environmental and social programs, the Youth Union involves young people in urban development in an effort to mobilize them around a shared nation-building project.

Originally named the Indochinese Communist Youth Union, the organization that today is known as the Ho Chi Minh Communist Youth Union was founded on March 26, 1931, by Ho Chi Minh as an anti-imperialist organization to fight for the independence of Vietnam. As a youth branch of the Communist Party, it also functioned as an institutional mechanism for recruiting, indoctrinating, and testing prospective Party members (Marr 1996, 36). Today, while it belongs to an umbrella organization, the Fatherland Front, the Youth Union is still under the direct control of the Communist Party. As defined by a ward-level chairman of the People's Committee, whom I interviewed,

> the Youth Union is the right arm of the Party, a pivotal force of the Party, and a leading organization in carrying out propaganda, urging people to fulfill their responsibilities. The role of the Youth Union is very important because they are well-trained, they are strong, and they play a leading part in organizing movements, especially cultural and social movements.

Although it declares itself a mass organization, the Youth Union is currently struggling to recruit new members, and its membership is restricted and controlled: young people are selected for it on the basis of school performance, behavior, morality, and family background. Such a strict selection process is necessary because of the Youth Union's function in preparing people for future Party membership. As described in the official rhetoric of the Party, the Youth Union is "the socialist school for youth."

Like other mass organizations in Vietnam (e.g., the Women's Union, trade unions, the Farmers' Union), the Youth Union represents a highly centralized political system, which is reflected in its multi-tiered organizational structure. Existing on different administrative levels (national, provincial, district, ward or commune, and group), the Youth Union recruits members on the basis of their affiliation with a specific ward or commune, educational institution, or workplace. Providing an efficient framework for political control, recruitment, and mass mobilization, this organizational structure allows the Youth Union, and ultimately the Party, to reach people in their everyday lives. As an administrative unit, every ward has a People's Committee, located in a local public building. In both Mai Ninh and Truc Tuyet, these buildings are centrally located on main roads and are visited throughout the day by local people who come for various administrative, legal, and social matters. Housing the local branches of the Youth Union, the People's Committees' buildings in the two areas are also frequent meeting points for the most dedicated Youth Union members, who go there to attend meetings, organize youth programs, and coordinate activities with other Youth Union branches at ward or district level.

The Youth Union plays several important roles in the formal organization of youth (Valentin 2007). First, the restriction of membership contributes to processes of social inclusion and exclusion, because membership in the Communist Party is key to following a political career and achieving high positions in the public sector. Second, the Youth Union represents a mobilizing force engaged in molding future citizens in accordance with the dominant national ideology, and in response to political, economic, and cultural pressures from both within and outside Vietnam. Here I focus on the latter to show how, in its efforts to mobilize young people and to make itself visible to the population in general, the Youth Union engages young people in a range of social activities and voluntary programs.

Most of the Youth Union's activities are voluntary, but a precondition for reaching the next step in a political career, namely membership in the Party, is a good record as an active member. Not all Youth Union members are necessarily driven by a belief in its political ideology; they may be pragmatically aware that membership will enhance their career opportunities within the public sector. Most of the Youth Union members we encountered, except for the local leaders, who were employed on a full-time basis by the People's Committee, were either studying or working during the day. They told us that it was often difficult to find the time to regularly participate in activities, especially during examination periods. A few said that the Youth Union had no attractions for their age group, and they considered it more appropriate for younger, school-age children.

Mai, a 22-year-old woman, explained her reasons for not attending meetings and activities very often. When we met her for the first time in spring 2003 she was working full-time in a beauty parlor, and when she was off duty she occasionally had to help her parents with their food stall. The following year, in summer 2004, she found a job in a travel agency, which required that she also take courses in accountancy three evenings a week. In her spare time she preferred to go out with her friends rather than participate in Youth Union activities, from which, as an ordinary member, she could not benefit much anyway. These activities took up much of the leisure time of the most dedicated members, such as the group leaders who were responsible for organizing subgroups of both the Youth Union and the Young Pioneers, the Communist Party's branch for children aged 9–15. Indeed, they spent most of their spare time organizing meetings and activities as well as recruiting new members. Moreover, some had personal interests, which they pursued in the name of the Youth Union: for example, 17-year-old Phuong, a dedicated aerobic dancer, represented the Mai Ninh Youth Union in both district-level and national competitions.

The activities provided by the Youth Union can be divided into three broad categories: one centers on community development and social work, the second on physical exercise and competitive games, and the third on the engagement of young people in national celebrations, such as Independence Day (September 2), Ho Chi Minh's birthday (May 19), and War Invalids and Martyrs' Day (July 27). Youth Union members participate in these activities, either as performers or as organizers of the Young Pioneers. The activities are highly institutionalized, with the intention of socializing, disciplining, and controlling youth in accordance with the dominant ideology. This results in a hegemonic discourse in which young people are the key actors in the process of nation-building and state-led modernization. Particularly relevant to this chapter is the way in which such activities are in various ways staged in the public domain and thus become visible in the urban landscape. Their performative dimension is very pronounced; games, physical exercise, and holiday parades are regularly occurring events involving teams of young people, who in different ways display discipline, collective spirit, and strength. Football matches, dancing contests, and summer games with competitions (such as singing, tug-of-war, or floral decoration) are performed in semi-public places such as stadiums, cultural centers, and schools. Participants are easily identifiable as members of the Youth Union or the Young Pioneers; Youth Union members wear the group's emblem on the sleeves of their white shirts, and Young Pioneers wear a red scarf.

One example of such events is the annual district-level song and dance contest, which I attended in summer 2004. It took place in a big assembly hall in the cultural center of the district, a large, grey, square building recalling the period of the Soviet-supported planned economy. It lasted two days, with groups of Young Pioneers representing each ward in the district, and, under the leadership of Youth Union members, performing group by group. The performances took place on a large stage overlooked by a bust of "Uncle Ho," one of which is to be found in every public institution. Each group wore the same dress and was choreographed in symmetrical, uniform patterns. The program consisted of a kind of calisthenics, traditional Vietnamese folk dances as well as solo performances, evoking associations with, on the one hand, the socialist principle of discipline and collective spirit, and on the other hand, nationalist sentiments grounded in the national history of Vietnam.

Young people's engagement in community development is a key element in the work and legitimacy of the Youth Union. The annual Youth Union reports for 2002 from Mai Ninh and Truc Tuyet, prepared by the local Youth Union secretaries, explicitly stated that young people should be encouraged to participate in so-called volunteer movements that seek to improve and protect the physical and social environments. In concrete terms, and according to the young people

Figure 4.4. Young Pioneers participating in a singing and dancing contest arranged by the Youth Union. Hanoi, 2004. *Photo: Karen Valentin*

we spoke to, such goals were pursued through, among other things, organized programs of street- and canal-cleaning, whitewashing of walls that had been illegally painted with graffiti, and planting trees, but also by contributing to the maintenance of local security. These goals were also expressed in the collaborative volunteer programs established between Youth Union branches in wards and universities, which encouraged students to contribute to community development in both rural and urban areas. Such a program had been running for about five years in Mai Ninh, through which students from the University of Construction spent their summer vacations doing volunteer work, cleaning the canals, playing sports with children, and, on War Invalids and Martyrs' Day, repairing the houses of war invalids and "heroic mothers," women who had lost at least three children during the revolution against the French or the American War. Dressed in bright blue canvas shirts with emblems, occasionally with a scout-like hat hanging from a cord around the neck, the students were made visible both by their presence in the neighborhood and by their interactions with Youth Union members from Mai Ninh.

Maintaining that such activities promote social responsibility and solidarity, both members and leaders of the Youth Union were concerned to engage young people in them to distract them from the temptations of "social evils." From the perspective of the Youth Union, engaging young people in community work was a way of controlling the social environment of the ward and, if necessary, reorienting young people who had started down the "wrong" track. The annual Youth Union report in Truc Tuyet clearly illustrates this, highlighting the need

> to put into operation programs to communicate the model of a Green, Clean, and Healthy cultural environment, so that the families of Youth [Union] members, Youth [Union] members themselves, and pupils won't throw litter into the street. And [a specific] street is registered to be the sample street. Controlling areas with many drug addicts [is important] to keep the environment clean.[5]

This passage reflects an interesting, implicit juxtaposition of different kinds of urban waste—litter and drug addicts—both of which should be kept away from the streets and which young people should learn to handle.

Offering young people "meaningful" leisure, that is, a set of formally organized and politically informed social activities, the Youth Union aims to turn young people into socially responsible persons, active participants in urban community development and other collective events. As an integral part of the Communist Party, the Youth Union also provides a way for the current one-party system to reproduce itself by recruiting new Party members and fostering loyalty to the existing political power. The Youth Union was established as an anti-imperialist organization in the 1930s, when Vietnam was still a French colony. When we spoke to elderly family members and official representatives, it was clear that the character and role of the Youth Union has changed since then. During both the war of emancipation against France and the American War, the organization's key role was to mobilize young people militarily and organizationally in order to fight for an independent Vietnam and to protect the country against the "enemy." Contemporary youth who have no personal experience of war have appropriated the nationalistic rhetoric, but it has become wrapped up in a discourse of "modernization" and "development," reflecting the changing historical conditions and the striving for economic progress and national development (see Valentin 2007).

Although the "enemy" is no longer an explicitly named foreign power, patriotism and nationalism are still key values in the Youth Union's ideological foundation. Relevant here is the principle of filial duty, which locates young people as inferior, and obedient, to their seniors. Because Confucian doctrine does not distinguish between the state and political relations on the one hand and society and familial relations on the other, the family and the state do not differ in essence, only in scale (Tuong Lai 1991, 5). Occupying a central position in Confucian morality, the category of the family is the foundation of the country; hence family morality permeates and rules all other relationships in society. When seen from this perspective, young people's loyalty to the Youth Union and the Party, and ultimately the nation, might be seen as a filial duty analogous to the loyalty they are expected to have to their parents and other seniors. It is open to debate how these strong authority structures, placing youth in positions inferior to both seniors and the nation, are likely to be affected as young people gradually become more and more oriented toward conceptions of popular, global youth cultures, which may—or may not—exist "out there."

Maintaining power for the Party is a challenge in a society that is undergoing profound transformations as a result of, among other things, the introduction of market socialism, increasing privatization, and integration into the global economy. The fact that it is difficult for the Youth Union to recruit new members is evidence of its declining legitimacy in the eyes of the young themselves. It is an open question whether this decline is due to ideology or the kinds of activities the Youth Union offers. On the one hand, most of the young people in this study were dedicated Youth Union members who acknowledged the advantages of membership, seeing it either as a necessary step toward a career as a state employee or politician, or as a means to gain social or organizational skills that could be useful in other spheres. On the other hand, a few complained that the kinds of activities offered by the Youth Union could not attract "modern" youth. Judging from the huge number of young people in the streets, cafés, karaoke bars, department stores, and discos, it is clear that Hanoi offers young people a wide range of opportunities for consumption and leisure that may challenge the centrality of the Youth Union in their everyday lives (see Wildermuth, this volume). And yet it is also crucial to acknowledge that for young people, membership in the Youth Union and participation in consumer-oriented leisure activities are not mutually exclusive. In particular, the young people in Truc Tuyet who had the purchasing power to position themselves in the cultural space of the emergent, consuming middle class certainly knew how to seek out the fancy cafés around Hoan Kiem Lake and yet remain loyal to the Youth Union.

Although membership in the Communist Party is still a prerequisite for higher positions in the public sector, the expansion of the private sector has created entirely new career opportunities beyond the domain of the Party. Because they are able to follow alternative routes into the labor market, young, educated people may have less need today to become Party members and consequently less need for a good record in the Youth Union. At the same time, however, unemployment rates among urban youth are reported to be higher than among any other groups of working age in Vietnam, which is partly explained by a mismatch between the skills taught in the educational system and those needed by the labor market (Dang Nguyen Anh, Le Bach Duong, and Nguyen Hai Van 2005). Another challenge to the Youth Union, and any other mass organization, is the rise of private civic associations (Kerkvliet 2003; Le Bach Duong et al. 2003), such as NGOs,

Figure 4.5. Focus group discussion with Youth Union members from Mai Ninh and volunteering university students. Hanoi, 2004. *Photo: Karen Valentin*

sports clubs, and computer centers, which provide alternative formalized settings where young people can interact and spend their leisure time. In short, the expanding private sector, with both its labor market and its civic associations, and the less-organized youth activities appearing in the public sphere are competing with the Youth Union for young people's social and political energy.

Conclusion: A Generational Perspective on Urban Youth

Unlike youths in the two other research sites—Recife and Lusaka—young people in Hanoi have grown up in an era of political stability and economic progress, and consequently under material conditions that by far exceed what their parents, who were young during the American War, ever experienced. Despite a general rise in living standards, the gap between the rich and the poor has widened since the introduction of *doi moi,* which is to a great extent a result of the different growth rates of urban and rural areas (Do Thien Kinh et al. 2001). The city offers young people and their families opportunities and prospects that are unavailable in rural areas, but it also confronts them with places that are considered morally illegitimate for young people. Using the Youth Union as an avenue for exploring young people's experiences of growing up in an urban environment and the inherent spatializing practices involved in this, I have focused on how young people, by virtue of their position in generational hierarchies and their particular status as youth, are assigned specific places and roles in the city.

A perspective on Hanoi as both text and context sheds light on the politicized nature of both the city and the young. It shows that the physical organization of the city is an outcome of political power and contestation in different historical epochs, but also that this organization has contributed to the shaping of different youth generations growing out of Hanoi. By interpreting the city as a text and approaching it from a generational perspective, we may be able to see the contours of different politico-ideological generations inscribed on the city and consequently the changing structural conditions of society. Reading the city as a context for social action, on the other hand, allows us to examine the specific conditions under which different generations of young people grow up and how they are formed as both individuals and historically produced categories. From a societal perspective, succeeding generations of youth correspond to and are constructed in response to changing politico-ideological systems, in terms of both dominant discourses of youth and counterdiscourses. However, individuals have to transcend the boundaries between these changing systems and, on the basis of personal experiences and life trajectories, negotiate what it means to be young at a particular point in history.

Acknowledgments

The Hanoi City study was conducted in collaboration with the Institute of Sociology, Center for Humanities and Social Sciences, Hanoi, under the guidance of Dr. Dang Nguyen Anh. Ms. Nguyen Thi Phuong and Mr. Duong Chi Thien worked as senior research assistants, and Mr. Phi Hai Nam and Ms. Nghiem Thi Thuy as junior research assistants. I am grateful to the entire research team for their support. My interpreter, Ms. Nguyen Chung Thuy, was invaluable in her efforts to translate as carefully as possible. I also thank Tine Gammeltoft for critical comments on earlier drafts of this chapter.

Notes

1. This is the case, for example, in formerly communist countries of Eastern Europe (Pilkington 1994; Riordan 1989; Kuebart 1989), socialist states in postcolonial Africa, such as Zanzibar in the 1960–70s (Burgess 1999, 2005), and countries under fascist leadership, such as Mussolini's Italy (Koon 1985) and Nazi Germany (Wallace and Alt 2001).

2. The Youth Federation is an umbrella organization of which the Youth Union is a core member. Whereas the latter is explicitly defined as a sociopolitical organization, the former is conceived of as a social organization whose membership is not so strictly controlled.

3. The quotations are taken from tape-recorded interviews, which were transcribed by the interpreter and later translated by people appointed by the Institute of Sociology. During the

interviews I carefully noted down people's answers as they were translated by the interpreter. These notes were later compared with the official translations as a way of cross-checking.

4. The legal age of marriage is 18 for women and 20 for men, though nationally the average ages at first marriage are higher, namely 23.1 and 26.2 (in 2003), respectively (Committee for Population, Family and Children 2005, 41).

5. This is an unofficial translation.

References

Appadurai, Arjun. 1995. The Production of Locality. In *Counterworks: Managing the Diversity of Knowledge,* ed. Richard Fardon, 204–25. London and New York: Routledge.

Bucholtz, Mary. 2002. Youth and Cultural Practice. *Annual Review of Anthropology* 31:525–52.

Burgess, Thomas. 1999. Remembering Youth: Generation in Revolutionary Zanzibar. *Africa Today* 46(2):29–50.

———. 2005. The Young Pioneers and the Rituals of Citizenship in Revolutionary Zanzibar. *Africa Today* 51(3):3–29.

Burr, Rachel. 2006. *Vietnam's Children in a Changing World.* New Brunswick, N.J.: Rutgers University Press.

Casey, Edward S. 1996. How to Get from Space to Place in a Fairly Short Stretch of Time: Phenomenological Prolegomena. In *Senses of Place,* ed. Steven Feld and Keith H. Basso, 13–52. Santa Fe, N.M.: School of American Research Press.

Chae, Suhong. 2003. Contemporary Ho Chi Minh City in Numerous Contradictions: Reform Policy, Foreign Capital and the Working Class. In *Wounded Cities: Destruction and Reconstruction in a Globalized World,* ed. Jane Schneider and Ida Susser, 227–48. Oxford and New York: Berg.

Committee for Population, Family and Children. 2005. Data on Population, Family and Children. Hanoi: Nha Xuat Ban Thong Ke.

Dang Nguyen Anh, Le Bach Duong, and Nguyen Hai Van. 2005. Youth Employment in Viet Nam: Characteristics, Determinants and Policy Responses. Employment Strategy Papers, International Labour Organization.

Do Thien Kinh, Le Do Mach, Lo Thi Duc, Nguyen Ngoc Mai, and Tran Quang, with Bui Xuan Du. 2001. Inequality. In *Living Standards during an Economic Boom: The Case of Vietnam,* ed. Dominique Haughton, Jonathan Haughton, and Nguyen Phong, 33–46. Hanoi: United Nations Development Programme and Statistical Publishing House.

Drummond, Lisa B. W. 2000. Street Scenes: Practices of Public and Private Space in Urban Vietnam. *Urban Studies* 37(12):2377–91.

Fong, Vanessa L. 2004. *Only Hope: Coming of Age under China's One-Child Policy.* Stanford, Calif.: Stanford University Press.

Gammeltoft, Tine. 2002. Being Special for Somebody: Urban Sexualities in Contemporary Vietnam. *Asian Journal of Social Science* 30(3):476–92.

Gammeltoft, Tine, and Karen Fog Olwig. 2005. The Anthropology of Children. In *To Make My Parents Happy: Anthropological Perspectives on Children in Vietnam,* ed. Tine Gammeltoft and Karen Fog Olwig, 11–36. Hanoi: Statistical Publishing House.

Hoang Huu Pee and Nishimura. 2000. The Historical Environment and Housing Conditions in the "36 Old Streets" Quarter of Hanoi. In *Shelter and Living in Hanoi*, ed. Trinh Duy Luan and Hans Schenk, 10–56. Hanoi: Cultural Publishing House.

Hy V. Luong. 2003. Postwar Vietnamese Society: An Overview of Transformational Dynamics. Introduction to *Postwar Vietnam: Dynamics of a Transforming Society*, 1–26. Singapore: Institute of Southeast Asian Studies; Lanham, Md.: Rowman and Littlefield.

Jamieson, Neil L. 1993. *Understanding Vietnam*. Berkeley: University of California Press.

Kerkvliet, Benedict J. Tria. 2003. Grappling with Organizations and the State in Contemporary Vietnam. Introduction to *Getting Organized in Vietnam: Moving in and around the Socialist State*, ed. Benedict J. Tria Kerkvliet, Russell H. K. Heng, and David W. H. Koh, 1–24. Singapore: Institute of Southeast Asian Studies.

Koon, Tracy H. 1985. *Believe, Obey, Fight: Political Socialization of Youth in Fascist Italy, 1922–1943*. Chapel Hill: University of North Carolina Press.

Kuebart, Friedrich. 1989. The Political Socialisation of Schoolchildren. In *Soviet Youth Culture*, ed. Jim Riordan, 103–21. Basingstoke and London: Macmillan.

Le Bach Duong, Khuat Thu Hong, Bach Tan Sinh, and Nguyen Thanh Tung. 2003. Civil Society in Vietnam. In *Voices from Southern Civil Societies: The Interplay of National and Global Contexts in the Performance of Civil Society Organisations in the South*, 91–119. Policy Papers 6/2003. Helsinki: Institute of Development Studies, University of Helsinki.

Logan, William S. 2000. *Hanoi: Biography of a City*. Sydney: University of New South Wales Press.

Marr, David G. 1996. Vietnamese Youth in the 1990s. Australian-Vietnam Research Project, Working Paper no. 3. Sydney: School of Economic and Financial Studies, Macquarie University.

Ministry of Health, General Statistics Office. 2005. *Survey Assessment on Vietnamese Youth*. With support from UNICEF and WHO. Hanoi: Ministry of Health, General Statistics Office.

Nguyen Quang and Hans Detlef Kammeier. 2002. Changes in the Political Economy of Vietnam and Their Impacts on the Built Environment of Hanoi. *Cities* 19(6):373–88.

Olwig, Karen, and Eva Gulløv. 2003. Towards an Anthropology of Children and Place. In *Children's Places: Cross-Cultural Perspectives*, ed. Karen Fog Olwig and Eva Gulløv, 1–19. London and New York: Routledge.

Pilkington, Hilary. 1994. *Russia's Youth and Its Culture: A Nation's Constructors and Constructed*. London and New York: Routledge.

Riordan, Jim. 1989. The Komsomol. In *Soviet Youth Culture*, ed. Jim Riordan, 16–44. Basingstoke and London: Macmillan.

Susser, Ida, and Jane Schneider. 2003. Wounded Cities: Destruction and Reconstruction in a Globalized World. In *Wounded Cities: Destruction and Reconstruction in a Globalized World*, ed. Jane Schneider and Ida Susser, 1–23. Oxford and New York: Berg.

Thomas, Mandy. 2002. Out of Control: Emergent Cultural Landscapes and Political Change in Urban Vietnam. *Urban Studies* 39(9):1611–24.

Tran Dinh Huou. 1991. Traditional Families in Vietnam and the Influence of Confucianism. In *Sociological Studies on the Vietnamese Family*, ed. Rita Liljeström and Tuong Lai, 25–47. Hanoi: Social Sciences Publishing House.

Trinh Duy Luan and Nguyen Quang Vinh. 2001. *Socio-economic Impacts of "Doi Moi" on Urban Housing in Vietnam.* Hanoi: Social Sciences Publishing House.

Tuong Lai. 1991. Introduction to *Sociological Studies on the Vietnamese Family,* ed. Rita Liljeström and Tuong Lai, 3–11. Hanoi: Social Sciences Publishing House.

Valentin, Karen. 2005. Hanoi. *Tidsskiftet Antropologi: BYER* 47:33–41.

———. 2007. Mass Mobilization and the Struggle over the Youth: The Role of Ho Chi Minh Communist Youth Union in Urban Vietnam. *Young: Nordic Journal of Youth Research* 15(3):299–315.

Wallace, Claire, and Raimund Alt. 2001. Youth Cultures under Authoritarian Regimes: The Case of Swings against the Nazis. *Youth & Society* 32(3):275–302.

Wyn, Johanna, and Rob White. 1997. *Rethinking Youth.* London: Sage.

5

Localities and Sites of Youth Agency in Lusaka

Karen Tranberg Hansen

Lusaka, Zambia's physically scattered and socioeconomically divided capital, presents itself to a first-time visitor with the visual props of development driven by neoliberal investment, in the form of several new shopping malls. The capital's religious topography is particularly striking, with the recent completion of a Catholic cathedral and the Cathedral of Faith of the Pentecostal Universal Church of the Kingdom of God.[1] But most visible are billboards about the "killer disease," HIV/AIDS. Indeed, in the name of development, HIV/AIDS is the main focus of NGO activity in Zambia, including in most matters pertaining to young people.

This chapter is about processes that both constrain and enable young people's efforts to change their life circumstances in Zambia's capital against the backdrop of sociopolitical and economic changes associated with neoliberalism. The focus is on activities in different locations, from politics to culture, that may contribute to altering long-held local meanings of youth, changing it from implying dependence to expressing agency. This complexity of young people's everyday lives is hidden from view by the almost exclusive preoccupation with reproductive health in HIV/AIDS research and media reporting in Zambia. The resulting "cover story" lacks contextual understanding of life on the ground. In a very deliberate effort to enlarge the characterization of young people from the narrow issue of HIV/AIDS, I include in my scope several settings of daily life where young people interact, with a variety of agendas. Indeed, as Mamadou Diouf has noted, young Africans "excluded from the arenas of power, work, education and leisure . . . construct places of socialization and new sociabilities whose function is to show their difference, either on the margins of society or at its head" (2003, 5).

Widespread urban inequality and a lack of jobs, housing, and social and medical services make young people in Zambia subject to the kind of violence that some have called structural (Galtung 1969; Farmer 2002). HIV/AIDS, and the structural violence that helps produce it, represent urban "wounds" that result from the general deterioration of urban life in Zambia since the 1970s (Schneider and Susser 2003). Lusaka's new shopping malls are visual evidence of young people's simultaneous inclusion in a global world of consumerism and their exclusion from it due to their limited economic means. Even so, as I demonstrate in this chapter, it is an oversimplification to present the situation of today's youth in Lusaka in dichotomous terms, because most young people's lives are deeply entangled with both these processes.

The challenges facing a large proportion of young people in Zambia's urban areas have a long history that is linked to the country's political and economic colonial history as a mining center. Lusaka is one of Africa's most rapidly growing cities, though its growth has slowed in recent years (Hansen 1997; Potts 2005). But continuities mask important differences. The predicament of today's youth is not so much a recycled legacy of past history (Schlyter 1999) as it is a product of more recent political and economic transformations. My concerns in this chapter belong to the present, to the era of neoliberal politics and economics that was launched when the one-party state yielded to multi-party rule in 1991. Changing local and global socioeconomic and political contexts give new meanings to youth, confronting long-standing cultural ideals that used to guide relations between the sexes and the generations. Affecting both the history and geography of opportunity, these transformations are inaugurating new times.

Zambia's 1991 multi-party elections introduced liberalized economic development priorities that have sharpened long-existing sociospatial polarizations, extending them in new ways that are particularly visible in urban areas. Today, shopping malls displace small-scale traders and street vendors, and changing property values relegate low-income residents to housing on the edge of the city. These processes form the backdrop for this chapter's exploration of how young women and men from different socioeconomic backgrounds negotiate their place in Lusaka.[2] I first offer background information and sketch some of the structural transformations that have reshaped Lusaka's landscape since the early 1990s. I then discuss the meanings that young people and Zambian society generally attribute to youth, as well as the significance that young urban residents attribute to space. The remaining sections focus on young people's efforts to gain access to important urban sites where they express their desire for participation and recognition, as I explain from the point of view of trainees in a vocational school. I next turn to spaces of political engagement where young people call dominant power structures into question. Finally, I approach cultural space as sites where young people are searching for identity and belonging. I consider two such sites:

religious movements and the popular music scene. Taken together, these different yet overlapping spaces of engagement provide rich evidence of young people reshaping and improving society's currently problematic view of them.

I launched my part of the youth project in 2001 by conducting a household survey of the backgrounds of young people between the ages of 15 and 25 in three different residential areas of Lusaka. I carried out participant observation in a vocational training center in 2002, examined church-related youth activities in 2003, and pursued youth political activities in organized and informal groups and NGOs in 2004. I briefly followed up some of these issues in 2005. My research included group discussions, student essays, and the tracking of the trajectories of a small cohort of young people whose lives I began observing in 2001. The inclusion of young people beyond the teenage years and the four-year duration of this study permit detailed insights into the experiences of young women and men along their diverse trajectories to adulthood.

Background

Zambia's economy has performed poorly since the mid-1970s, yet the country continues to export copper and other minerals. In recent years, its agricultural exports have increased through diverse connections to the global economy, in which South Africa and China are important investors. Because it is the capital of Zambia, Lusaka has significant relationships with the World Bank and the International Monetary Fund (IMF), development agencies, and international political organizations. These relationships, together with Lusaka's national and regional trade and other factors, demonstrate its importance as an administrative center and exchange hub for goods and services from across the country and the world. Although it is not a "global city" (Sassen 1994), Lusaka is very much a part of the changing global economy of the twenty-first century. Indeed, even with their dilapidated infrastructure and poor amenities, cities such as Lusaka are globalizing rapidly.

Lusaka's new shopping malls and Internet cafés do not hide either the country's prolonged economic crisis or the ravages of HIV/AIDS, malaria, and cholera; the latter recurs in sprawling urban markets and townships almost every rainy season. In the first half of the 1990s, Zambians were worse off than they were in the mid-1970s (GRZ and UN 1996). With more than two-thirds of the population living on less than US$1 a day, Zambia continues to perform poorly on standard indicators of development: education, health, longevity, child mortality and nutrition, formal employment, and wages (UNDP 2004). Fifteen percent of the primary school-age cohort does not attend school (CSO 2000). The HIV/AIDS prevalence rate for the 15–49 age group is high (estimated at 16.5 percent in 2003), higher in urban than rural areas, and five times higher for young women between 15 and 19 years of age than for young men in the same age group. The chance that a 15-year-old will die from AIDS is estimated at one in two. And most of them will die by the age of 35 (SIAPAC 2004, 2).

Lusaka's population is approaching two million, and close to half the country's total population of about eleven million is urban. According to 2004 UNDP projections, young people below 25 years of age constitute 64 percent of Zambia's total population, whose average longevity is estimated to be 32.7 years. To be sure, young people are central to the reproduction of society and its future. Where do they fit into this process? Formal employment declined from 17 to 11 percent, offset to some extent by an increase in informal activities, between 1992 and 1999 (CSO 2000). But the reference to the enormous growth of the informal economy since the 1970s glosses over inequalities in terms of gender and age, activity, location, and organization. Privatization of the economy has pushed many adults into the informal economy. Competition with adults limits the entry of young people into the informal economy, placing them in low-level jobs with few prospects for upward mobility or the acquisition of higher qualifications. There is no doubt, as Jennifer Cole and Deborah Durham have pointed out (2007), that one of the most conspicuous fault lines in the new millennium is generational.

Socioeconomic Inequality across Space and Class

Structural adjustment programs (SAPs) and recent neoliberal reforms are contributing to the transformation of urban space, changing the distribution of economic opportunities throughout individual cities, between cities in Africa, and globally (Zeleza 1999; Pugh 1995; Riddell 1997). Such policies have important ramifications across urban space, affecting the livelihoods of different population segments in different ways, sharpening and extending social and spatial inequalities.

Two decades of SAPs (since the early 1980s) and one of neoliberal reforms (since the early 1990s) have altered the nature and availability of urban space in Lusaka, including land, infrastructure, and access to markets. In the wake of these reforms, changes in land values have adversely affected both access to housing and its location, as well as the place and nature of commercial activity. Because housing markets have been privatized and no low-cost government housing constructed since the 1970s, more than 75 percent of Lusaka's population lives in informal or squatter settlements, locally called compounds, in the peri-urban areas (Mulenga 2001; Nchito and Myers 2004, 109).[3] Inadequate provision of electricity, water, sanitation, and transport reduces the chance that services and small-scale manufacturing activities will develop in such areas. And large-scale business developments, including the international airport, commercial farms, and cattle ranches next to Lusaka's low-cost housing areas, limit the possibility of peri-urban expansion.

Foreign investment, especially by South African firms, in a variety of commercial activities, mostly retail, has resulted in new patterns of spatial segregation in Lusaka. Chinese investment is growing, especially in the urban wholesale and retail sector, where Chinese-owned and -managed shops selling low-cost housewares and apparel are pushing a competitive wedge into a commercial sector that Indians and Zambians dominated in the past. A highly visible consequence of these developments since the mid-1990s is the displacement of small-scale trading and service activities from the city center to areas on the periphery in order to free up space for shopping malls and stores. Violent confrontations between urban authorities and street vendors over the use of public space for commerce continue to take place, and street vendors, most of them male youth, are intermittently removed. Such young men are regarded as a public health nuisance who disrupt established businesses, or else as criminals or illegal immigrants (Hansen 2004b).

The privatized market economy has also helped introduce shifts in Lusaka's religious geography. President Frederick Chiluba's declaration in 1991 that Zambia was a "Christian nation" prompted the registration of many new churches. In effect, the city has turned into a religious resource as places of worship have multiplied, sometimes taking place in schoolrooms and tents. Both mainline and Pentecostal churches have mobilized mass communication technologies such as radio, television, and video to make spiritual and social resources available to believers.

These transformations are evident also in cultural space and in how, where, and with whom young people spend their time away from home. Some of these spaces are significantly gendered and highly charged in sexual terms. The transformations of both the economy and space in Lusaka have complicated ramifications for young people of different class backgrounds. Young people's responses to these changes depend on their gender, socioeconomic situation, geographical location, and cultural outlook, including religion, and are affected by the kinds of skills and resources they can draw on from within the organization of everyday life in their own households and in the wider setting.

Youth and Its Meanings

People in Zambia broadly define youth chronologically as the period from age 12 or 15 to 35.[4] But what youth means is a cultural question. Many parents distinguish youth from children by their maturity, which they define both socially and sexually. In their view, maturity arrives earlier for young women than for young men. Young women and men refer to sexual activity when they distinguish between childhood and youth.

Young people and adults generally agree that the chief meaning of youth is dependence or being "kept," which means relying on others for food, shelter, and clothing. This is certainly how some young secondary-school students in grade 12 put it in essays they wrote for me about being a young person in Lusaka. A 17-year-old young woman wrote in 2001, "Being a young person in Lusaka today means no freedom; even when it is given to you, it is given in a way that reminds you of your limitations. You are reminded that you are becoming an adult and are supposed to act responsibly yet get treated as a child. It seems that you never have time to live your own life." A 19-year-old male fellow student had this to say: "In Lusaka, if you are young, you are considered to be a child who has no say in the issues of the country. In some parts of Lusaka, you are considered a nuisance . . . a bad image of the young people."

The impatience in these young people's voices is palpable. The young woman wants to be considered as an individual, to be able to experience youth as a distinct phase of life, with its own outlook, a youth mentality. The young man alludes to how young people who are out and about in the city, especially young men, are viewed in negative terms, even as dangerous. Their statements converge in one observation: Zambian society does not regard youth as social actors with whom it must reckon. The government and many parents view young people as subordinate to their authority, in a hierarchical, patriarchal, and gerontocratic understanding of how society ought to work.

The cultural terms for adulthood in Zambia, in the view of both youth and parents, revolve around independence from others, responsibility toward others, and the ability to take care of a household. But attaining social adulthood in Zambia is difficult, for schools do not provide education for all, secondary-school graduates face difficulties in obtaining formal jobs, and even young people with university degrees no longer expect to find jobs easily. The housing situation is abysmal, except for the rich. Young people out of school, in informal or insecure formal jobs if they are working at all, cannot afford to rent rooms or houses. If they are poor, many remain where they are, in crowded compounds. As I explain below, young people from middle-income backgrounds are particularly conscious of their restricted exit options and try to improve their chances by acquiring business or trade skills. And although not all youth from well-off backgrounds can expect to proceed straight from higher education into formal employment, they are financially cushioned against a hard life. Some of them turn to entrepreneurship in business and culture.

"Where You Are": Youth and Urban Space Attachment

The household survey I conducted sampled young people in three different residential areas: very poor, middle-income, and well-off.[5] Although this categorization conceals heterogeneity in household size and organization within each

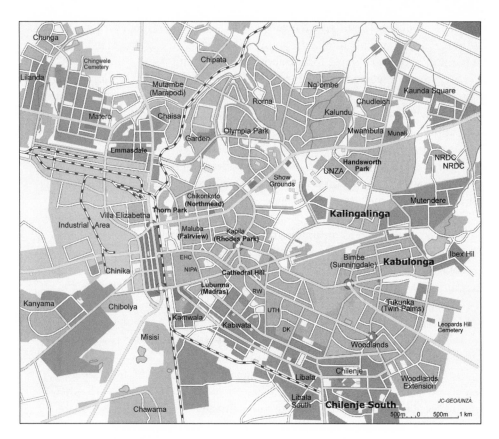

Map 3. Map of Lusaka

of these areas, it captures their contrasting socioeconomic resource bases. Most households were extended, but crowding was extreme in many poor households. All these young people were very conscious of disparities in wealth. They experience life in Lusaka in spatial terms, in relation to "where they are" (Beall 2002, 48). The young people from the poorest areas distinguished "where they are" in the compounds from the high-income residential areas. Some of them worked hard devising ways to get away, yet felt trapped in the compounds. Many blamed their lack of job prospects on their limited education. Others thought that life might be better if they received more training, though few had the means to pay school fees. Young people in the middle-income area struggled not to "slide down" and "get caught in the compound" (Hansen 2005). They were particularly busy taking courses to improve their situation.

Young people from *apamwamba* backgrounds, as the well-off are called (the

word is a Nyanja term meaning "those on the top"), live in high-income residential areas and constitute a tiny segment of Lusaka's huge youth population.
Because most of them had educational prospects and financial support to ensure a
smoother transition into adulthood than their poorer age-mates, they were better
placed to take advantage of the capital's resources. Their concerns were somewhat
different. Our interviews revealed three priorities: continuing with education in
order to become independent, postponing marriage but having active relationships, and having a good time. Studying at colleges, training institutions, and
universities, sometimes in Australia or the United States, many of these young
people have the means—usually because of well-placed parents—to hang out with
friends at Lusaka's new shopping malls, pool halls, gyms, bars, and parks. They
can afford the party scene and have the means to travel, including to Zambia's
game parks and lodges as well as abroad. Many came from households with the
kind of amenities their poor age-mates see as the yardstick to measure "where
they are" not themselves, because their lifeworlds do not include well-appointed
houses, cars, satellite dishes and Internet access, and the latest fashions. These
young people live comfortable lives and enjoy a degree of freedom that poor
young people admire.

Trajectories of Space, Class, Gender, and Sexuality

Young people's experiences are affected by the socioeconomic situations of their
households, their levels of education, labor market conditions, and, last but not
least, their cultural outlooks and individual strategies. Together these factors
help us understand how distinct groups of young people become socially and
economically involved in different ways. Drawing on interviews and conversations with young women and men enrolled in vocational training courses in
2002, I now explore the place attachments of students from poor households,
many of whom were living with guardians rather than with their parents. This
particular training institution, the Kanyama Youth Programme Trust (KYPT)
Technical Institute, charged lower fees than many similar institutions in Lusaka;
it also sponsored some students with funding from NGOs, particularly young
women from "vulnerable homes," that is, households where a parent or parents
had died from AIDS.[6]

These young students emphatically wanted to leave their compounds. They
described Lusaka's compounds in graphic terms as overcrowded, dirty, and
disease-ridden. They saw unemployment and hunger governing life in the compounds. When describing the corollaries of these circumstances, they referred to
drinking, drugs, prostitution, theft, and gangs. According to 20-year-old Sarah,
who was studying hotel management and catering, these circumstances make it
"easy to do unwanted things like prostitution and drinking."

Figure 5.1. Young women and men at a carpentry course. Lusaka, 2001.
Photo: Karen Tranberg Hansen

Some young men agreed with the women that there are "too many temptations" in the compounds. Mwansa, a 33-year-old automotive mechanics student,
expressed this categorically when he said, "Don't live in the compounds." For
many years he had scraped together a living by pushing a *zamcab* (a wheelbarrow
for hire) in a Lusaka market. At 33 years of age, he was still considered a youth
because he was not economically self-sufficient. When I met him, he lived in a
rented room in a compound. Wishing to use his creative skills in writing and
performance, Mwansa explained that he needed a trade just to get by.

The young women trainees did not have as clear personal agendas as the young
men. Some women assumed that they would be able to obtain skilled jobs after
graduation and that they would marry and have children. Many had boyfriends.
Most male students had girlfriends. The young men, unlike the young women,
drew a distinction between girlfriends and lovers (or fiancées); girlfriends, they
explained, are just friends, while lovers (or fiancées) are sexual partners. The
young men complained that girlfriends want sex because they believe it might
lead to marriage and maintenance. In the view of young men, these young women
considered sex a means of luring boyfriends into marriage.

If young women hold this attitude, it is not surprising that Peter, a 19-year-old
carpentry student, told me that "girlfriends disturb our minds." Young men like

him live in the time of the "killer disease," AIDS, and they know it. Several of them were concerned with the difficulties involved in restraining their sexuality while preparing themselves for adulthood through training courses. Widespread cultural ideals in Zambia construe successful manhood as entailing strong heterosexual desires that are difficult to control and therefore pursued actively and aggressively both outside and within marriage (Ndubani 2002; Simpson 2005). Some young men viewed women as actively searching for partners, that is, as predatory. A group of football players between the ages of 18 and 21 in Kalingalinga compound told me in 2001 about their difficulty "refraining from girls." "There is a chain of them," one said; "you must have many" (Hansen 2003, 39).

Transactional sex has been widely reported in Zambia. When people live on less than US$1 a day, the link between poverty and sex is strong. Young girls from their mid-teens have sex with older men in exchange for money and gifts (Fetters, Mupela, and Rutenberg 1997; Kambou, Shah, and Nkhama 1998; Remes et al. 2003; Webb 1997). Young male trainees complain that they do not have the money to sustain relationships with girls. Some of them try to avoid sexual activity. Twenty-year-old Alick, a student in the automotive mechanics course, emphasized that he had a girlfriend, not a lover. Speaking of the great need for self-control, he said he could manage because "I have the fear of God" (he was an active member of a Pentecostal church). Nineteen-year-old Stephen, in the carpentry course, said that he was trying to "keep" himself, a formulation I had previously heard mainly from women. He would give himself five years, he explained, during which he hoped to build a house and furnish it, before he considered himself ready for marriage. The widespread assumption in Zambia that men are in charge of households weighed heavily on these young men. They talked about organizing their lives, building themselves, having a program, and achieving their goals in a more purposeful way than the young women.

These young people's experience of "where they are"—that is, in the compound—mediates their understanding of what it takes to leave such a place, and those requirements are clearly gendered. This experience of "where you are" shapes how poor youth view the city. Many of them lack economic means and are not often able to pay for public transportation to visit relatives or friends elsewhere in the capital. For this reason, many are reduced to just "sitting at home," as they told me, when I asked how they spent their time when not attending courses. Many young women, and some men, had a hard time naming Lusaka attractions other than general landmarks, such as the parliament and high-rise buildings, probably because shopping malls, sports clubs, and hotels are associated with a way of life to which they have no access.

The distinctions these young people drew between "where they are" in the compound on the one hand and Lusaka's center and high-income residential areas on the other did not refer primarily to physical space but to ways of liv-

Figure 5.2. Young men and women at a tailoring course. Lusaka, 2001.
Photo: Karen Tranberg Hansen

ing, "the way we stay." This is the language of space, money, and social relations.
Sarah told me that she did not like "the way we stay" when she explained how she
lived with her brothers and sisters in Chawama compound. Her mother had left
her and her siblings when their father died. Enes, a tailoring student of 19, said
that her role model was "someone who stays nicely, is comfortable, and doesn't
face problems like we do." According to 18-year-old Abijah, in the hotel management and catering course, a person who "stays nicely" is someone "who has
everything," someone who has completed school and additional training, owns
a home with electricity and running water, an indoor toilet, and private rooms
for the household's young people, and has clothes to wear and enough food for
the whole household. Such a person is "working," which in Zambian English
contrasts with self-employment and small-scale trading. People who work are
"respectable," said 20-year-old Precious, in the tailoring course, and "at home we
are not." Both her parents have died, so she lives with an older brother, his wife,
a young brother, and a cousin in two rented rooms in a compound.

Today in Lusaka, disparities in wealth are more conspicuous than ever, against
the backdrop of shopping malls and the visibility of "global goods" that are out
of the reach of most of the young people I quoted above. They talk about Lusaka
as a "divided" city, drawing the "boundary" as Andson, a grade 12 student, did

in 2004: "between people from the compounds and those from the [high-in-come] residential areas," between the "low-class" or "common man" and "the high-class people," the type of people who work in offices, eat at restaurants, and enjoy shopping in the malls. To him and many others, consumer goods are about power and possession. It is striking that the contradictions between the material circumstances under which these young people live and how they desire to live their lives are negotiated through commodities and particular constructions of social relations and of space.[7] In their discourse, consumer goods bridge the opportunity gap. The difficulty of crossing that bridge provokes both admiration and anxiety. This is evident in the desires of the young people I have quoted, whose imaginations involve gender conventions and a household ideal whose normative vision very few people in Zambia in fact live up to.

Exclusion and Inclusion in Political Space

Young people's chief concern is jobs. Zambia's growing youth unemployment often features in political speeches, yet is rarely addressed in practice. Only a few of the young people from the cohort I met at the technical and vocational training center in 2002 found jobs after completing their training, and then only in the informal economy, and not always ones that used the skills in which they had been trained. Graduates from higher-level technical and vocational training institutions such as Lusaka's state-sponsored trade training institute fared little better. Scraping together the money for fees, some have begun new lines of study in information technology or business administration, hoping that these skills might open up alternative job opportunities.

In an effort to qualify the notion, propagated by the international media, that people in Zambia are politically docile, my assistants and I explored the political scene in relation to youth in 2004, from the level of party politics, to alternative institutions, to interaction with young people in the three residential areas where the household survey was conducted. Although many of the young people I have come to know through this research were disenchanted with formal party politics, some found other spaces for different forms of political expression. Their general disenchantment is evident in the observation that "youth are seen but not heard," made by a 22-year-old woman from an *apamwamba* household who was enrolled in a computer training course. She referred to politicians as "not very interested [in youth], they just mention it." Many young people see party politics as almost irrelevant to their personal situation.

Although these young people voted in the presidential elections in 2001 and 2006, they had little regard for party affiliation or formal party politics. Young adults who were active in mobilizing people to vote in the 1991 election that dismantled the one-party state and brought the Movement for Multiparty

Figure 5.3. Self-employed hardware vendor in his makeshift stall. Lusaka, 2002.
Photo: Karen Tranberg Hansen

Democracy (MMD) to power told me how disappointed they were once multi-party rule was put into place and they were sidelined. From their viewpoint, today's political parties revolve around "big men" who exploit young people as mobilizers and crowd-controllers rather than as participants in formulating and implementing programs to improve their living conditions.

In 1991 Zambia launched a course of multi-party politics, yet the legacies of nearly twenty years of one-party rule (1972–91) remain evident. The new constitution adopted after 1991 permitted several political parties but retained considerable executive control in the presidency. Constitutional reforms in 1996 subjected the powers of the president to scrutiny, a process that remains a key to ongoing constitutional reform debates. The electoral victory of the MMD at every election since 1991 has intensified its control of the state's resources, including externally sourced funds. Other political parties include the United National Independence Party (UNIP), formerly the sole party, which has survived the transition to multi-party rule, and several small parties that come and go, some of which have yet to achieve political institutionalization.

The MMD's control of state resources has given rise to the "big man" syndrome and personalized politics. These resources rarely trickle down to the poor through patronage networks but tend to stay in the hands of a narrow political

Figure 5.4. Graduates of an auto mechanics course with a wrecked car they have reconditioned for use as a pirate taxi. Lusaka, 2004. *Photo: Karen Tranberg Hansen*

elite (van de Walle 2003, 312–13). With both public and private employment severely restricted, the political elite can make very few material gains by using the civil service to attract political clients. In such a situation, commerce and trade might provide settings for patron-client relationships to develop through access to business licenses, tax concessions, and import facilities.

From the point of view of many, including the young, you need to know someone in power in order to get anywhere in society. But economic constraints have reduced the possibilities for mass party patronage. This is why many of the young people I talked to consider party politics at the presidential and constituency levels useless. "There is nothing in it for us," they say. At the party constituency level there is little youth involvement, even though some parties have youth constituency chairs. Constituency chairs whom I interviewed in 2004 complained of the lack of funds to ensure youth participation in shaping political agendas and programming youth-oriented activities. Throughout the Chiluba years, much of the money set aside for a Constituency Youth Fund was in fact used by the ruling party. There is little doubt that economically astute party members benefited from these funds by receiving public sector contracts, and allegations of past misuse are widespread.

Young people are mobilized at political rallies to carry posters, control the crowd, and intimidate others. They are also deployed at times to promote political violence against the supporters of opposition parties and their property. "Political piece-work" of this kind is usually paid in cash or kind. Such young people are called "cadres," a term that harks back to the days of the one-party state and the disciplinary, vigilante functions of its youth wing. Yet my young friends also reminded me that "cadres" rarely obtain support for candidacies for political office or public appointments.[8]

Disappointed by their exclusion from program formulation in party politics, some young people have approached NGOs as an arena in which to promote a democratic political culture.[9] In the past some leaders of NGOs, among them members of the Women's Lobby Group, became political entrepreneurs and were brought into the first MMD government. Several externally funded NGOs in Zambia are active in political capacity-building, promoting accountability, transparency, and democratic leadership.[10] Such democracy-oriented NGOs typically organize regional workshops aimed at empowerment, communication skills, and networking, as well as raising awareness about problematic issues such as education, poverty, and HIV/AIDS.

In 2003 these NGOs and several others (a total of twelve) merged into a network, the National Youth Constitutional Coordinating Committee (NYCCC), in an effort to include the views of young people in a review process that was intended to lead to the formulation of a new constitution. Some of the NGOs making up the NYCCC were also involved in the review process that took place in 2004 in preparation for a new national youth policy that was passed into law in 2006.

External donors prefer networks rather than small organizations that come and go. The activities of networks such as the NYCCC are easier to track because there is more accountability and transparency. The NGO scene has generated career trajectories for well-educated young people that the downsized civil service and the reduced formal sector cannot supply. The fragmenting of smaller organizations makes it easy to shift allegiances from one to another. In the process, politics has become less concerned with public goods and society, and more concerned with individuals, their progress, and personal networks. This is issue-oriented politics. Helping to transform local expressions and meanings of politics, the NGO scene has been instrumental in launching political careers and incorporating youth issues into broader agendas. Yet these processes are double-edged. For while developments outside conventional political structures may open alternative channels for influencing politics, they may also disperse the conventional location of power from within the state to the fragmented NGO scene with its externally imposed agendas, ultimately disenfranchising young people from the heart of local politics.

Negotiating Cultural Space

Church movements and the popular music scene constitute dimensions of space, not only in a physical sense but also as social practices that define place and belonging (see introduction and Valentin's chapter in this volume). A range of authorities in society at large, including parents, schools, police, the courts, and the churches, devise rules that organize the population across space in terms of age (Massey 1998, 127). In addition, recent processes of socioeconomic restructuring have transformed the capital's urban space. While these processes affect the ways in which young people experience the city, they in turn assign particular meanings to specific spaces, in the process turning space into place (Gupta and Ferguson 2002, 67). As I discuss below, moving about with a religious outlook in this changing urban setting, young people sometimes redefine the spaces others have created for them by the ways in which they use or refrain from using them. Still other spaces they create themselves, as in the music scene, which is not tied down to specific localities.

Religious Space and Inclusion

Religious beliefs are a resource that forms an important part of some young people's engagement with urban life (Hansen 2004a). Providing spiritual modes of being and belonging, religious movements help construct new visions of the individual and the community, promising young people "a future that already exists" (Diouf 2003, 7). In Lusaka, young people are joining churches in growing numbers. Most of Zambia's mainline churches have considerable social engagement, including schools and clinics, lay involvement, women's and children's programs, and increasingly a variety of youth activities (Carmody 1999). The Catholic Church in particular has addressed public issues on diverse topics, including the constitution, SAPs, and HIV/AIDS (Komakoma 2003). While the Catholic Church is the largest and fastest-growing denomination, Pentecostal theology appears to offer a strategy for urban living that has a special appeal to young people in their formative age. Much like the mainline churches, many of the Pentecostal churches have recently involved themselves in skills training and programs for street children and orphans.

In order to learn about the attractions and meanings of youth involvement in church activities, in 2003 my assistants and I worked in the three different residential areas where I had launched this research project, this time focusing on the involvement of young people with mainstream and Pentecostal churches. We also participated in a variety of youth activities and meetings. Going beyond these specific residential areas, we conducted surveys in three very popular Pentecostal churches that attract middle-income, upwardly mobile individuals: the Northmead Assemblies of God, Bread of Life International, and Winners' Chapel. We also took part in youth meetings.[11]

The young people, both women and men, who participated in youth activities in the denominations that have been established in Lusaka for a long time tended to come from households where a parent or guardian attended the same church. This pattern did not hold among the young people who attended the Pentecostal churches. Many young members of those churches had joined within the last three to four years. Their decisions to join were prompted by visits to churches that their friends attended, by curiosity, and also by television shows. Several of the young people we spoke to were attracted by the Pentecostal style of preaching and manner of worship. The preaching style is interactive, dialogic, with frequent use of call and response. Many Pentecostal pastors and bishops are highly charismatic and have great performance skills. The manner of worship includes music, often English-language gospel singing accompanied by electric keyboard, guitar, and drums amplified by loudspeakers, a choir, and above all, individual praise-singing and praying as prelude and conclusion to the service. Some services feature speaking in tongues and possession. This rich ambience of devotion generates a sense of nearness to God that appears to touch and "transport" some people and to be conducive to the infilling of the spirit. It also provides an inclusive setting where pastors, bishops, and their assistants actively reach out to draw visitors into their congregations. Many young people experience this ambience as very welcoming.

Regardless of whether they remained with the church they grew up with or joined a Pentecostal church, youth at specific life stages appeared to obtain different things from their affiliations. Many young people under 20 talked about the importance of activities ranging from choir practice and Bible reading to social outings and spiritual retreats. In short, some churches keep young people very busy. They spoke of how much they enjoyed participating in choir practice, praise-singing, and dramatic productions. Somewhat older youths, those in their twenties, talked more about the significance of spirituality. While they might not participate in as many church activities as the younger crowd, their spiritually based faith had implications for many other domains of their lives, from their domestic settings to the public world, from work to leisure. Spirituality to them did not connote a set of specific activities, but rather an attitude or outlook, a stance. The explanation of a 23-year old woman who had switched from the UCZ to Bread of Life International when she began studying at the University of Zambia (UNZA) three years previously is not unusual: "I have learned the truth and live according to the Word," she said; "this spiritual growth assists me keep my stance while I am at UNZA."

Regardless of denomination, all these churches exert authority over their members, stressing morality, responsibility, discipline, and hard work. Their organization is hierarchical, and they tend to be male-dominated. Women are auxiliaries in most churches, except at the level of lay involvement and outreach. The blueprint for family living that most denominations advocate stresses marriage as a precursor to child-bearing and puts the husband in charge of households as the chief provider for his wife and children.

But Pentecostals have an additional edge: the "fear of God." In Pentecostal theology, once you confess your sins, you become born again, saved. God is your personal savior. With this faith in God, you accept the Bible as his Word, considering it to be the guiding authority on how to live.

Through God, young Pentecostals explain, everything is possible, and this possibility offers hope. He is the provider; he has a plan for you. Living according to his Word will make your expectations come to fruition. This faith gives you the willpower and strength to carry on. In short, the faith that is nourished by the "fear of God" both encourages and empowers you, enabling the success that many Pentecostal pastors and bishops promise their congregations. It also helps relieve young people like Alick from the peer pressure that many of them experience as restricting their options. The "fear of God" liberates them, in the sense that it frees them to fashion their own futures. Subordinating oneself to God's authority, placing him first in all decisions, and not following what others are doing does not restrict your actions. It is rather your own will not to do what others are doing or to do it differently. This is one of the meanings of power of which Anthony Giddens speaks (1983, 88–94). The self-respect that such decisions foster gives you the spiritual strength to handle yourself and to control your body in a variety of situations, including sexual relationships.

Incorporating space into expressions of their religious experience and influencing how they orient themselves toward urban life and its temptations, Pentecostal faith and the "fear of God" help young men like Alick and Peter to fashion, at least temporarily, a construction of masculinity that differs from the aggressive, sexually active version that is so prevalent in urban Zambia. They subordinate this dominant version to a notion of manhood as disciplined, careful, hardworking, and not "indulging," that is, not drinking, smoking, taking drugs, or pursuing casual sex.

Some young women's expressions of religious belief were tinged by their fear of failure because of their difficulties in following "the Word." While young women who were active in Pentecostal youth activities talked about abstinence, invoking God and the Bible, they did not do so in quite the same manner as the young men. Indeed, many young women try to be responsible and careful, yet their efforts are easily challenged. "Being young in Lusaka means making or breaking your life," according to a 17-year-old woman student in a tailoring and design course who

Figure 5.5. Private school run by a Pentecostal church. The sign reads, "The Fear of God Gives Wisdom and Knowledge." Lusaka, 2004. *Photo: Karen Tranberg Hansen*

attended the Word of Life church in Kalingalinga compound. "Life in Lusaka is too competitive, especially on the girls' side," complained another 17-year-old woman who just had graduated from secondary school and was about to begin law studies at the university. Such sentiments were shared by many other young women, who argued that there is "too much" to admire in Lusaka. Competition is rife, life is exaggerated and too fast, the demand for fashion is great. Young women's frequent reference to "admiration" and "fashion" is a discourse about desire revolving around consumption and a lifestyle that many of them cannot afford.

The way young Pentecostal men and women talk about the challenges and temptations of life in Lusaka embeds the city in a moral geography of good and evil. This moral topography is distinctly gendered. The women were more ambivalent about how to maneuver in such spaces than the young men, perhaps because they experience greater pressure to engage in sex than young men. Their ambivalence arises from two widespread but conflicting models of youth transitions: for young men the avenue to adulthood is work, while for young women it is sex. Viewing young women as sexual predators, these young men did not consider their female age-mates to be in "their market." Invoking "the fear of

God," some young men defer their sexual desires while they plan and prepare themselves for male adult responsibilities as heads of households.

While religious belief does not amount to an explicit criticism of the institutional workings of Zambian society that have excluded so many youths, it does demonstrate the power of the notion of salvation to put young believers in charge of their own lives. Much like the democracy NGOs that promote an individualized understanding of society, these movements instill a sense of personal responsibility. In this way, the "fear of God" provides skills and strategies for young people to draw on during a specific stage in their lives that may open a pathway for individual endeavors, a space for youth agency to fashion different trajectories toward adulthood.

The Music Scene: Freedom and Constraints

Zambia's popular music scene offers rich scope for young people's desire to inhabit a global world on local terms. The music scene provides a cultural space that is characterized by desires for recognition and presence, reaching far beyond the country. Yet even in its global aspirations, Zambia's popular music is intertwined with the experiences of everyday life in ways that resonate with their time and place. The popular music scene in Zambia attracts considerable attention from young people and adults of both sexes across the country. Music blasts loudly from radios in minibuses, where most passengers will readily tell you which artists are in the top ten. While urban nightclubs attract an audience of those with better means, some well-known local artists make a point of performing in the compounds, where they present themselves as ambassadors for public issues such as child labor. Democracy NGOs recruit popular musicians around election time for live performances in cities and provincial towns to rally young people to register to vote. NGO networks concerned with HIV/AIDS frequently hire musicians to sing about abstinence and condoms on events such as World AIDS Day. Such concerts have been hugely successful, with thousands of young people attending (*Sunday Mail* 2001). Outside such organized events, radio makes music available to everyone, and the music stations are eagerly listened to.

Zambia's popular music creatively incorporates many outside influences, with lyrics in several local languages and English. Today's music includes rumba and zoukous from the Congo, kwaito from South Africa, Afro-pop from Nigeria, Zam-ragga, hip hop, and rap. Gospel has become important over the last decade, with pop gospel and funky gospel in local languages and English. Gospel music is even played in nightclubs. The widespread use of *kalindula*-style instrumentation produces a unique Zambian sound consisting of acoustic guitar, a two-string bass, drum(s), and percussion.[12]

Figure 5.6. Party time. Young couple dancing. Lusaka, 2003. *Photo: Karen Tranberg Hansen*

Over the course of two months in 2004, every weekly top-ten chart included songs by two gospel groups, the Glorious Band and Hosanna, performing in local languages and English with *kalindula* instrumentation among their presentations. Other top-ten works were by a changing list of male and female performers, mainly singing in local languages. Many lyrics focus on love, such as number four on the Radio Four Top Ten chart on August 13, 2004, Winston's "Natenga pensulo," in which a young man grabs a pencil and a piece of paper and writes a love letter to his sweetheart (Winston 2004). Number three on the chart, Exile's "Kumwela ni mwela" ("I am a good guy"), features a young man asking his parents for forgiveness because he has indulged in smoking dagga and in drinking. The "good guy" sings, "I don't think that there is anyone in the world who was born a savage, a prostitute, or a drunkard with beer in their mouth. Some children are born in very difficult situations such as poverty; does it mean to be born is wrong? Now listen, Mother . . ." (Exile 2004). Number one on that chart was Nalu's "House, Money, Car," with *kalindula* instrumentation. Nalu's conversational song, in English, Bemba, and Nyanja, tells about a young woman and man who are talking. The man believes that he can get the woman because he has a house, money, and a car. "Don't pretend," goes the lyric, "don't be difficult, babe, money is life." Yet the woman argues that money and material goods do not constitute happiness, only true love does: "That English you are speaking is yours—the fact is that love and poverty/hunger are enemies" (Nalu 2004).[13]

The treacherous trajectory toward adulthood is an important theme in recent popular music. The lyrics quoted above depict young people as the creators of their own problems and the authors of their own solutions. Some hits admonish young people about the dangers of indulgence, including sex and consumption. Already in 2000, Black Muntu alluded to them, blaming sex and clothes for death (meaning AIDS) in their rap song in Nyanja, "Chi manso manso" (literally "of the eyes, eyes," meaning approximately "admiring" and connoting that admiration causes problems) (Black Muntu 2000).[14] One verse describes a young woman named Jane putting on a miniskirt. "When you see [this], you look at her soft body and complexion, you feel she's the right person. Stop it! You are just inviting death."

In an ideal world, the desires for consumer goods and for sexual relationships pertain to two separate areas. But in today's Lusaka, the two easily become mixed. Young women know that money and transactional sex can jeopardize their chance of economic improvement because of the economic pressures of everyday life and challenges about the future. Poverty easily drives them into risky sexual relations that threaten their health and social status. Some of the criticism so evident in music from the mid-1980s—for example, in P. K. Chisala's songs about dishonest policemen, immoral husbands, hypocritical church elders, and corrupt politicians in Kaunda's regime—has been replaced by a focus on the individual. As on the political scene, where the patronage system excludes young people from participation and leaves them to their own devices, popular music tells young people to get on with their lives, for the state is not going to help them. This parallels the tenor of the Pentecostal message, conveying a politics of self-promotion that may or may not lessen the hierarchical hold of Zambia's party politics and the institutional structures that underpin it.

Conclusions: Healing Urban Wounds?

A first-time visitor to Lusaka, a member of the Youth and the City project, commented on the aggressive poverty she encountered. The human costs of more than twenty years of SAPs, aggravated by recent liberalized market-oriented policies, have been enormous and are strikingly evident on the urban scene. They manifest themselves in the shortage of jobs and housing, growing poverty, low or declining levels of education, and poor health that is aggravated by the high prevalence of HIV/AIDS (Poku 2001). With Zambia near the bottom of the UNDP's Human Development Index, the great majority of Lusaka's young population experience urban life as structural violence. Conditioned by a colonial background of restrictive economic policies, and driven today by externally prescribed development policies, these urban wounds constrain youth agency on many fronts.

Even then, recent transformations of urban space and economic opportunity are changing the contexts of young people's lives and thus the meaning of youth, from being dependent to taking charge. Young people are the source of much of Lusaka's energy and vitality. Some young people have begun to challenge long-held and widespread constructions of aggressive male sexuality and female subordination. As this chapter demonstrates, there is evidence from many sites of young urban people working hard to make a difference: in vocational training institutions, informal political activity, NGO relations, and church settings, on the music scene, and of course in many other spaces not alluded to here. When we study sites other than that of HIV/AIDS and reproductive sexual practices, we may in fact reveal numerous overlapping contexts where young people are working hard to change their locations in social space in order to take charge of their own lives. Demonstrating their difference from their predecessors and wanting inclusion, these young residents are profoundly marking today's urban landscape with a view to changing it tomorrow.

Acknowledgments

In conducting my part of the Youth and the City project in Lusaka between 2001 and 2005, I collaborated with the Institute for Economic and Social Research (INESOR) of the University of Zambia, where I enjoy the status of research affiliate. Dr. Chileshe L. Mulenga, acting director of INESOR for most of this time, provided invaluable advice and input. Chris Simuyemba, a research assistant from INESOR, worked alongside me in previous projects and during the first phase of this project; he died of AIDS in 2001. I want to thank the many others who have assisted me in this research in innumerable ways, who are simply too many for me to list them all individually. Chief among them were, in 2001, Edith Ndubani and Joseph Tembo, and for the rest of the project's duration, Maurice Pengele, Wilfred Manda, and Tamara Nkhoma. Jennifer Cole provided valuable criticism of my desire to take on too many issues, as did LaRay Denzer, who offered much constructive advice.

Notes

1. The Universal Church was established in Zambia by a pastor from Brazil in 1995. It has been banned from operating several times, first in 1997 and again in November 2005, when

allegations of satanism and sexual abuse prompted the destruction of church property at the new cathedral and at church branches in some compounds. In each case, a judicial review allowed the church to resume its activities.

2. The discussion is also informed by my long-term research engagement with urban life in Lusaka, which I have examined over time and from a variety of angles (e.g., Hansen 1989, 1997, 2000).

3. "Compound" was a common term throughout the southern African region, and was first used for the racially segregated housing institution adopted on the gold and diamond mines in South Africa in the late 1980s (Rex 1974; Turrel 1984).

4. When asked to define youth in terms of age, Zambians of all ages often place the upper limit at 35 years. This may be a legacy of the age range of the youth league of the former one-party political system. I have also been told that civics classes define age 35 as the end of youth.

5. The first, a very poor area, was the oldest section of Kalingalinga, one of the oldest squatter areas in Lusaka, which was not upgraded until recently. The second, Chilenje South, was built immediately after independence in 1964 by the government to provide family housing to the city's growing working class; here the housing stock has now been privatized and sold, by and large to people who are better off than the original tenants. The third, Kabulonga, is a high-income, low-density area, whose large plots and houses today are inhabited by Zambians in elite positions and by expatriates. The household survey comprised fifty interviews in each of these areas.

6. KYPT Technical Institute, supported by NORAD, GTZ, FINIDA, and others, offers training in vocational skills and entrepreneurship. I observed the training in four courses in 2002 and interviewed 15 students in hotel management and catering, 10 in tailoring, 13 in automotive mechanics, 5 in carpentry, and 1 in bricklaying. The first two courses enrolled largely women, the rest largely men. Students' ages ranged from 18 to 24 years for women and from 18 to 32 years for men. The majority of the students had dropped out of school after grade 9, although a few had completed grade 12.

7. See Ansell and van Blerk 2005 for a discussion of children's preoccupation with the social and economic aspects of urban life in informal housing areas.

8. One exception was the 2004 appointment of the deputy minister as minister of Youth, Sport, and Child Development and the 2005 election of the mayor of Lusaka, both of whom had moved up through the political hierarchy. They did not last. The deputy minister was assigned another portfolio and the mayor was not reelected.

9. I am not referring to the vast majority of NGOs in Zambia that work on HIV/AIDS issues, because this is where the money is; so much so, in fact, that the country lacks the capacity to absorb it all.

10. The external institutions funding such efforts include the EU Election Unit, the Friedrich Ebert Foundation, GTZ of Germany, DFID of the UK, USAID, Irish Aid, UNICEF, and others. Among the major NGOs dedicated to democracy projects are the National Youth Constitutional Assembly, Young Politicians for Change, Youth Forum Zambia, Operation Young Vote, the Anti–Voter Apathy Project, the Youth Forum for Peace and Justice, and the Youth Association of Zambia.

11. We also attended other churches. While I went to service at a different church every Sunday to increase my exposure, I also attended some Catholic youth activities in the parish in which I lived. For a while, I accompanied a young woman who had recently joined a new, locally founded Pentecostal ministry, the Yahweh Global Ministry. Part of a group of young people whose lives and activities I have observed since this project began in 2001, she was an active evangelist and intercessor.

12. *Kalindula's* characteristic sound "arises from the bass. . . . Kalindula has a continuous rhythm over which the voice sings. The drum has to adjust to the voice" (Bender 1991, 147).

13. Translations by Maurice Pengele and Wilfred Manda.

14. I thank Pieter Remes for information about this song.

References

Ansell, Nicola, and Lorraine van Blerk. 2005. "Where We Stayed Was Very Bad . . .": Migrant Children's Perspectives on Life in Informal Rented Accommodation in Two Southern African Cities. *Environment and Planning A* 37:423–40.

Beall, Jo. 2002. Globalization and Social Exclusion in Cities: Framing the Debate with Lessons from Africa and Asia. *Environment & Urbanization* 14(1):41–51.

Bender, Wolfgang. 1991. *Sweet Mother: Modern African Music.* Chicago: University of Chicago Press.

Carmody, Brendan. 1999. *Education in Zambia: Catholic Perspectives.* Lusaka: Bookworld.

Cole, Jennifer, and Deborah Durham, eds. 2007. *Generations and Globalization: Youth, Age, and Family in the New World Economy.* Bloomington: Indiana University Press.

CSO (Central Statistical Office). 2000. *Living Conditions in Zambia, 1998.* Lusaka: Central Statistical Office.

Diouf, Mamadou. 2003. Engaging Postcolonial Cultures: African Youth and Public Space. *African Studies Review* 46(2):1–12.

Farmer, Paul. 2002. On Suffering and Structural Violence: A View from Below. In *The Anthropology of Politics: A Reader in Ethnography, Theory, and Critique,* ed. Joan Vincent, 424–37. Malden, Mass.: Blackwell.

Fetters, Tamara, Evans Mupela, and Naomi Rutenberg. 1997. "Don't Trust Your Girlfriend or You're Gonna Die Like a Chicken": A Participatory Assessment of Adolescent Sexual and Reproductive Health in a High Risk Environment. Lusaka: CARE Zambia.

Galtung, Johan. 1969. Violence, Peace and Peace Research. *Journal of Peace Research* 6(3):167–91.

Giddens, Anthony. 1983. *Central Problems in Social Theory: Action, Structure and Contradiction in Social Analysis.* Berkeley: University of California Press.

GRZ and UN (Government of the Republic of Zambia and the United Nations Systems in Zambia). 1996. Prospects for Sustainable Human Development in Zambia: More Choices for Our People. Lusaka: Pilcher Graphics.

Gupta, Akhil, and James Ferguson. 2002. Beyond "Culture": Space, Identity, and the Politics of Difference. In *The Anthropology of Globalization: A Reader,* ed. Jonathan Xavier Inda and Renato Rosaldo, 65–80. Malden, Mass.: Blackwell.

Hansen, Karen Tranberg. 1989. *Distant Companions: Servants and Employers in Zambia, 1900–1985.* Ithaca, N.Y.: Cornell University Press.

———. 1997. *Keeping House in Lusaka.* New York: Columbia University Press.

———. 2000. *Salaula: The World of Secondhand Clothing and Zambia.* Chicago: University of Chicago Press.

———. 2003. Target Group Interventions among Youth in Zambia: Research Constructions and Social Life. *Anthropology in Action* 10(1):34–40.

———. 2004a. Gudsfrygt og fremtidsplanlaegning i Lusaka, Zambia (Fear of God and planning for the future in Lusaka, Zambia). *Den Ny Verden* 37(3):63–72.

———. 2004b. Who Rules the Streets? The Politics of Vending Space in Lusaka. In *Reconsidering Informality: Perspectives from Urban Africa,* ed. Karen Tranberg Hansen and Mariken Vaa, 62–80. Uppsala, Sweden: Nordic Africa Institute.

———. 2005. Getting Stuck in the Compound: Some Odds against Social Adulthood in Lusaka, Zambia. *Africa Today* 51(4):3–18.

Kambou, Sarah Dergnan, Meera Kaul Shah, and Gladys Nkhama. 1998. For a Pencil: Sex and Adolescence in Peri-urban Zambia. In *The Myth of Community: Gender Issues in Participatory Development,* ed. Irene Guijt and Meera Kaul Shah, 100–10. London: Intermediate Technology Publications.

Komakoma, Joe. 2003. *The Social Teachings of the Catholic Bishops and Other Christian Leaders in Zambia: Major Pastoral Letters and Statements, 1953–2001.* Ndola: Mission Press.

Massey, Doreen. 1998. The Spatial Construction of Youth Cultures. In *Cool Places: Geographies of Youth Cultures,* ed. Tracy Skelton and Gill Valentine, 121–29. London: Routledge.

Mulenga, Chileshe L. 2001. Peri-urban Transformations and Livelihoods in the Context of Globalization in Lusaka, Zambia. Peri-urban Research Network, Working Paper 3. London: Faculty of the Built Environment, South Bank University.

Nchito, Wilma, and Garth Andrew Myers. 2004. Four Caveats for Participatory Solid Waste Management in Lusaka, Zambia. *Urban Forum* 15(2):109–33.

Ndubani, Phillemon. 2002. Young Men's Sexuality and Sexually Transmitted Infections in Zambia. Ph.D. dissertation, Karolingska Institutet.

Poku, Nana K. 2001. Africa's AIDS Crisis in Context: "How the Poor are Dying." *Third World Quarterly* 22(2):191–204.

Potts, Deborah. 2005. Counter-urbanisation on the Zambian Copperbelt? Interpretations and Implications. *Urban Studies* 42(4):583–609.

Pugh, Cedric. 1995. International Structural Adjustment and Its Sectoral and Spatial Impacts. *Urban Studies* 32(2):261–85.

Remes, Pieter, Caroline Njue, Frederick Kaona, Lydie Kanhonou, and Severin-Cecile Abega. 2003. African Youth, Sex and the City: A Multisite Perspective from Yaonde, Cotonou, Kisumu and Ndola. Paper presented at the annual meeting of the African Studies Association, Boston, Mass., October 30–November 2.

Rex, John. 1974. The Compound, the Reserve, and the Urban Location: The Essential Institutions of Southern African Labour Exploitation. *Southern African Labour Bulletin* 1:4–17.

Riddell, Barry. 1997. Structural Adjustment Programmes and the City in Tropical Africa. *Urban Studies* 34(8):1297–1307.

Sassen, Saskia. 1994. *Cities in a World Economy.* Thousand Oaks, Calif.: Pine Forge.

Schlyter, Ann. 1999. Recycled Inequalities: Youth and Gender in George Compound, Zambia. Research Report no. 114. Uppsala, Sweden: Nordiska Afrikainstitutet.

Schneider, Jane, and Ida Susser, eds. 2003. *Wounded Cities: Destruction and Reconstruction in a Globalized World.* Oxford: Berg.

SIAPAC (Social Impact Assessment and Policy Analysis Corporation). 2004. Impact Assessment of HIV/AIDS on the Education Sector in Zambia. Final Report for the Ministry of Education. Lusaka.

Simpson, Anthony. 2005. Sons and Fathers/Boys to Men in the Time of AIDS: Learning Masculinities in Zambia. *Journal of Southern African Studies* 31(3):569–86.

Susser, Ida, and Jane Schneider. 2003. Wounded Cities: Destruction and Reconstruction in a Globalized World. In *Wounded Cities: Destruction and Reconstruction in a Globalized World,* ed. Jane Schneider and Ida Susser, 1–23. Oxford: Berg.

Sunday Mail. 2001. Shatel Prop Up Voter Registration Exercise. July 22, p. 9.

Turrel, Robert. 1984. Kimberley's Model Compounds. *Journal of African History* 25:59–75.

UNDP (United Nations Development Programme). 2004. *Human Development Report 2003.* New York: Oxford University Press.

van de Walle, Nicolas. 2003. Presidentialism and Clientelism in Africa's Emerging Party Systems. *Journal of Modern African Studies* 41(2):297–321.

Webb, Douglas. 1997. Adolescence, Sex and Fear: Reproductive Health Services and Young People in Urban Zambia. Lusaka: Central Board of Health and UNICEF.

Zeleza, Paul T. 1999. The Spatial Economy and Structural Adjustment in African Cities. In *Sacred Spaces and Public Quarrels: African Cultural and Economic Landscapes,* ed. Paul T. Zeleza and Ezekiel Kalipeni, 43–72. Trenton, N.J.: Africa World Press.

Discography

Black Muntu. 2000. "Chi manso manso." *Wisakamana.* Lusaka: Mondo Music.

Exile. 2004. "Kumwela ni mwela." *So Lucky.* Lusaka: Mondo Music.

Nalu. 2004. "House, Money, Car." *House Money Car.* Lusaka: Mondo Music.

Winston Moyo. 2004. "Natenga pensulo." *Love yamuti.* Lusaka: Mondo Music.

Part 3. Youth Making Meaning

6

Youth and the Home

Katherine V. Gough

The home plays an important role in people's lives as a key site for personal development. While some people are able to spend vast sums of money styling their homes, for others the maintenance of home, both physically and emotionally, remains a daily struggle. Since the home is not only a physical space but also a symbolic concept and a contested site, connotations of home vary widely both culturally and over time. As Alison Blunt and Ann Varley (2004, 3) claim, geographies of home "are located on thresholds between memory and nostalgia for the past, everyday life in the present, and future dreams and fears." The home is where young people form many of their values and ideals, but it is also a place where they struggle over power relations. The concepts of home and youth are closely connected, as it is often only on moving out of their childhood home that young people are considered to have become adults.

The homes young people live in are the product of the cultures and resources of the households they grow up in, as well as housing policies at the national and global levels. In this chapter I explore the relationship between youth and the home in the three very different urban settings of Recife, Hanoi, and Lusaka. The central issues I address are the experiences of young people growing up in their homes, how they attempt to set up homes of their own, and the meaning of home to them. The ways in which class and gender cut across these issues within the three sites run through the chapter. Following this introduction, I conceptualize youth and the home, and offer a brief account of the fieldwork conducted. I then examine each city in turn, starting with Recife and moving to Hanoi before finally ending up in Lusaka. Within each location, I explore the experiences and aspirations of youth in both low-income and middle-income residential areas in relation to the home.

Conceptualizing Home and Youth

In conceptualizing the home, it is useful to distinguish between the house, the home, and the household. The house is a material, spatial entity; the household is the people who live together and make up a social and economic unit; and the home is a sociospatial concept that often represents the fusion of the physical unit of the house and the social unit of the household (Saunders and Williams 1988). Physical aspects of the home, such as its location, size, internal layout, and material quality, not only reflect cultural values and traditions, but also enable and constrain activities and relationships within it. The social construction of home consists of the twin concepts of home as an ideal and home as a reality, hence notions of home embody both the material and the symbolic. The concept of family, more common in everyday life, further complicates matters, and as family relationships are so central to ideas about home life, the concepts of home and family are sometimes used interchangeably. However, as Gill Jones (2000) argues, the conflation of home with family is confusing. Although a family consists of people in close relationships, this is not necessarily true of a home. The home can thus be seen as "a material and an affected space, shaped by everyday practices, lived experiences, social relations, memories and emotions" (Blunt 2005, 506).

Since home is a term imbued with personal meanings, "different people are likely to understand 'home' to mean different things at different times and in different contexts" (Easthope 2004, 135). The differing meanings of home are influenced by residential location, housing tenure, class, and ethnicity. Gender and age are key factors that differentiate household members' perceptions of the meaning of home (Mallett 2004). These perceptions are affected by power differentials within the household, especially perceived rights to make decisions within the home and the nature of the relationships between household members. The home is thus a site of inequality where, underlying the domestic idyll, power relations are expressed and reinforced through rules that control space and behavior.

Young people in particular are subject to rules that control their behavior within the home and their movement outside of the home. Although the home is generally considered to provide a refuge from the pressures of the outside world, where young people have little domestic power, the parental home does not necessarily constitute a safe haven (Abbott-Chapman and Robertson 1999; Jones 2000). The parental home plays an important role as the launching pad for transition to adult living, and for young people it may become the site of tensions surrounding the struggle for independence and adulthood (White 2002). In many, though not all, societies, becoming emancipated from parental control requires physically moving away and establishing one's own home. What constitutes a legitimate way of leaving home is culturally embedded and may be supported by government polices (Jones 2000). As I show in this chapter, the relationship between youth and the home is complex, varying by culture, class, and gender.

Building on the issues raised above, I discuss the following questions in relation to the three study sites. What is the physical nature of the homes lived in by young people and how does it affect their experiences of living at home? What possibilities do young people have to set up their own homes? What is the meaning of home for young people and in which ways do they link the concepts of youth and home? Before considering these issues in relation to the cities of Recife, Hanoi, and Lusaka, I present a brief account of the methods used in this research.

Researching Youth in the Home

In Recife, Hanoi, and Lusaka, I conducted research on youth and the home in the low- and middle-income residential areas selected by the anthropologists (see Dalsgaard and Valentin, this volume, for further details on the project methodology). The areas I studied in Recife were Vietnã (low-income) and Torre (middle-income); in Lusaka they were Kalingalinga (low-income) and Chilenje South (middle-income); and in Hanoi they were Mai Ninh (low-income) and Truc Tuyet (middle-income). I conducted the fieldwork between March 2002 and October 2004.

The primary research method I used was informal interviews with young people. During the interviews, I covered a range of prespecified topics, usually starting with questions related to the home, then the neighborhood, the city, and finally the informant's prospects for setting up his or her own home. Although I introduced similar topics in each interview, in practice the interviews varied widely, with space being given to the young people to talk about any issues they wished to raise. I interviewed between forty and fifty young people in each city, some individually and others in small groups. Where possible, I interviewed young people with whom the anthropologists had already been in contact. This meant that informants were already aware of the project, and some basic information on their families and living situations was available. I contacted other young people for interviews through the "snowballing" technique. I always took notes on the location of the plot, the physical nature of the house, and the house's contents, and in some cases drew sketches of its interior layout.

I selected a range of youth for the interviews, varying by age, level of schooling, occupation, household composition, and marital status. Most of the interviews took place in the young people's homes, though a few were held in the street, a school, or a bar. I conducted all of the interviews myself, working together with a local research assistant, except in Lusaka, where a Danish research assistant conducted half of the interviews together with a local assistant. The majority of the interviews were taped and subsequently transcribed. I also conducted many informal discussions with the young people, members of their family, and others while walking around the neighborhoods.

Youth and the Home in Recife

In an editorial to a special issue of *Geoforum* on urban Brazil, Edésio Fernandes and Márcio Valenca (2001, v) write, "What first comes to mind when thinking about Brazil is the striking contrast between the rich and the poor. This is, before anything else, a very visual and visible phenomenon." The urban poor live predominantly in *favelas* on land which has been obtained through a range of informal and often illegal means and on which the occupiers construct their own houses (De Souza 2001). Vietnã, in Recife, is a *favela* which originated as a land invasion in the late 1960s. Despite its subsequent legal recognition, Vietnã still has a bad reputation and is considered to be a violent neighborhood, especially by those who do not live there. The houses are predominantly single-story, though many have been extended to accommodate family members or to rent out rooms to tenants, resulting in a high population density (see figure 3.2). Most young people in Vietnã were born and have grown up in the same house, though a few tenants have moved into the area more recently. It is a neighborhood where people know each other and are constantly in and out of each others' homes. One elderly woman we spoke to refused to believe that neighborhoods could exist where the neighbors did not know each other; having always lived in a *favela*, she could not comprehend such a thing.

The young people of Vietnã grow up in crowded housing. Not only do they tend to have little or no space they can call their own within the home, they usually share a bedroom with several others, and sometimes even a bed. This lack of space is problematic for many of them, and they complain bitterly, especially about younger siblings always going through their belongings. Sharing a bed becomes more problematic as young people reach puberty, but often there is no alternative. It is not only the lack of space that is an issue for young people, but also privacy more generally. As many of the houses do not have wooden interior doors but only curtains, noise travels throughout the home. Most of the houses in Vietnã have a living room with soft furniture and large display units, often featuring a television set, which serves as a focal point in the home (figure 6.1).

The amount of time young people spend in the home varies greatly, but clearly reflects gender differences. Young men tend to spend very little time in the home, preferring to hang out on the streets. This is partly because of the lack of space in the home, but such hanging out is also an important part of their identity formation. As a group of three young men explained, "Boys who stay at

Figure 6.1. Interior of a home in Vietnã. Recife, 2002. *Photo: Katherine V. Gough*

home end up like girls; they go nuts and get silly." Young women have to assume domestic responsibilities at an early age, being in charge of domestic work by the time they reach their teens. Parents try to make young women spend their free time within the home, partly in an attempt to reduce teenage pregnancies. Young women who spend time in the street are judged to be in danger of following the "wrong path." However, the young women themselves do not passively accept having to stay at home but resort to a range of strategies of resistance. For example, where possible young women will sit on the veranda of a home, which is usually protected by metal bars but opens onto the street. In this way they can be in the home, yet be able to converse with those out on the street. Another strategy used by the young women is to chat with friends while on their way to carry out an errand in the neighborhood for their mothers, then find an excuse for their long absence. As well as parents restricting their movements, the young women complain that their neighbors watch their every step. Gossip is rife, which at times makes young women reluctant to leave home. Luciana (aged 19) explained, "Over where I live it's like this. Everyone is always looking at me, more than they would the president of the Republic. If I go out with somebody, everyone looks, asking, 'Who can that be? Where are they going?' So to avoid this I prefer not to go out. I choose to stay at home to avoid the comments and the worries in people's little heads."

Many of the restrictions placed on young people by their parents are related to a fear of violence in the street. The overriding concern of adults and youth alike in Vietnã is violence, for many young men and some young women lose their lives while still teenagers. People are afraid not only of being robbed, hurt, or even killed by criminals or the police, but also of having a son, a friend, or a brother killed because he is involved in crime (Gough and Franch 2005). Many young people, even young men in their late teens and early twenties, reported that they had to be home at a certain time, and if they were delayed their parents would become very concerned. Despite being very aware of the dangers, many young people resent the restrictions placed on them by their parents, and some leave home at an early age in order to try to escape parental control. However, this strategy does not always work, as Patricia, an 18-year-old mother, found out: by moving in with her husband she merely exchanged parental control for that of her husband. "I used to think, 'When we're married we'll go out a lot because we won't have problems with my parents.' But when it's not the parents [restricting you], it's the husbands." Patricia had moved into the house of her future parents-in-law when she was 16. She said that she had had to leave her family home as her father would beat her; initially he did it only when he was drunk and angry but later he did it "all the time," so she left. Her experience demonstrates how the home can be a violent rather than a safe place.

Young people have a range of strategies for leaving the parental home. As they have grown up in a *favela,* many consider paying rent to be a waste of money,[1] and most cannot afford to pay rent anyway. The opportunities for land invasions are limited nowadays, especially in the vicinity of Vietnã, and buying land or a house is prohibitively expensive. Moreover, many of the youth do not want to leave the neighborhood. Consequently, subdividing or extending the parental home becomes a popular option. Patricia's two elder sisters had followed different housing strategies. Marita, the eldest, had married at 16, and her husband, Roberto, had moved in with her. Initially he was treated as an additional member of the household, but following the birth of their first child the three of them started to live as a separate household. The separation was reinforced by altering the structure of the family home so that they could enter their room directly from the outside. After Roberto became unemployed, they again formed a joint household with her parents, Marita being responsible for the majority of the housework. Thiago, the husband of the middle sister, Clécia, also moved into his wife's parents' home following their marriage. He and Clécia lived there for two years, during which, although his parents-in-law made him feel very welcome, Thiago did not feel at home, as he "could not take his shirt off." When a small area of land adjacent to Vietnã was invaded in 2001, Thiago saw the opportunity to establish his own home. He built a wooden shack on a very small plot of land, and he and Clécia moved into it. A year later, when Clécia was six months pregnant, they moved back into her parents' home while Thiago rebuilt the house using permanent materials. The family of three then returned to the one-room house, which was almost filled up by a double bed, with just enough space for a toilet and kitchen at the back and a stereo along the wall. They professed to be very happy in their home as, although illegal and very small, it was their own space where they could make all the decisions.

Some young people established their own home by building on the family plot. The original plots were long and narrow, allowing houses to be extended at the back. Some of the young people were planning to build or had already built a room for themselves and their partners behind the parental home. When there is no more space to build on the plot, another possibility is to add a second floor onto the parental home. Luciana and her 23-year-old fiancé were building a second floor on top of her parents' house, which they planned to live in following their wedding. They had decided on this solution to their housing situation as her fiancé was living with his stepfather, where they could not build, they could not afford to buy a plot, and they did not want to rent. As Luciana said regarding rent, "Today you pay and tomorrow you owe already." They had bought the building materials with money from a friend whom they were paying back, and the extension was being built by her uncle and cousin free of charge. As the original house had not been built to support a second floor, supporting pillars had to be built onto its exterior. On completion they would have an 18-m^2 home with a living room, kitchen, bedroom, and bathroom.

The wealthy residents of Recife live in more affluent areas of the city in apartment blocks, as these offer greater security than houses. The middle classes tend to live in apartment blocks of a slightly lower quality or in old villas, such as those in the residential area of Torre (see figure 3.3). Although the rich and the poor live in very different residential areas, which are clearly demarcated spatially, because of the nature of the terrain in Recife no one lives more than a kilometer from a *favela*. In Torre there are some pockets of *favelas* located along the banks of the Capibaribe River. Most middle-income youth living in Torre have their own bedroom within their home, and although some have to share a room with siblings, none has to share a bed. The apartments and houses are furnished and decorated like many middle-class homes in the West, complete with televisions, DVD players, computers, and books (figure 6.2). As most families have maids, daughters do not have many domestic obligations.

The young people of Torre see the home as a safe place, especially in comparison to the street, which they see as a dangerous space to be avoided. Torre youth fear that they will be victims of robbery, assault, or kidnapping rather than that they will themselves become, or know someone who becomes, a perpetrator

Figure 6.2. Interior of a home in Torre. Recife, 2002. *Photo: Katherine V. Gough*

(Gough and Franch 2005). Consequently the young people spend much of their time in the home, studying, relaxing, or hanging out with friends. As Nathalie (aged 15) said, "I prefer to spend my time at home. I have stopped going out into the street as I don't spend time any more with those people. I spend my time on the Internet and inside my home listening to music and studying." When they do leave the house, young people are usually driven by their parents, or drive themselves, to places considered safe, such as school, extracurricular activities, and shopping centers. Young people have little contact with their neighbors and meet their friends principally through their private schools.

The young people we met in Torre were all still living in their parents' home and had no immediate plans to move out.[2] Most of them planned to either rent or buy an apartment when their incomes became sufficient, the location depending on where they found employment. They still considered themselves to be youth as they were financially dependent on their parents and living in their parents' home. The link between the concepts of youth and the home was more complex in Vietnã, where the housing situation and life stages of the young people were much more diverse. One young man (aged 18) explained, "Young people hang out at corners chatting, go out with their friends, whereas adults have certain norms, they spend more time in the home, have responsibilities, spend time with the family, but a young person does what he [*sic*] wants." Young people in Vietnã generally agreed with this statement, though in practice the distinction between youth and adulthood is far from clear-cut. Many young people become parents at an early age and live in housing arrangements where they are neither fully part of the parental home nor totally separate from it. Consequently, many feel that they are both youth and adult at the same time, with only a tenuous link between how they feel and their status in the home.

Youth and the Home in Hanoi

Under communist rule, the planning process in Vietnam followed the top-down Soviet style, with residential neighborhoods built to house workers. The apartment blocks were homogeneous in appearance and located in close proximity to workplaces, shops, schools, and recreation areas (Nguyen Quang and Kammeier 2002). Mai Ninh is one such residential area, consisting of seventeen parallel apartment blocks built by the state in the 1960s and 1970s (for further details see Valentin, this volume). In the area of Mai Ninh where we interviewed young people, the apartments housed workers from a nearby textile factory. Many of the occupants were retired workers and their families, some of whom have now purchased their apartments under a government policy giving tenants the right to buy. There are also a number of young tenants and owners who have come to Hanoi to study or work who share an apartment.

Young people growing up in Mai Ninh live in very compact spaces. In the older blocks the apartments consist of just one room of 18 m² with one floor (eight to ten apartments) sharing a communal kitchen and toilet. In the newer blocks the apartments measure 24 to 28 m² and have two rooms, a kitchenette, and a toilet (Hoai Anh Tran and Dalholm 2005). Many households have expanded their apartments by adding a loft within the room, which serves as a sleeping area (figure 6.3), or by building extensions on the outside of the apartment blocks, often hanging in mid-air, to provide extra space (see figure 4.3). After visiting one apartment, I took down the following description: "The apartment consisted of one room divided in half by a tall dresser, with a mat on the floor. The parents slept in a loft bed above where we were sitting. Three sisters in their twenties slept in a large bed behind the dresser, though if it is hot one sister may sleep on a mat in the living room. The kitchen was in a building out the back. There was just one small window at the back, not giving much light, as the kitchen was just behind. Two motorbikes were stored against a wall in the living room." Many apartments lack furniture, though this partly reflects a preference for sitting on mats on the floor. One young man explained that, when talking to relatives, his family will sit on the floor, but if business partners visit they invite them to sit

Figure 6.3. Interior of a
home in Mai Ninh. Hanoi,
2004. *Photo: Katherine V.
Gough*

around a table. He was of the opinion that a bed occupies too much space, so he
chooses to sleep on the floor, which he also claimed to find more comfortable.
Many young people have to share a bed with siblings.

The young people interviewed in Mai Ninh spend a considerable amount
of their time in the home, studying and helping with household chores. One
schoolgirl described her typical day as follows: "I get up at 5:45, do the housework until 7:15, then I go to extra classes and get home after class at about 10:30.
After helping finish prepare the food I have a meal with my family, then I cycle
to school at 12:15. I am home again at 18:00 and help cook, then have dinner at
19:00. I study from 19:30 and go to sleep at 22:00 after watching some television."
There appeared to be little gender difference in the amount of time that youth
attending school spent in the home, though the young women spent more time
doing domestic work. Young people who were employed typically worked long
hours, leaving home by 7 AM and not returning until 7 PM or later, usually seven

days a week. Their long working day made it difficult to interview them, as the little time they were in the home was mainly spent eating or sleeping.

The difficulty of finding the space, and the peace, to study was an issue raised by many of the young people attending school or university. Because of noise during the day they resort to studying at night, sometimes until the early hours of the morning. A young man who was a university student explained that he studied late into the night "because it is more convenient. I can prolong the time and am not being controlled by anyone else." This shows that he was not studying late just in order to have peace, but also because he had a sense of having greater control when the rest of the family was in bed. He was able to temporarily create freedom in the space because of the nighttime absence of other people awake.

Truc Tuyet is located to the north of the old quarter of Hanoi and is predominantly an area of narrow-fronted houses several stories high. There are also some large colonial houses built by the French, which were subsequently taken over by the state and subdivided into apartments. Most of the houses have been in the same families for several generations, and in many instances large houses have now been subdivided because of the increasing pressure on accommodation. The land behind the houses that front onto the streets has been extensively infilled, resulting in a dense maze of narrow winding passageways with no public space or gardens. A considerable degree of gentrification has occurred as older properties have been bought up and demolished, and new houses, up to five stories high, constructed in their place. Many of the first residents of Truc Tuyet were engaged in handicraft production, though today many are professionals with higher education.

Truc Tuyet has a range of inhabitants and living spaces. Families who go back several generations often live in subdivided dwellings, some of which are remarkably small. For example, we interviewed one young woman who was living with her parents and sister in a 9-m^2 house with a loft area accessed by a ladder. The original house had belonged to her grandparents, who had subdivided the plot for their seven sons and daughters. There were currently six families living on the plot, a total of about twenty-four people. The father slept in the living room, which doubled as a kitchen and dining room and was also where his motorbike was stored, while the mother and two daughters slept in the loft area. They shared bathroom facilities with five other families. Not all subdivisions end up this small, though. One young woman was living with relatives while her parents built a house in Truc Tuyet. She explained that her grandparents had bought a large plot which had been subdivided into five parts for the children. Her parents have only 25 m^2, but as they are building a five-story house she will have her own bedroom. Despite the small area of some homes, they generally had more space and more furniture than did the apartments in Mai Ninh. The living rooms had intricately carved wooden furniture, and often televisions and computers (figure 6.4).

Figure 6.4. Interior of a home in Truc Tuyet. Hanoi, 2004. *Photo: Katherine V. Gough*

For all the young people we spoke to in Hanoi, the home is an important site for living and learning and a place where they gain a range of skills and knowledge. They mainly mentioned learning social and life skills in the home, rather than practical skills. A 15-year-old young woman explained, "My mother teaches me what is good and bad, what I should and should not do. I should help people and not just think of myself." Another young woman (aged 19) said, "I learn from my parents the nature of hard work. My parents have to work very hard, therefore I have to study harder." Finally, a 20-year-old young man said, "My parents teach me the correct way to behave. They guide me to show me how to get a good job in the future." As well as guidance in good behavior and how to get a good job, the young people and their parents often talked about how to avoid "social evils." Concern with social evils, especially drugs (see Valentin, this volume), partly restricts young people's movements outside the home as they attempt to avoid certain areas, especially those where drug use is reported to be widespread. Their parents also impose restrictions on where they can go and what time they have to be home. Despite these restrictions young people have considerable freedom of movement, as most of them own a bike or motorbike, or can hitch a lift with a friend. They can thus quickly get to places away from the watchful eyes of those who know them.

In Vietnam, the eldest son is traditionally expected to live with his parents and care for them in their old age. His wife will move in with him, the younger siblings being expected to move out of the family home on marrying. Setting up home, given the rapidly rising land and house prices in Hanoi, is difficult for these young people. In recent years, the shift away from Soviet-style master planning to a more market-driven system has resulted in a breakdown of the linkages between industrial and residential areas and the increasing privatization of state-owned housing (van Horen 2005). In both Mai Ninh and Truc Tuyet, young people's plans for their future homes often include subdividing the parental home. A young man in Mai Ninh explained that, with his low salary, it would take him twenty years to buy a house. His family have already planned to divide up their ground-floor apartment between the three brothers. Currently the eldest brother, who is married, lives at one end of the apartment, with his own entrance. The youngest brother has one room, the parents sleep in the living room, and he himself sleeps in the front of the apartment in a room that is used to store eighteen motorbikes at night, an important source of income. After he and his brother marry, they will stop storing motorbikes and will subdivide the remaining rooms to create separate apartments.

Housing young women in the future was not seen as such a problem, as Vietnamese women are expected to live in their husband's home on marrying. One young woman was interviewed the day before she was due to marry and move in with her husband and his parents. She explained that she would have to live with her husband's parents as long as they live, as her husband is the eldest son in the family. She was aware that it would take some time to adjust to living in her in-laws' home: "Getting married and living in the husband's family, I have to be on the look-out. It won't be as comfortable as living in my home. I shall have to demonstrate good behavior in everything I do." It is not always possible for women to live with their in-laws, either for economic or social reasons. A woman we met in Mai Ninh told us that she and her family had been living with her parents-in-law in the countryside, but the arrangement was "too complicated." After her parents died, the apartment she had grown up in in Mai Ninh was divided into two and occupied by her elder brothers. They later allowed her to convert the entranceway, which measured 6 m^2, into a home for herself, her husband, and their two teenage daughters. The space was very neat and tidy, consisting of a living area with a wall dividing it from a toilet and kitchen, and a sleeping loft extending halfway across the room, at head height, for the daughters. When I arrived, Thuy, aged 15, was doing her homework sitting cross-legged on the bed, which she shared with her sister. At night not only did the small living area become the parents' sleeping area, it was also where the family's bicycle and motorbike were stored. As there was a metal door and only one very small window high up, their home became very hot in summer. However, they expressed satisfaction with their small home, as it was their own space.

Many of the young people in both Truc Tuyet and Mai Ninh were attached to the neighborhoods they were growing up in, and many claimed that they wished to live there as adults. A young woman in Truc Tuyet was so adamant that she wanted to continue living there that she said, "If I can't get married to a boy from Truc Tuyet, I'll convince my husband to come and live in Truc Tuyet." However, some of the young people expressed a wish to move away from their neighborhood, claiming that it was too crowded. Young people are aware that they are likely as adults to live in even smaller spaces than those they are growing up in. Even when a group of young people were asked about their dream home, one young man said, "My dream house is one that has a *small* space, trees, and a means of transport passing by easily, equipped with services such as water and electricity." When questioned about the limited space in the home, one young woman said, "What is more important is how people in the family treat each other."

Young people mainly saw the transition between youth and adulthood in terms of acquiring a stable job or getting married. They rarely mentioned setting up a home of their own. One young woman from Mai Ninh (aged 23) said she felt like an adult, although she was still living at home with her parents, as the money she earned from teaching dancing was enough to cover her daily expenses. Yet a young man (aged 22), also from Mai Ninh, said, "I am not an adult because I dare not escape outside when my father does not agree." The same young man later explained that "Vietnamese youth are different from foreign youth in terms of independence. Young Vietnamese are dependent on their parents. Parents probably decide 50 percent of their affairs."

Youth and the Home in Lusaka

Squatter settlements initially arose in Lusaka during the British colonial period, when the growing African urban population had to find its own solution to the shortage of housing. The compound of Kalingalinga was one such settlement, established in the early 1940s on abandoned farm land, where the Indian owners allowed Africans to build houses (Tait 1997). Plots were large and the houses were single-story and owner-occupied. By 2004, many of the houses had become multi-family dwellings. Some owners have extended their homes by adding rooms which they rent out, whereas others have changed the layout of their homes to enable them to rent out existing rooms. Typically three to four households live in one house, but the number can be considerably higher, with up to eleven households living on one plot. Some gentrification has occurred, and the families who have a house to themselves have usually moved from better-off areas; some sold their previous home and bought one in Kalingalinga, some have rented out their home in another area and are renting a cheaper one in Kalingalinga, and others have moved into the area following retrenchment which resulted in their losing both their jobs and their employer-provided accommodation. With the worsening economic situation, rent has become an important source of income for many homeowners.

Most young people in Kalingalinga are living in multi-family houses, of which their household occupies only one or two rooms. The living space often has to double as a sleeping space, which can be especially problematic for young people needing a place to study. As one young man living in a rented house, where he shares a bedroom with three brothers, complained, "My brother was writing his final exams for grade 12, so he was disturbing us a lot in the night. He used to study at night. He would switch on the light when I would be enjoying my sleep. Whenever I wanted to play music, he would tell me, 'Switch off the radio; I want to study.'" Many young people share not only a bedroom but also a bed. Although some said they liked the company, many complained about the inconvenience. In order to obtain more space and avoid the danger of incest, posed when youth of both sexes sleep in the same bedroom, some families rent rooms in other houses where young men would go to sleep at night.

Despite the lack of space, some occupants clearly take pride in their homes, which they decorate with care. Mary (aged 23) lived in a single rented room of approximately 6 m² with her two young children and her mother. A curtain separated the bed from the living area, which was decorated with photographs, a clock, stacks of plates, and cupboards (figure 6.5). The room was decorated in blue and yellow and was immaculately kept. Many domestic activities, such as cooking and washing, take place outdoors on the plot. Performing tasks outdoors both extends the space of the home and results in increased contact with neighbors, thus making such activities more sociable. Living in such close proximity with other households, however, can lead to conflict. The young people told of arguments over issues such as the playing of loud music or cleaning the yard. Competition also arises between households regarding the clothes they wear, the food they eat, and the possessions they have in the home.

Some of the young people we met in Kalingalinga were still in school, some of the young women were selling food items from small table-top stalls or working as maids, and some of the men were doing casual work, though many were unemployed. Many of the young people talked of just sitting at home with nothing to do, though the women usually did housework, whereas men often sat in a bar rather than at home. Indeed, in order to find young men in Kalingalinga to

Figure 6.5. Interior of a home in Kalingalinga. Lusaka, 2004. *Photo: Katherine V. Gough*

interview, we had to go to a bar, even in the morning. The young men explained that they were not at home because they were trying to find some way of earning money. In the words of one young man, "Men don't find it good to stay at home because then they just think of all the problems even more, so it is better to move around so you don't think about the problems of money, food, and clothes." Some young men's lives revolved around the bar. A young man described a typical day as waking up at 8 AM and going to the bar for drinks. Then he goes to the video parlor,[3] back to the bar, home for lunch, back to the bar, sees another video if possible, then back to the bar before going home to sleep, the time at which he leaves depending on his pocket.

As Karen Tranberg Hansen (1997) also found, many young people's lives are centered on the compound, which they rarely leave except to visit relatives, as they do not have the financial means. Some young people leave Kalingalinga only once a month, or even once every two months, and have never been to the shopping centers of Manda Hill and Arcades. As one young man (aged 25) said, "These places are just too expensive, so there's no use going there. I can't afford anything there. I am afraid to even go window-shopping as I may be tempted to steal, so it's best to avoid the place." Other young people, however, frequently made the long journey, walking or taking a bus into the center of Lusaka in an often futile search for work.

A wide range of household forms are found in Lusaka, as households adopt their urban arrangements "in pursuit of both economic and social ends" (Hansen 1997, 70). Raising children has never been seen as the exclusive domain of parents, however, and the increasing number of deaths from HIV/AIDS has resulted in many children becoming orphans at a young age. The young people of Kalingalinga are growing up in a range of household types, in nuclear or extended families with their parents, grandparents, and other relations or friends. Many of them have already lived in several households, often moving because of educational opportunities or changing family circumstances.

Mackson (aged 26) was born on the Copperbelt, where he lived for nine years before moving to Lusaka with his parents, who passed away five years later from HIV/AIDS. He subsequently moved to Chipata to live with his grandparents, until an aunt sponsored him to attend a boarding school in another district. Mackson returned to Lusaka in 2004 to stay with his aunt and uncle in the hope that they would sponsor him to extend his studies further. As they did not have the means, he was planning to return to Chipata to farm and try to save to fund his own studies. Meanwhile he was running his aunt's small stall selling foodstuffs, but he did not plan to stay long as he did not feel comfortable in a household with two rooms housing five people. This high degree of residential mobility is common among the youth of Lusaka (see Gough 2008).

Many of the orphans who lived with relatives felt that they were a burden, both financially and because of the space they took up in the home. There is often no money for them to continue schooling and they are unable to find any work. One young man (aged 17), who was living with his sister and family in two rooms in a rented house, told us, "I am not very comfortable living here because I am just being kept by my sister. There are times when she does not have money and she is complaining that I am here. I feel uncomfortable when she is complaining as I think that I am contributing to her being broke."

One phenomenon associated with the HIV/AIDS pandemic is young people heading households themselves. Many of those who inherit houses from deceased parents or guardians take in tenants and become landlords. Although rent is an important source of income, the transition from living in a single-family house to occupying a small part of it along with several other households is far from easy. At 18, Gloria was the youngest landlady we encountered. While her parents were still alive the family had lived in a five-room house, though before he died her father had built some rooms for tenants to supplement his income. Following her parents' deaths, the house was subdivided into eleven housing units. Gloria was living in a small room at the front which had been the kitchen. Although the house showed signs that it had once been a fine house with a walled garden, it was now in a dilapidated state and lacked electricity. Nonetheless it provided Gloria with a source of income and a degree of independence which she would not otherwise have had.

In recent years, home ownership has been encouraged in Lusaka through the sale of formerly council-owned rental houses and flats. This has been occurring in the residential area of Chilenje South, which was established by the Lusaka City Council soon after independence in 1964. Several hundred houses, with two to four bedrooms, a living room, a kitchen, and a bathroom, were built and rented out at rates affordable for the lower middle class. All the houses in Chilenje South are still single-family dwellings, though they often accommodate greatly extended families, and in some cases extensions have been built. The youth of Chilenje South have much more space in their homes than those living in Kalingalinga, sometimes even having their own room. We found the young people hanging out in their homes chatting, watching television, and playing computer games. The kitchens and bathrooms are fully equipped, and the living rooms are furnished with soft furniture and a range of electrical goods (figure 6.6). Although originally the houses were surrounded by low metal fences, many of the owners, especially the newcomers, have since built high brick walls. One young man, Alfred (aged 19), said that before new people moved in and some started building high walls, there was much more of a sense of community in Chilenje South. Neighbors used to know each other, whereas now there is an increasing tendency for residents, especially the newcomers, to isolate themselves both spatially and socially.

Although the houses they live in are quite different from those in Kalingalinga, many of the young people in Chilenje South also have complex housing histories. These are typically related to the ability of relatives to sponsor education, or to the passing away of relatives. George (aged 15) was living in his grandparents' house in Chilenje South. After his parents died when he was very young, he moved to the Copperbelt to live with his uncle, but following his death George moved to his grandparents' house. He was sharing the three-bedroom house with twelve other members of his family. His elder sister had recently moved in with her three children, following her husband's death. Together with her husband she had built a small house on the plot of his parents' house, but following his death she and her children had been forcibly removed from their home. She had taken her in-laws to court in an attempt to regain possession and was awaiting the outcome. As Karen Tranberg Hansen (1997) has shown, women's property rights in Zambia have become increasingly insecure, as the deteriorating economic situation has reduced the number of "proper marriages," which involve paying a dowry.

Many of the young people from both Kalingalinga and Chilenje South have already moved home several times and have experienced changes in their households during their childhood. Consequently, actually moving out of the

Figure 6.6. Interior of a home in Chilenje South. Lusaka, 2004. *Photo: Katherine V. Gough*

parental home may not be such a psychological challenge as it is in many other circumstances. Young people's greatest concern is finding the financial means to set up their own home. Some young people were remarkably optimistic, believing that if they obtain educational qualifications they will find employment and the means to rent their own accommodation. Others are more pessimistic about their future and the possibility of finding work. They told us that they had to be the best students or know someone to find a job after qualifying. As one young man said, "It is tough unless your father owns a company or your father works for someone and can push for you." We only met a couple of youths in Chilenje South who had jobs, and in both cases they had obtained them through contacts. Although none of the young men in Kalingalinga was in regular employment, George (aged 26) had previously worked as a cleaner in an international school where his sister was working. While working there he had rented two rooms in Kalingalinga, where he lived with his wife and baby daughter. After three years he lost his job and had to give up his home, as he could no longer pay the rent. Both he and his wife moved back in with their respective mothers, as it was not possible for the whole family to move into either home. Four years later George had still been unable to secure another job and his marriage had broken down, which he partly attributed to the lack of their own home.

Many of the young people considered a good home to be one in which both parents were still alive and working. Those who had become household heads at a young age particularly stressed that their lives had been very different when their parents had been alive. Young people emphasized the importance of the social side of home life more than the spatial (see also Hansen 1997 and Schlyter 1999). They defined a good home as one where there is love, respect, cooperation, and communication. According to one young man, "The physical structure of the house is not important. You can find that there is a nice big house, but the people who live there are evil in their hearts. You can't consider that a good house. I would respect a home that is bad physically but with good people." This does not mean that the spatial aspect of the home does not matter to young people. Some explained that a good home should have a clean yard, a good building, and enough space: "It should not be very tight." Such idealized descriptions do not reflect the type of home in which most young people in Kalingalinga are living.

Some young people drew a direct link between youth and home, claiming that "young people like moving around, but adults sit at home." Others felt that they would only consider themselves adults when they were able to establish their own homes. However, one young man (aged 25) had his own home, which he had inherited from his deceased parents, but felt that he was still a youth because he could not find adequate employment: "I am still a youth. To be an adult, you would know how to get a good job to get a better life. Without a good job, I feel like a youth. . . . Being married and having a house does not make me an adult." The feeling of being a youth or an adult is not necessarily constant. One young woman (aged 27) spoke of feeling like a youth and an adult at different times and in different places: "Sometimes I feel like a youth and sometimes like an adult. When I'm with my mum, I realize that I'm young. When I go back to my own home, I feel like an adult because I'm in my own house and I'm a parent. Basically being a youth or an adult is just a feeling." Although some of the young people wanted to stay in the compound, as they considered it to be their home, others were adamant that they would move out as soon as they had the chance. In the words of one young man, "I do not feel at home here. . . . I have to move out of here so I can experience a higher kind of life than I am living here." Unless the economic situation improves, though, his chances of doing so are relatively slim.

Concluding Comments

For young people in Recife, Hanoi, and Lusaka, the home plays an important role in their transition from childhood through youth into adulthood. The types of housing that they live in and their experiences of home vary greatly both between and within the three cities, though there are some common features. Many young people, especially but not exclusively those in the low-income group, experience home as a cramped place. Such physical crowding has implications for their daily life and social relations in the home. Some young people share not just a bedroom but also a bed, which becomes problematic as they grow older.

Although the home is a safe and secure place for some young people, it is a place full of conflict and contradictions for many. The contradictory image of home as both a safe and a dangerous place was especially evident in Brazil, which is a much more violent society than Vietnam or Zambia. Parents are often anxious to keep their youngsters off the streets to avoid violence, yet the home is not a sanctuary, as young people may experience violence there too. Domestic violence is no doubt more widespread than we could uncover, because of the dominant image of home as a safe place. The violent nature of society in Recife struck us especially when, within six months of our interviews, two of our male informants had been murdered in Vietnã, one on the street and one in the home of a friend.

For young people in all three cities, home is a place for living and learning, and, in Hanoi especially, for studying. Although it can be difficult for young people to find a place to study, they devise strategies to overcome the lack of space, such as studying at night. Home emerged as a particularly important place for studying in Hanoi for two reasons: the nature of Vietnamese society, and some of the methodological restrictions on our study. First, schooling in Hanoi is highly competitive (see Madsen, this volume). Young people want (and feel they are required) to be able to support their parents in their old age, and the two-child policy has increased the pressure to succeed. It is also realistic to expect educational qualifications to lead to a job. This is often not the case in Lusaka and Recife, especially for the low-income youths. Second, our research process was highly controlled in Vietnam, with the result that most of the young people we interviewed were selected for us by the People's Committee, so we principally met "model" youth (see Dalsgaard and Valentin, this volume).

People's homes change over the life course. The dwelling itself may be expanded or contracted as occupants or their fortunes change. Moving out of the family home and establishing a home of one's own is often associated with the transition from youth to adulthood. Home was especially variable in Lusaka. Many young people in Lusaka experience changes in the physical structure of their homes, especially reductions of living space, either because it is subdivided or because the household moves to a smaller, often rented house. Some young people who have lost both their parents subdivide the family home in order to live off the rent. The theme of home as a changing place is dominant in Lusaka for two reasons. First, supporting the extended family has always been very important, with children being raised by a range of relatives. Second, the impact of HIV/AIDS has accentuated the fluid nature of the home, resulting in an increase in the number of dependents, the rise of youth-headed households, and a corresponding reduction in dwelling sizes. There are also changes over time in those who live in the home: siblings grow up and move out, grandparents and parents die, relatives, friends, and increasingly dependents, many of whom are orphans, move in. For some of these young people, home is an alienating place where they feel they do not belong.

These varying experiences of home are aptly summarized by Alison Blunt and Ann Varley (2004, 3) when they claim that home is "a space of belonging and alienation, intimacy and violence, desire and fear." Although, as Blunt and Varley argue, experiences and relationships in the home "lie at the heart of human life," establishing a home of their own is beyond the reach of many young people. In fact, many of the young people we met will find it much more difficult to set up their own homes than their parents did. The increasing privatization of state housing means that young people in Lusaka and Hanoi are unlikely to obtain housing linked to their employment or be able to rent state-owned housing. In Recife, the opportunities for land invasions arise prior to elections. As the city grows, available land is located further and further from the center. Many youth whose parents are owner-occupiers extend or subdivide the parental home in order to create space for newly formed households. This option is not available to young people who grow up in rental housing. Many low-income youth have only a remote chance of ever becoming homeowners, and even the cheapest rented accommodation may be beyond their means. Their inability to establish their own homes can result in a prolongation of the period of youth, as young people continue to live in the home of parents or guardians as financial dependents. As the home is potentially a source of income, a place of work, and an asset, not becoming a homeowner means more than simply not owning accommodation. The future looks brighter for many middle-income youths, especially in Recife and Hanoi, who are deferring leaving the family home until they have completed their studies and found employment. In time, they are likely to be in a position to rent or buy a dwelling.

There are clearly associations between the concepts of "youth" and "home," yet the links between them are far from clear-cut. Some of the young people in all three cities, of different socioeconomic backgrounds and both genders, described the behavior and roles of youth and adults in relation to the home. Adults spend more time in the home, whereas young people, especially young men, move around more outside the home. The idea that a young person living in the family home is still a youth, as adulthood is associated with establishing one's own home, is an oversimplification. The oldest son in a Vietnamese family is expected to stay in the parental home and start his own family, gradually assuming the role of household head; not leaving the parental home does not mean that he is not an adult. Conversely, although some young people in Lusaka have become homeowners following the deaths of their parents, they do not feel like adults as they are unable to find employment. Most young men in Lusaka find it very difficult to establish their own home because of the economic situation, and young women are expected to find a husband before moving out of the family home. The teenage households established by the low-income youth of Recife are often unstable, so that young people leave the parental home only to return to it later. Some of the middle-income youth in all three cities live in the family home until they have finished their studies, while others may leave the home in order to study elsewhere. In neither case is the choice necessarily considered to be linked to being either a youth or an adult.

Exploring the link between youth and the home illustrates how, as Gill Valentine (2003, 37) has argued, the transitions between youth and adulthood are not a "one-off or one-way process." The changes associated with growing up, such as setting up one's own home, may occur once, more than once, or not at all. As I have illustrated in this chapter, the relationship between youth and the home is complex, being intersected by social differences brought about by culture, gender, and class.

Acknowledgments

As this chapter is based on field research in three countries that were new to me, it would not have been possible without the support of the three anthropologists in the project, Anne Line Dalsgaard, Karen Valentin, and Karen Tranberg Hansen, and their local counterparts, Russell Parry Scott, Dang Nguyen Anh, and Chileshe Mulenga. I remain hugely indebted to all of them for making the research possible. In Recife, I worked together with Mónica Franch, who became more of a research partner than an assistant; in Hanoi, Nghiem Thi Thuy kindly assisted in arranging the interviews and Nguyen Chung Thuy was a very competent interpreter; and in Lusaka, Marianne Haahr, Joseph Silavwe, and Elizabeth Mwansa participated in the interviewing and showed a lively interest in the findings. I thank them all for assisting me in the field and teaching me much in the process. I am also grateful to all of the Danish research team and to Tracey Skelton for their constructive comments on successive drafts of this chapter.

Notes

1. As homeowners in *favelas* have invaded the land on which they build their homes, they do not pay rent.

2. Elsewhere as well, young people may live in the parental home for an extended period of time while completing their studies (White 2002).

3. There are several video parlors in Kalingalinga. They are housed in wooden shacks which contain rows of benches, a television, and a videocassette player. A small fee is paid to enter the parlor and watch the videos, which are typically violent or pornographic foreign films.

References

Abbott-Chapman, Joan, and Margaret Robertson. 1999. Home as a Private Space: Some Adolescent Constructs. *Journal of Youth Studies* 2(1):23–43.

Blunt, Alison. 2005. Cultural Geography: Cultural Geographies of Home. *Progress in Human Geography* 29(4):505–15.

Blunt, Alison, and Ann Varley. 2004. Introduction: Geographies of Home. *Cultural Geographies* 11:3–6.

De Souza, Marcelo Lopes. 2001. Metropolitan Deconcentration, Socio-political Fragmentation and Extended Suburbanisation: Brazilian Urbanisation in the 1980s and 1990s. *Geoforum* 32:437–47.

Easthope, Hazel. 2004. A Place Called Home. *Housing, Theory and Society* 21(3):128–38.

Fernandes, Edésio, and Márcio Valenca. 2001. Editorial: Urban Brazil; Past and Future. *Geoforum* 32:v–ix.

Gough, Katherine V. 2008. "Moving Around": The Social and Spatial Mobility of Youth in Lusaka. *Geografiska Annaler* 90(3).

Gough, Katherine V., and Mónica Franch. 2005. Spaces of the Street: Socio-spatial Mobility and Exclusion of Youth in Recife. *Children's Geographies* 3(2):149–66.

Hansen, Karen Tranberg. 1997. *Keeping House in Lusaka.* New York: Columbia University Press.

Hoai Anh Tran and Elisabeth Dalholm. 2005. Favoured Owners, Neglected Tenants: Privatisation of State-Owned Housing in Hanoi. *Housing Studies* 20(6):897–929.

Jones, Gill. 2000. Experimenting with Households and Inventing "Home." *International Social Science Journal* 52(2):183–94.

Mallett, Shelley. 2004. Understanding Home: A Critical Review of the Literature. *Sociological Review* 52(1):62–89.

Nguyen Quang and Hans Detlef Kammeier. 2002. Changes in the Political Economy of Vietnam and Their Impacts on the Built Environment of Hanoi. *Cities* 19(6):373–88.

Saunders, Peter, and Peter Williams. 1988. The Constitution of the Home: Towards a Research Agenda. *Housing Studies* 3(2):81–93.

Schlyter, Ann. 1999. Recycled Inequalities: Youth and Gender in George Compound, Zambia. Research Report no. 114. Uppsala, Sweden: Nordiska Afrikainstitutet.

Tait, John. 1997. *From Self-Help Housing to Sustainable Settlement: Capitalist Development and Urban Planning in Lusaka, Zambia.* Brookfield, Vt.: Avebury.

Valentine, Gill. 2003. Boundary Crossings: Transitions from Childhood to Adulthood. *Children's Geographies* 1(1):37–52.

Van Horen, Basil. 2005. City Profile: Hanoi. *Cities* 22(2):161–73.

White, Naomi Rosh. 2002. "Not Under My Roof!" Young People's Experience of Home. *Youth and Society* 43(2):214–31.

7

Toward Eduscapes:
Youth and Schooling in a Global Era

Ulla Ambrosius Madsen

In various ways the dynamic interplay between sphere, site, and self is brought together in the chapters on youth and city in this volume. While "sphere" is an overall concept comprising a blending of policies, ideologies, and history that constitute urban space, "site" is the physical manifestation of sphere, places where young people negotiate their position and struggle to find meanings. Analyzing the multiple meanings of *juventude,* Anne Line Dalsgaard, Mónica Franch, and Russell Parry Scott (chapter 3 of this volume) study how youth in Recife "steer" toward adulthood in a context marked by huge social differences, unemployment, and the collapse of institutions. Exploring the interplay between the city as a physical location where young people live and youth as a structural category, Karen Valentin (chapter 4) analyzes the relationship between young Hanoians and "politicized space." Karen Tranberg Hansen (chapter 5) investigates young people's efforts to gain access to different urban spaces in Lusaka in times of neoliberal politics and economics. My aim in this chapter is to further explore the interaction between sphere, site, and self in the context of local schooling, which becomes the lens through which I analyze young people's responses to modernization processes and neoliberal reforms that condition societal realities. Theories of youth, schooling, globalization, and comparative education are central to the analytical framework that I apply to this study.

Studying youth as a structural and an experiential category implies a focus on young people's practices, interpretations, and responses to what it means to be a student in a particular historical and local context (Nilan and Feixa 2006; Honwana and De Boeck 2005). Inspired by Arjun Appadurai's concept of "scape," Sunaina Maira and Elisabeth Soep suggest using "youthscapes" to study youth as a social achievement rather than a psychological stage (2005, xviii). The study of youthscapes reveals how "youth are drawn into local practices, national ideologies, and global markets while always occupying an ambiguous space in and between them" (xix). Youthscapes are a useful heuristic for studying young people in the field of education, and I use the concept as an approach to analyzing the positions youth create and occupy "within and between" power structures as they materialize in school.

The classical distinction between education and schooling suggests that the "educated person" should be understood as a contextual cultural construction, and a school as "a state organized and regulated institution of intentional instruction" (Levinson, Foley, and Holland 1996, 2). Since my focus is on institutionalized practices, I will refer to education as activities and policies that are elements in the cultural construction of the educated person (Bourdieu and Wacquant 1992; Levinson 2000; Stambach 2000). When we apply the dynamics inherent in the concepts of youth referred to above, schooling turns into a concept that embraces agents' (i.e., teachers', students', and parents') interpretations of and responses to the organization and regulation of time, space, and place.

Building on cultural theories of globalization and education, this chapter attempts to explore ways of understanding and studying schooling across national, cultural, and social boundaries (Appadurai 1996; Arnove and Torres 1999; Inda and Rosaldo 2002; Tabulawa 2003; Tomlinson 1999). In his analysis of education reform in Botswana, Richard Tabulawa (2003) argues that since the collapse of the Soviet Bloc, education has become central to democratization processes and liberal reforms around the world. He demonstrates that international political declarations as well as national policies are marked by a discourse of pedagogy, teaching, and learning that can be traced back to Jean-Jacques Rousseau and the early Enlightenment: learner-centered education, child-centered teaching, and participatory, democratic, and inquiry-based methods of learning (2003, 9). While Tabulawa's focus is on how ideas and values from the Western Enlightenment spread with globalization, Nicholas Burbules and Carlos Alberto Torres (2000, 15) investigate how new policies and steering strategies, with particular demands for evaluation, financing, assessment, standards, teacher training, curriculum, instruction, and testing, set a global agenda for schools to respond to and implement neoliberal education reforms.

Although Appadurai does not explicitly deal with educational issues, I argue that we can use his notion of ideoscape as a point of departure for further exploring the dynamics of globalization processes (Appadurai 1996, 33). Ideoscapes are connected to ideologies and counterideologies of the state and are, according to Appadurai, constituted by ideas of the Enlightenment, i.e., freedom, welfare, rights, sovereignty, representation, and democracy. Emphasizing that imagination is social practice as work and negotiation of meanings and order (1996, 31), Appadurai points to what he sees as something critical and new in global cultural processes: the ability of an increasing number of people in ever more parts of the world to consider a wider range of lives. From this perspective, school is an interesting institution to study. Following Appadurai's ideas of ideoscapes as global flows, I suggest the "eduscape" as an analytical concept with which to understand and study the increased interconnectedness of schools across national, cultural, and social contexts.

There is a long tradition of ethnographic studies in education and comparative education, but few contributions cut across ethnography and comparative studies in investigating educational phenomena (e.g., Alexander 2000; Arnove and Torres 1999; Anderson-Levitt 2003). Comparative education developed originally out of a positivist and functionalist approach to education that aimed to understand factors that determine academic achievement, in order to develop models for the transfer of educational systems from one context to another (Crossley and Watson 2003). Several contributions have challenged the positivist understanding and positivism's belief in value-free social inquiry: the classical methodological dispute with positivism on assumptions of value-free knowledge and objectivity, the postmodern questions of representativity and legitimacy, and the postcolonial focus on embedded constructions of dichotomies, hegemony, superiority, and the "triumph of the West" in the discourses of non-Western cultures (Gupta and Ferguson 1997; Marcus 1998; Welch 1999). Central to the comparison in this study are the meanings and practices young people construct around schooling, between local realities and global projects (Madsen 2006). While how to construct site is disputed (Gingrich and Fox 2000; Gupta and Ferguson 1997; Ferguson 2006; Stronach 2006), this study is in accordance with the traditions of theoretical and empirical work in the project and is grounded in physical locations: secondary schools and classrooms in the three cities. On the basis of a parallel presentation of ethnographic material, the conclusion attempts to cut across site in order to compare findings from the three sites.

Brazil: School—A Safe Alternative to Hanging Out?

The current educational system in Brazil was established in the aftermath of a military regime that governed the country from 1964 to 1985. This was an era of Brazil's history dominated by the violation of human rights and persecution of political minorities (Gomes and Capanema 2001; Sherif 2001). Brazil declared a policy of "education for all" in the beginning of the 1990s, and between 1990 and 1998 enrollment in primary schools more than doubled. This growth placed pressure on the secondary educational system, as well as postsecondary professional training programs.

A 1996 law reorganized schools on the basis of democracy and autonomy, creating governing bodies consisting of the head teacher and representatives of teachers, pupils, and parents: a significant break with the highly centralized organization of the previous educational system (Birdsall and Sabot 1996; Marteleto and Rodrigues 2002). Participation is a keyword in contemporary reforms, and attempts to decentralize schooling have been followed by innovation in pedagogy and changes emphasizing cross-curricular themes, values inherent in ethics, the environment, cultural pluralism, health and sexual education, work, and consumption.

The National Educational Plan approved in 2002 aims at strengthening the connection between education and "the world of labor and social practice," personal development, intellectual autonomy, and critical thinking (Brazil, Pernambuco Ministry of Education 2000). The national parameters for secondary education emphasize that a shift in competencies is required for democratic citizenship—from "discipline and obedience" to "creativity, curiosity, the ability to think multiple alternatives to a given problem." Many Brazilian states have implemented these reforms over the last decade. From a critical theoretical point of view, Louis Armando Gandin and Michael W. Apple argue that experiences from Porto Alegre, the capital of Rio Grande do Sul, the southernmost state of Brazil, reveal how neoliberal and neoconservative policies can be "stopped" by democratic educational alternatives (2002, 260). The "Citizen School" project attempts to involve poor and marginalized people in the decision-making processes at all levels through school councils. We find similar efforts in Pernambuco, a much poorer state than Rio Grande do Sul. Educational reforms in Pernambuco have increased access to education and reduced illiteracy rates (World Bank 2003a).

With "Open Schools" projects in Pernambuco, efforts have been made to establish school councils and to open up the schools to the large number of unemployed young people and adults who had never completed basic education. In the school where I conducted most of my fieldwork, dropping out and failing to finish were clearly problems, but enrollment in secondary school was increasing, albeit primarily in afternoon and evening classes. It was not a problem to get access to the school or to the classrooms. I was allowed to move around and talk to students and teachers as long as I informed the management of the appointments I made. The headmaster of the school told me enthusiastically how the school had developed from "a not so good school to a good school," thanks to a school development program supported by the ministry in which she and some of the teachers had participated. Its aim was to develop models of how to open the school to the community and to learn new pedagogical methods, with a focus on cross-curricular and participatory teaching and learning methodologies (Kempner and Jurema 2002).

The school was located in the outskirts of Recife, close to a poor residential area.

Walls surrounded the yard and students, teachers, and visitors entered through a gate where security guards searched the students who were entering for drugs and guns. Opposite the school was a café where young people, claiming they had nothing else to do, would "hang out," listening to music, playing cards, drinking, and smoking. Teachers and students considered the café a "risky" place, since students liked to spend their time there rather than attending classes: "It is the first phase in dropping out," a student told me. The following is an extract from my field diary covering an average day at school.

> Friday, and the first lesson is mathematics. Students who come too late keep inter-rupting the teaching. The teacher gives the students some tasks and walks around in the class to the students who ask for help. Some wait for help but the majority talk about something different in small groups. Next lesson is physics, but the teacher does not come. After a while some go to the café while others hang around in the classroom. Third lesson is Portuguese and the students have been told to prepare for a test. The teacher is punctual. The first 5 minutes the teacher and the students talk about the coming election. The teacher tells them that he votes for Lula. "I want to see Brazil burning. We have to burn before we can flourish." Writing the tasks on the blackboard, the teacher explains the rules and almost gives the solution of the problems they are supposed to solve alone. Some complain that this is new to them. "That is not true. We have had this many times. I cannot make it easier for you. This is easier than taking candies from a child. But for those of you who are not interested, I cannot do more." Fourth and fifth lessons are biology. Two out of the five students who left for the café show up again. It is a young female teacher and the topic is sex, AIDS, contraception, and the female body. The students are very interested and focused—listen and ask questions related to everyday life experi-ences: violence, pregnancy, and childcare. After 60 minutes the lesson stops and some of the students bring out soft drinks, cakes, and a boom-box. For the next 30 minutes they have a small party, singing and dancing and enjoying themselves. "That is what we do every last Friday of the month," the teacher explained. "I like to see them happy and relaxed."

My diary notes clearly demonstrate that the atmosphere in school was extremely relaxed. The students walked in and out of the classrooms, sometimes without asking permission, in order to take a break, chat with other students, flirt, smoke a cigarette, or go to the toilet. Inside the classroom the atmosphere between teachers and students was remarkably informal, not least in relation to academic issues. As my observations indicate, students favored the biology lessons for two reasons: first, because sexuality appeared a relevant and urgent topic to young students of this age; second, because the biology teacher was committed to developing good social relations.

Some of the teachers claimed that it became difficult for students or teachers to distinguish between a relaxed relationship and a lack of discipline and interest, since young people considered the school to be a "kind of home" where they could do whatever they liked. It could be difficult for teachers to discipline the students for their behavior or their academic performance. It was explained to me that dissatisfied students and relatives were liable to react physically to poor marks and exam results, and therefore teachers carefully considered the marking and evaluation of students.

Many of the teachers had been educated during the military regime, when pedagogy was centered on discipline, order, and the rote memorization of a huge amount of material. The content and structure of teacher education had undergone fundamental changes since the education reforms commenced in 1995. Secondary education had shifted toward reform-oriented pedagogy, with an emphasis on bridging theory and practice, critical thinking, and participatory learning, and these ideas and theories were also included in teacher training (Lûdke and Moreira 1999). Unlike their colleagues in private schools, teachers in public schools were paid poorly, in some cases not enough to maintain a family. While teachers in private schools were vulnerable to parents and students who went "shopping" for education, teachers in public schools could not be fired, and that made the work attractive to many in times when unemployment was high.

> The school thinks of itself as democratic, but we are very exclusive. There are not many black students, if you just look around, and only students from the middle class or the rich classes will make it. (Female social science teacher, 28 years old)

> I sometimes feel that this is the end of time for the young people: there is no religion, no hope. Violence, drugs, and gangs, and that is what is there for them, and that is why young people do not care about going to school. But we, the teachers, have to explain the reason why [they should]. (Male Portuguese teacher, 54 years old)

> It is a liberal school, but whenever it feels threatened it is highly repressive. The liberal school is also lost because it does not have good results. It is a paradox: it is very difficult to work without having discipline. You do not learn well without discipline. And that was well done by the authoritarian school (they just knew how to do it). So the school is looking for its identity. What does it want? What can it be? (Male history teacher, 34 years old)

Presenting the school as an institution divided against itself, teachers pointed at a number of contradictions and dilemmas in their work. On the one hand the school appeared democratic and liberal, but on the other hand it was exclusive and incapable of obtaining good results, since, according to the history teacher, students and teachers lacked discipline. Teachers often empathized with the young people in difficult circumstances, regarding them as victims in the "end of history," exposed to violence, drugs, and gangs.

The students in grade 10 were from poor or lower-middle-class backgrounds.

While students in the private schools came from privileged family backgrounds with access to a challenging and well-equipped learning environment, students in public schools had to deal with a scarcity of everything from food to textbooks and teachers. As a teacher from a private school said, "The tragedy is that poor people have never been to school, and when they come it is bad, incomplete, and ignorant of who they are and what they need."

> What is the use of going to school? Even if we get better teachers, better materials, better schools, it will not change the living conditions of young people in this country. We are suppressed by powers that we cannot control: unemployment, violence, inequality, poverty. So what is the use of learning? I think students in schools understand the problems better, they can see what is happening today: government pretends it is paying the teachers; teachers pretend they are teaching; students pretend they are learning. (Roschinaldo, 18 years old)

> I think education is very important for your future. I go to school and I also work, and that is why I can manage. . . . If I did not go to school I would have no work . . . that is how it is. I would just be hanging out and I do not want to do that, although many of my friends do . . . but I want an education . . . I really want. (Josepha, 19 years old)

> This is a good school. But I think poor people might as well forget about education . . . it is just waste . . . it will lead to nowhere. But where else is there to go? (Maria, 17 years old)

As these quotations suggest, students were quite ambivalent about the school. On the one hand, they perceived attending school as necessary for gaining an education that would make possible a safe future and a secure job. On the other hand, they also saw school as a waste of time, feeling dominated by forces beyond their control. Roschinaldo and Maria both emphasized that despite these problems the school was a good place—or the only place—to stay. It provided them an opportunity to better understand some of the structures and dynamics of the society in which they lived.

According to Anne Line Dalsgaard and her colleagues (chapter 3 of this volume), students in grade 10 were in a life phase between adolescence and youth. In the school—during classes—they were in principle defined, positioned, and treated as pupils and adolescents, and thus were subordinate to teachers and had certain duties to fulfill according to the curriculum. Although students in the classroom actively challenged the allocation of roles and positions to teachers and students, they nevertheless depended on the teachers' support, preferences, mood, and expertise. It was different outside school, in the home and the streets (Katherine V. Gough, chapter 6, and Norbert Wildermuth, chapter 9 of this volume). Outside classrooms the students changed their attitude and behavior.

Figure 7.1. Taking a break in Recife, 2003. *Photo: Anne Line Dalsgaard*

They smoked, flirted, and argued and used school as a space to exercise *juventude,* taking the role of young people rather than that of adolescents.

To these young people school represented the belief and dream that social change and progress could be possible through education. In attending school, the students participated in an educational project that was defined rhetorically as democratic, emphasizing ideals of equality, inclusiveness, and individual rights. Inside the school, however, the project was undermined by irregular attendance, and students dropped out because of poverty or loss of motivation and interest. Social relations between teachers and students, and acquaintance with people who had managed to secure an education despite harsh living conditions, reemphasized the potential of schooling. Outside the school, unemployment, racism, and violence determined students' lives and futures. School appeared as one of the few relatively safe alternatives—perhaps the only one—these young people had to a life in the streets, unemployed.

Zambia: School—A Shelter from Hunger and Poverty?

Formal education in Zambia is linked historically to British colonialism, dating from the late 1880s, and its efforts to control the development of Africans, their abilities and skills, in order to serve and reproduce the social order laid down by white settlers and the colonial power. The Christian mission and the colonization of Africa had from the very beginning the goal of civilizing and Christianizing what missionaries and settlers perceived as a heathen and undeveloped people (Osei-Hwedie and Ndulo 1989; Snelson 1974, 11). Formal schooling was established as an alternative to cultural learning through family, kin, and community. This early era of education was characterized by ignorance and rejection of the ways in which Africans had hitherto transmitted "wisdom, knowledge and experience from one generation to the next. . . . As a result schools were alien to the local culture from the outset—they were foreign to the people, western-inspired and -conceived" (Kelly 1999, 31).

At independence in 1964, Zambia found itself with a large illiterate population, despite the fact that Western formal education had been established in the country for a period of almost seventy years (Serpell 1993). With the new political regime and the ideas of humanist socialism launched by President Kaunda, education was seen as the key to social transformation. In 1991, elections led to a multi-party political system and a political realignment with the West after years of one-party rule and a command economy. Structural adjustment, liberalization, and privatization shaped public policy throughout the 1990s. In the wake of the declarations of "education for all," a national conference was held. The result was a new policy focusing on three key areas: quality, access, and management. A fourth concern was teaching processes, with a shift in pedagogy toward "learning" and the "child" (Carmody 2004; Boesen 2000). With this focus, Zambian education changed from the structures of a command economy and the ideology of humanist socialism toward a liberal economy and a democratic ideology. Liberal reforms, introduced in 1991, aimed to increase efficiency and financing, and were supported by a number of donors involved in the education sector. The most recent policy statement, "Education in Zambia 2002," addresses critical issues such as the HIV/AIDS crisis and unemployment, concerns that largely determine whether Zambian educational reforms can be successfully implemented. The number of secondary schools is insufficient. What its more, they tend to be located in and around urban areas where enrollment has increased. A huge problem is the increase in the dropout rate, due to poverty and disease (Zambia, Ministry of Education 2001). This chapter explores current educational reforms in Zambia with reference to students at a secondary school on the outskirts of Lusaka.

The school was first established in 1929. Counting a number of prominent citizens as alumni, not least the former president, Kenneth Kaunda, the school is still widely known and respected as an outstanding educational institution in Zambian society. However, cuts in education have adversely affected its infrastructure, limiting the teaching equipment and materials available. What previously had been well-equipped laboratories and classes are now in very poor condition, with broken doors and windows and damaged blackboards, chairs, and tables. This disintegration corresponded well with teachers' and students' lack of interest and limited resources and opportunities to commit themselves to school and education (Bassey 1999; Carmody 2004; Musonda 1999).

I was allowed access to students, classrooms, and teachers, and no one demanded that I inform staff or the authorities of my whereabouts. This free and open access reflected, I felt, a touch of cynicism. I could not escape the feeling that the situation at school was so desperate, and shaped by so little hope, that almost nothing mattered any more, least of all my presence.

I made an appointment with an English teacher to observe his grade 11 class. Before the lesson started, we discussed the conditions for education and young people in Zambia and he said, "They are trapped—between the images of America and the realities of Africa. They are running after something that they will never reach. Only a handful of students graduating every year will get a seat in the university and it is very difficult, almost impossible, for them to find a job." This critique of what he saw as the dominance of American or Western culture in Africa stood in sharp contrast to the content and methodology of the teaching that I subsequently observed and that exposed some of the contradictions and paradoxes inherent not just in his class but in Zambian schooling in general. Extracts from my diary illustrate some of these contradictions:

> The teacher distributed copied sheets including exercises. There were not enough copies and 3–4 students had to share one sheet. A student was asked to read: "My mother thought she was giving the best care to her children by feeding us eggs and sausages for breakfast, sandwiches prepared with slabs of cheese, bologna, or ham bracketed in slices of white bread smothered with mayonnaise and topped with a leaf of lettuce for lunch. For dinner we feasted on roasted beef hamburgers, hot dogs, pork chops or fried chicken always with potatoes, baked or boiled or mashed, and portions of canned vegetables. And every meal was washed down by glasses of milk."
>
> The story was about a teenager who grew up in the States in the 1950s, and who later in life faced problems with overweight, which caused serious heart problems and strokes. . . . Studying at the university, he could not keep himself from eating "hotdogs with chili sauce every night before going to bed." The final sentence was as follows: "Thousands of teenagers in the States are dying every year due to too much food and affected by strokes."
>
> After reading the full text the teacher wanted to focus on three words: rebellion, distress, disoriented.
>
> The teacher wrote the words on the blackboard and subsequently asked the students to find them in the text and read the sentence in which they were mentioned.
>
> The teacher: "Rebellion." A student reads: "By the time I was six or seven years old, my body was already rebelling against some food I was given." The teacher:

"Who is a rebel?" The student: "Someone who fights." The teacher: "Yes, a rebel is a person who fights against the society; if he is suppressed he fights for his rights. Rebellion is a movement, a group of people, often young people, who fight for their rights."

The teacher: "Distress." A student: "Neither I nor my family connected the signs of distress with the meals served in our home." The teacher: "What is distress?" No one answers. The teacher: "Distress . . . distress is when a person, a young man cannot get his needs fulfilled. When hunger . . . diseases, HIV/AIDS, then a person is distressed."

The teacher: "Disoriented." A student: "I suddenly woke up, it was dark and I did not feel, I was disoriented and could not find my way to the bathroom." The teacher: "Disoriented, what is that?" A student: "Disoriented means that you are confused, that you cannot find out what to do in your life. Where to go, what to be or how to be without a future." The teacher: "Yes, many people here in Zambia or in Africa, they are disoriented, they do not know what to do, because many think they have no future. They do not know what will come. That's what makes them disoriented.

I was surprised that the historical contradictions and problems in African education were presented so clearly and unambiguously: African teachers teaching English to African students in one of the poorest nations on the continent used a text about problems of obesity and overeating among American teenagers in the 1950s. I was struck by the class's lack of reaction, especially since the teacher had been so critical of American culture's domination of African youth. There were no signs of embarrassment either in the teacher's body language or in that of the students. I knew that only a minority of the students had had breakfast before coming to school, that few would have any lunch, and that not all of them would have a full meal on returning home from school.

The teacher used the text as a point of departure for elaborating on critical issues related to young people's lives and to the larger society. He encouraged the students to interpret the concepts of rebellion, distress, and disorientation independently of how they were used in the text, directing the lesson to questions of power, suppression, and resistance. This interchange demonstrates how teachers and students used the school as a space to critique forces that constrained them: The lesson was first and foremost about hunger, poverty, and inequality. Connecting "Americanization" to the local context and the students' lifeworlds, the teacher, by interpreting and contextualizing what he defined as key concepts in the text, encouraged the students to respond to power structures that affected them. In this way the lesson became a place where power structures and strategies for resistance were negotiated.

There is the thing about Africa: You have to be able to look after yourself, otherwise you are lost . . . just lost, ma'am. (Caroline, 17 years old)

When I am in the school I can still hope that things will change . . . when you are in a school you have a hope . . . educated people give you hope, outside there is nothing. (Joseph, 19 years old)

The government has put a lot of focus on HIV/AIDS programs so that they have neglected other sectors, like education. I know we need to fight AIDS but all the attention is focused on AIDS; what happens to schools? Who is going to maintain them? For example, collection of garbage in schools, if this is neglected then diseases will start breaking out, leading to greater problems in schools. Government needs to have balance and focus in its activities. (Robert, 19 years old)

According to Robert, a problem in Zambian schooling is that the government has concentrated on AIDS, ignoring in the process the "big problems" in the education sector, which no one felt responsible for solving. The school's decayed infrastructure clearly indicated the consequences of the current political priorities. Joseph attended the lesson described above, and his emphasis that education and "being educated" provide "hope" reflect very well the paradoxes of schooling: despite a devastated learning environment, students occasionally experienced teaching that opened up discussions and understandings beyond the immediate realities. Going to school was a way for students to insist on a position in the society that was not limited by unemployment, disease, or poverty, and to escape the "nothing" which they felt was waiting for them outside the school. For Caroline this "nothing" was the general living condition of people in Africa: "you have to be able to look after yourself." The expectation and hope that young people and their parents attached to education was, however, daily undermined by the teachers' irregular attendance, caused by poor living conditions. A huge problem among teachers in Zambia is increased mortality due to AIDS.

Many of the teachers at the school had been educated during the previous government, which had a different philosophy of education (Carmody 2004; Reagan 2005) and under which textbooks were free and "the government looked after everything. Now it does not look after anything," as the headmaster explained. The teachers often touched upon differences between the former system and the current. "In the previous regime, grade 12 was enough to get a life, a good job and a future. . . . The teachers were respected and paid well in those days; now they are becoming poor, a new proletariat, if you like." Some of the teachers conducted extra classes, for which the students had to pay fees, as a way of securing an extra income. Students, parents, and management complained that these classes were often unnecessary and that teachers only conducted them in order to earn money, and would punish the students with bad marks in school if they did not attend the extra courses.

In towns, memory is fading away. You can forget. In schools you can pretend that everything is all right: Chatting, having fun, being together. It is still worthwhile, both for teachers and students. (Male history teacher, 44 years old)

Figure 7.2. After-school event in Lusaka, 2002. *Photo: Karen Tranberg Hansen*

> Education gives hope, but takes it back again. (Male literature teacher, 47 years old)

> Children become adults at a very early age in Africa. They have to look after themselves. But in schools we can make a difference. We can allow them to be children. That is the most important thing for me in my job. (Female English teacher, 38 years old)

Moving between resignation and critique, the teachers I talked to all expressed concern that education would be worth almost nothing in young people's search for employment and further schooling. For teachers, hope was crucial, and they emphasized (like the literature teacher quoted above) that it was "given and taken back" by education itself. Many of the teachers were resigned to the problems facing schooling in their country, but emphasized that the school was one of the few places where young people could forget the realities of life and enjoy friendship.

While students continually emphasized the importance of going to school, they nevertheless argued that it was a waste and misuse of time, energy, and resources. The making, breaking, and remaking of the dream of school are clear in the following example.

Adam, a student in grade 11, supported me a lot during my fieldwork. He introduced me to his mother, grandparents, uncles, and friends, and showed me around town. He was a friendly young man and very smart, which all his teachers commented upon. Adam did not have any textbooks, notebooks, or anything else to indicate that he was a student. The only signs were the t-shirt he wore with the inscription "Only the best is good enough for secondary school students" and a pen that he kept in his torn trousers. I knew he was good at, and very interested in, mathematics, but without the textbook he had no chance to earn good marks in the exams. I gave him some textbooks as a farewell gift and he was very happy, telling me that he wanted to "study in order to catch up" on what he had missed.

The next day, on my way to the airport, I realized that I had forgotten something at the school, so I stopped and rushed onto the campus to find the teacher. In the crowd of students whom I had worked with for almost a month, I saw a boy that I had not seen before. He had new clothes, a fancy Calvin Klein belt, and a black and shiny schoolbag. I recognized him when he turned around, though luckily he did not notice me. There he stood, Adam, with stylish clothes and a schoolbag, which he had always wanted so much—but it was empty. I realized he had sold the books and, with the proceeds, bought the things that would make him look like a real student in order to hide the painful reality that this experience was beyond his reach.

Vietnam: School—Toward New Values?

Gaining access to classrooms in Brazil and Zambia had been fairly straightforward, yet in Vietnam it proved to be a complicated issue. It was almost impossible for me get inside schools and classrooms, no doubt largely because of problems related to language, time management, and planning. The people that I had an opportunity to talk to had all been appointed by someone else. The students were appointed by the teachers, the teachers by the headmaster, the headmaster by the Youth Union and the People's Committee, and the various educational planners and researchers by government institutions. By following the hierarchy in this appointment system, I acquired insights into how the system wanted me to see its young people in schools.

Although it was difficult for me to meet young people inside the school system, I had no difficulty in reaching them outside the school, in the cafés or on the streets. The observations I draw on in this section stem mainly from interviews with headmasters, teachers, and students, all of which took place in the headmaster's office. In addition I conducted interviews with students in more informal settings away from school.

Vietnam reacted to the collapse of the Soviet Union in 1989 by rejecting pluralism, the multi-party system, and tolerance for a fledging group of political opposition parties. The country has maintained a communist structure even as the market has opened up, and the government still exercises tight control over social and political developments. Education reform has been a high priority in Vietnam since the 1990s, and has been seen as a vehicle for social and economic development and a way of supporting the current social reforms, termed *doi moi* (Cheng 2001; Duggan 2001; Vietnam, Ministry of Education and Training 2003; Thanh Minh Ngo, Lingard, and Mitchell 2006).

Compared to other countries in the region, Vietnam is known for its high educational standards. Net enrollment increased significantly in primary and secondary schools from 1993 to 2002, and the country has achieved remarkable increases in literacy and school enrollment and reductions in dropout rates (Pham Minh Hac 1998; World Bank 2003b, 62). Officially schooling is free, but the reality is somewhat different (Bélanger and Liu 2004). Costs for education do not differ by income so poor people, the middle class, and the rich pay the same—except for the richest, who pay slightly more. Tuition for extra classes is one major cost connected to schooling. These classes are meant to give students additional academic support in certain subjects, but students, parents, and teachers see them as a precondition for good marks and high exam scores. Students who want to make it through the educational system almost invariably take them.

Economic growth and development is one dimension of the educational reform; changes in pedagogical orientations are another (United Nations 2000). While the educational reform process includes a new teaching methodology that represents a break with the existing teaching culture, the reforms nevertheless attempt to balance the past, the present, and the future, which is emphasized in the following elaboration on the pedagogical implications of the education reform.

> Unlike previous centuries, in which the function of education was to transmit knowledge from one generation to the next, the knowledge at the disposition of the predecessors is probably now of less practical value than that acquired at the present time. This is an undeniable fact, even though we do not neglect the value of past knowledge. To prepare young people for the "learning society" of tomorrow, education needs to teach them how to learn, how to solve problems and how to unite new knowledge with that passed down from previous generations. (Phan Dinh Dieu 2003, 45–46)

The key categories introduced alongside the new teaching methodology—independence, the learning society, and problem-solving—represent an alternative to teaching traditions and practices inherited from Confucianism and from a centralized educational system with a science-based curriculum (Pham Minh Hac 1998; Rydstrøm 2001).

A large banner covered the entrance to a secondary school that I visited a couple of times: "Students of Mai Ninh: Be Obedient, Study Well, Behave, Be

Civilized, Be Polite. Topic of the School Year 2003–2004: Follow Uncle Ho's Teaching for DunBien Young Patriots, Study Well, Train Well, and Together Become Youth Union Members."

The Youth Union has as its most important goal the support of young people's moral and scientific education, in order to improve their place in the development of the nation and the Communist Party. Political ideology is personified in narratives about Ho Chi Minh and the political symbols that refer to his historical achievements. The Youth Union is a popular organization among school-going youth (Valentin, chapter 4 of this volume). Despite the *doi moi* reforms and the changes that Vietnamese society has undergone since their introduction, the Youth Union still has a firm grip on young people and continues to serve as an essential factor in socialization in Vietnamese society. Teachers and students explained to me that to be a member of the Youth Union, one must have good marks and recommendations from one's teachers and from the community. Young people who did not have a satisfactory record with the People's Committee could not be members of the Union, which meant that their chances of obtaining promotion in society were limited. A bad record might result from a young person's behaving improperly, not in accordance with the morals and ethics of communist ideology. In principle, only students with very good marks could be considered for membership. The marking system in Vietnam takes into account not only academic performance but also behavior, and to some extent excellence in behavior could compensate for academic weakness. Class monitors had to be exemplary students, good in all aspects of their lives, and members of the Youth Union, a fact that reflected the close relationships between schools and the party.

The headmaster of a secondary school was a woman who had been employed in the education sector for thirty-two years. According to her, the teaching methodology had changed twice—in 1996 and in 2002. "Vietnam is integrated into the world now and therefore we have to adjust to other Asian countries." The last changes were the most profound ones. Traditionally teaching and learning had been characterized by memorization, but *doi moi* had caused a shift toward a focus on children's activities. She emphasized that a major problem was the change in discipline in schools and classrooms. "Earlier students just had to respect and obey their teachers but now it is different; teachers have to respect their students and they should not punish so much." According to her, the students and the young teachers were very interested in the new methodology. For the older teachers it was difficult to "change their professional understanding and the role teachers have had for centuries. It is important also not to forget the past, and many young people seem to ignore history; that will be a big problem for society in the future." Like her, teachers and parents that I talked to were also concerned

Figure 7.3. Young people outside a school in Hanoi, 2004. *Photo: Karen Valentin*

with the need to balance the old and the new. The younger teachers were eager "to learn to be participatory," while the older generation worried that history would be forgotten in times dominated by a new media culture:

> All the media and the shows that young people watch these days are only for enjoying. They grow up in a society where the history will soon be forgotten. That is not right, that way, and I think the school should pay attention to that. (Male history teacher, 47 years old)

> The school has changed completely since I was a student. We have to make children active, to promote problem-solving and critical thinking. It is very exciting for me but also difficult. I have no experience, as people do in other countries, in how to be participatory, so we the teachers are also learning. To change, change it, is important, because now Vietnam is coming into the world. (Female music teacher, 27 years old)

The students I talked to were in grade 10. They worked hard for good grades, which they hoped would bring them closer to their ultimate dream: the university. Their parents were likewise struggling to manage the increased costs of education and expected that investment in education would come back one day in the form of support when they became too old to work.

It is important to study well and to become a good patriot. You cannot become a good patriot if you do not study well. Therefore strict discipline is important, and good morals. Then we can support our fatherland when we move into the world. That is also why *doi moi* is important. (Nam, male, 17 years old)

We can see on the Internet and in the media that young people are more independent in the world than we are. We depend on our parents: we have a traditional society. And that is also the case in the school. We cannot change that. Maybe those who set up their own business can. In my country, you cannot be independent. In my opinion, school should give you the basic knowledge to enter life, and then students should orient themselves. But this does not work in Vietnam. We depend on our families. I would like to study abroad and to learn about the world. Then I would like to come back and help my country develop. (Li, female, 17 years old)

Maybe you noticed when you watched us exercising in the break, but I do not move my body very much. I do not like it. I prefer to talk with my friends and not to do the exercise. But we have to; they require that we follow the instructions. But I do not like it, I just move my body a little. (Ning, female, 17 years old)

This young woman referred to physical exercises led by a teacher during the lunch break. In long rows, students moved their bodies, following the teacher's lead, and the young woman had seen me on my way to the headmaster's office. I had not seen her, but she used this opportunity to signal to me her critique of the school culture: she wanted to spend her time as she chose and to decide her own movements.

Both students and teachers appeared ambivalent toward the changes taking place at school. While the majority of the students expressed loyalty to the school and the system, there were some critical voices, such as the two quoted here. Following Phuong An Nguyen's analysis of the relationship between youth and the state in Vietnam (2005), school can be seen as an arena where changes in this relationship are exposed. The young people I met were struggling to find a place in the reform processes they experienced at school. While some took a position that was in accordance with the state rhetoric with which they were familiar, others, like the two girls above, critiqued the present and challenged the new policy, pointing at contradictions between the ideology of the past and the demands and prospects of the future.

Conclusion: Researching School in a Global Eduscape

By bringing together the dynamics of sphere-site-self across contexts, this chapter has exposed both the contextual and situational character of youth and school and an increased interconnectedness of youth and schools across the sites of this study. I argue that a global eduscape spreads across national and cultural boundaries as a consequence of neoliberal education reforms and actors' (i.e., students', teachers', and parents') interpretations of the changes that manifest in school and everyday life.

While the school in Brazil is struggling to find its identity as an institution between the authoritarian past and the democratic future, the school in Vietnam is strong and has a clear and unambiguous identity as a state institution intended to shape citizens prepared to support and develop the political order of the socialist state. The situation in Zambia is quite different. Zambian youth see an educational system in total dissolution as a result of severe cuts in the education sector as part of economic reforms and neoliberalism. There is no "system"; the school is mainly symbolic and a place where students wait. Living in a society where poverty is widespread and escalating and the tragedy of AIDS is overwhelming, students find in school a respite from their daily struggle to survive. In a sense such schools become orphanages; places to dwell and sites where orphans can deny their reality and dream of a different future. In contrast, the Vietnamese school constrains what students experience and learn. That is not the case in Brazil, where the school has turned into a more or less voluntary project and where young people are treated as adults—with no possibilities. Yet living in a modern and industrialized state in the Third World, attending a school that is itself part of a historic process of democratic reform and the fight for equality, the young people in this study are in principle able to choose what they will be, but are in reality constrained by mechanisms of social exclusion. I claim that diverse messages float from the enormous wealth, neoliberal reforms, democratic rhetoric, and poverty that these young people witness in their society, and that this diversity produces the confusion they articulate so clearly. Ultimately, these young Brazilian actors have little freedom to choose among the possibilities confronting them: gang membership, victim status, or a secure position in the wage economy. Students in Vietnam do not endure this type of confusion. While the communist state of Vietnam is in profound transition, the examples from this study demonstrate nevertheless that Vietnamese schooling is intended to foster conformity by balancing the old and the new.

"Youth" and "schooling" are, per se, modern phenomena and modernity is an irreversible, contingent process, which produces promises, hopes, and changed realities (Fuller 1991; Popkewitz 2000). Across the contexts of this study youth are connected through their engagement with the promises of schooling. School is an important imaginative space where young people participate in making sense out of possible worlds linked to the ideologies of democracy and individualization. Modernity, globalization, and imagination have a split character, since they reinforce control and suppression on the one hand and suggest new designs for collective lives on the other (Appadurai 1996). Subjected to structures that emerge with neoliberal reforms, poverty, and global inequality, the young people of this study are constrained by forces that are outside their reach and connected to the state and the market. As actors in schooling, they are negotiating and resisting power and designing visions and dreams that transcend the realities of their lifeworlds.

Across the world today, young people "carry the brunt of the spatial and temporal contradictions" of modernity and, regardless of their physical location, they are all attempting to "construct (and enact) futures that are not already appropriated by the state or the forces of consumer modernity" (Liechty 2003, 246). This chapter has illustrated how young people in three urban settings seek to acquire the imaginative tools to create their own futures. Although such tools may be shaped by historical, state, and transnational narratives about the individual, the citizen, and the state, they are never entirely controlled by them. Schooling, then, becomes one important site, and perhaps the most visible one, where local, state or national, and global forces intersect, and where increasingly reflective and interconnected actors respond to them.

Inspired by Appadurai's analysis of global flows and drawing on experiences from this project, I suggested at the outset that the term "eduscape" may capture these complex interactions. In effect, young people in Recife, Hanoi, and Lusaka are tied together in an eduscape that is a product of the interconnectedness of schools, educational reforms, and actors across the world.

Acknowledgments

I want to thank my colleagues and the research teams in Recife, Lusaka, and Hanoi for many good discussions over the years. A special thanks to Ms. Mónica Franch, Ms. Elisabeth Mwansa, and Ms. Nguyen Chung Thuy, who worked as my research assistants. Their support in all matters during my fieldwork has been invaluable.

I am indebted to my colleague Stephen Carney for our discussions on comparative education research and for his comments on earlier drafts of this chapter.

References

Alexander, Robin. 2000. *Culture and Pedagogy: International Comparisons in Primary Education.* Oxford: Blackwell.

Anderson-Levitt, Kathryn M., ed. 2003. *Local Meanings, Global Schooling: Anthropology and World Culture Theory.* New York: Palgrave Macmillan.

Appadurai, Arjun. 1996. *Modernity at Large: Cultural Dimensions of Globalization.* Minneapolis and London: University of Minnesota Press.

———. 2000. Grassroots Globalization and the Research Imagination. *Public Culture* 12(1):12–19.

Arnove, Robert F., and Carlos Alberto Torres, eds. 1999. *Comparative Education: The Dialectic of the Global and the Local.* Oxford: Rowman and Littlefield.

Bassey, Magnus O. 1999. *Western Education and Political Domination in Africa: A Study in Critical and Dialogical Pedagogy.* Westport, Conn., and London: Bergin and Garvey.

Bélanger, Danièle, and Jianye Liu. 2004. Social Policy Reforms and Daughters' Schooling in Vietnam. *International Journal of Educational Development* 24(1):23–38.

Birdsall, Nancy, and Richard Sabot. 1996. Opportunity Foregone: Education in Brazil. Washington, D.C.: Inter-American Development Bank.

Boesen, Inger W. 2000. Growing Up as an Educated Zambian: Primary Education and Cultural Identity in the Context of Change; A Study of Four Local Communities in the Copperbelt. Ph.D. dissertation, Royal Danish School of Educational Studies.

Bourdieu, Pierre, and Loïc J. D. Wacquant. 1992. *An Invitation to Reflexive Sociology.* Oxford: Polity.

Brazil. Pernambuco Ministry of Education. 2000. *National Educational Plan.*

Burbules, Nicolas C., and Carlos Alberto Torres, eds. 2000. *Globalization and Education: Critical Perspectives.* New York and London: Routledge.

Carmody, Brendan. 2004. *The Evolution of Education in Zambia.* Lusaka: Bookworld.

Cheng, Kai Meng. 2001. Changing Cultures and Schools in the People's Republic of China. In *Values, Culture and Education: World Yearbook of Education 2001,* ed. Jo Cairns, Denis Lawton, and Roy Gardner, 249–59. London: Kogan Page.

Crossley, Michael, and Keith Watson. 2003. *Comparative and International Research in Education.* London and New York: Routledge.

Duggan, Stephen. 2001. Educational Reform in Viet Nam: A Process of Change or Continuity? *Comparative Education* 37(2):193–212.

Ferguson, James. 2006. *Global Shadows: Africa in the Neoliberal Order.* Durham, N.C.: Duke University Press.

Fuller, Bruce. 1991. *Growing Up Modern: The Western State Builds Third-World Schools.* New York: Routledge.

Gandin, Luis Armando, and Michael W. Apple. 2002. Challenging Neo-liberalism, Building Democracy: Creating the Citizen School in Porto Alegre, Brazil. *Journal of Education Policy* 17(2):259–79.

Gingrich, André, and Richard G. Fox, eds. 2000. *Anthropology, by Comparison.* London: Routledge.

Gomes, Alberti Candido, and Celia de Freitas Capanema. 2001. Changing Cultures and Schools in Brazil. In *Values, Culture and Education: World Yearbook of Education 2001,* ed. Jo Cairns, Denis Lawton and Roy Gardner, 145–58. London: Kogan Page.

Gupta, Akhil, and James Ferguson, eds. 1997. *Anthropological Locations: Boundaries and Grounds of a Field Science.* Berkeley: University of California Press.

Honwana, Alcinda, and Filip De Boeck, eds. 2005. *Makers and Breakers: Children and Youth in Postcolonial Africa.* Oxford: James Currey.

Inda, Jonathan Xavier, and Renato Rosaldo, eds. 2002. *The Anthropology of Globalization: A Reader.* Oxford: Blackwell.

Kelly, M. J. 1999. *Planning for Education in the Era of HIV/AIDS.* Paris: UNESCO.

Kempner, Ken, and Ana Loureiro Jurema. 2002. The Global Politics of Education: Brazil and the World Bank. *Higher Education* 43:331–54.

Levinson, Bradley A. U., with Kathryn M. Borman et al. 2000. *Schooling the Symbolic Animal: Social and Cultural Dimensions of Education.* Lanham, Md.: Rowman and Littlefield.

Levinson, Bradley A., Douglas E. Foley, and Dorothy C. Holland. 1996. *The Cultural Production of the Educated Person: Critical Ethnographies of Schooling and Local Practice.* Albany: State University of New York Press.

Liechty, Mark. 2003. *Suitably Modern: Making Middle-Class Culture in a New Consumer Society.* Princeton, N.J.: Princeton University Press.

Lûdke, Menga, and Antônio Flávio Barbosa Moreira. 1999. Recent Proposals to Reform Teacher Education in Brazil. *Teaching and Teacher Education* 15(2):169–78.

Madsen, Ulla Ambrosius. 2006. Imagining Selves: School Narratives from Girls in Eritrea, Nepal and Denmark; Ethnographic Comparisons of Globalization and Schooling. *Young* 14(3):219–32.

Maira, Sunaina, and Elisabeth Soep, eds. 2005. *Youthscapes: The Popular, the National, the Global.* Philadelphia: University of Pennsylvania Press.

Marcus, George. 1998. *Ethnography through Thick and Thin.* Princeton, N.J.: Princeton University Press.

Marteleto, Leticia, and Clarissa Rodrigues. 2002. School Quality: Is Quality Only Enough to Explain Educational Inequalities in Brazil? Conference paper.

Musonda, Lawrence W. 1999. Teacher Education Reform in Zambia . . . Is It a Case of a Square Peg in a Round Hole? *Teaching and Teacher Education* 15(2):157–68.

Nilan, Pam, and Carles Feixa, eds. 2006. *Global Youth? Hybrid Identities, Plural Worlds.* London and New York: Routledge.

Osei-Hwedie, Kwaku, and Muna Ndulo. 1989. *Studies in Youth and Development.* London: Commonwealth Secretariat.

Pham Minh Hac. 1998. *Vietnam's Education: The Current Position and Future Prospects.* Hanoi: GIOI Publishers.

Phan Dinh Dieu. 2003. Renovation and Education. In Science, Education and Culture: Extending the Promise of Doi Moi, ed. Tran Doàn Lãm, special issue of *Vietnamese Studies* 148(2):41–47.

Phuong An Nguyen. 2005. Youth and the State in Contemporary Socialist Vietnam. Working Paper no 16. Centre for East and South East Asian Studies, Lund University.

Popkewitz, Thomas S. 2000. Reform as the Social Administration of the Child. In *Globalization and Education: Critical Perspectives,* ed. Nicholas Burbules and Carlos Alberto Torres, 157–87. New York and London: Routledge.

Reagan, Timothy. 2005. *Non-Western Educational Traditions: Indigenous Approaches to Educational Thought and Practice.* Mahwah, N.J., and London: Lawrence Erlbaum Associates.

Rydstrøm, Helle. 2001. "Like a White Piece of Paper": Embodiment and the Moral Upbringing of Vietnamese Children. *Ethnos* 66(3):394–413.

Serpell, Robert. 1993. *The Significance of Schooling: Life Journeys in an African Society.* Cambridge: Cambridge University Press.

Sherif, Robin E. 2001. *Dreaming Equality: Color, Race and Racism in Urban Brazil.* New Brunswick, N.J.: Rutgers University Press.

Snelson, P. D. 1974. *Educational Development in Northern Rhodesia, 1883–1945.* Lusaka: National Education Co. of Zambia.

Stambach, Amy. 2000. *Lessons from Mount Kilimanjaro: Schooling, Community and Gender in East Africa.* New York: Routledge.

Stronach, Ian. 2006. Enlightenment and the "Heart of Darkness": (Neo) Imperialism in the Congo and Elsewhere. *International Journal of Qualitative Studies in Education* 19(6):757–68.

Tabulawa, Richard. 2003. International Aid Agencies, Learner-Centered Pedagogy and Political Democratization: A Critique. *Comparative Education* 39(1):7–26.

Thanh Minh Ngo, Bob Lingard, and Jane Mitchell. 2006. The Policy Cycle and Vernacular Globalization: A Case Study of the Creation of Vietnam National University—Hochiminh City. *Comparative Education* 42(2):225–42.

Tomlinson, John. 1999. *Globalization and Culture.* Cambridge: Polity.

United Nations. Economic and Social Commission for Asia and the Pacific. 2000. *Youth in Vietnam: A Review of the Youth Situation and National Policies and Programmes.* New York: United Nations.

Vietnam. Ministry of Education and Training. 2003. *National Education for All: Action Plan 2003–2015.*

Welch, Antony. 1999. The Triumph of Technocracy or the Collapse of Certainty: Modernity, Postmodernity and Postcolonialism in Comparative Education. In *Comparative Education: The Dialectic of the Global and the Local,* ed. Robert Arnove and Carlos Alberto Torres, 25–50. Oxford: Rowman and Littlefield.

World Bank. 2003a. Next Steps for Education in Four Selected States in Brazil. Report no. 24343-BR. Washington, D.C.: World Bank.

———. 2003b. *Vietnam Development Report 2004: Poverty.* Hanoi: World Bank.

Zambia. Ministry of Education. 2001. *HIV/AIDS Education Strategic Plan, 2001–2005.* Lusaka: Ministry of Education.

8

The Work of the Imagination:
Young People's Media Appropriation

Norbert Wildermuth

This chapter explores some of the diverse practices of media appropriation through which young people in Recife, Hanoi, and Lusaka make sense of the world around them and their place within it. This conceptualization of the media as fundamental tools through which young people understand themselves and their environment goes hand in hand with the attempt to explore and analyze their use of the media within the context of the other leisure activities they engage in. As this is too formidable a task to complete in a single research project, I will focus on the question of the skills and knowledge that young people acquire from the media. I understand skills and knowledge primarily in terms of the lifestyle and identity projects that the media permit young people and inspire them to experiment with and to approach playfully. Young people make use of images of lives both different from and similar to their own, which the media represent in both realistic and fictional modes. In contemporary modern societies, this "work of the imagination" (Appadurai 1996) constitutes a fundamental resource in their struggle to make sense of their lives, to define themselves in relation to others, and to inform the choices and decisions demanded by their present lives and their plans for the near and distant future.

With Kirsten Drotner (1996, 20), I approach the media as resources that enable experience-based forms of knowledge, which allow young people to explore the drafts and projects of identity in which they are engaged. That is, the practices of media consumption and reception by which young people engage the media are understood as a form of cultural and aesthetic practice through which they seek to comprehend, define, and create themselves (Drotner 1991, 58). As Steven Miles argues, young people use global and local media in their ongoing attempts to make sense of their lives and "construct opinions about what lifestyles might be *deemed* to be appropriate" (Miles 2000, 69).

174

In the context of three cities as different as Recife, Hanoi, and Lusaka, the global-local dynamics that characterize mediated texts and their consumption make the empirical study of young people's situated media appropriations both promising and challenging. Behaviorist studies tell us what media specific groups of young people typically consume, and where and when they consume them. However, we learn little about what these media mean to them, nor about the structural and cultural processes through which they are constituted as an audience (Ang 1989, 96). To put the point more concretely, although studying the TV viewing patterns of teenage lower-class girls in Recife will provide us with a basis for further enquiries and understanding, in itself this is not sufficient for an analysis of their practices of media consumption, understood as a site of cultural struggle in which a variety of forms of power are exercised and resisted. While the active production and attribution of meaning is a fundamental and unquestionable quality of young people's appropriation of media, the textual and social determinations of media use, which structure the conditions under which this interpretative agency has to be realized, deserve equal attention. Thus the relationship between young people and media cultures, which increasingly pervade (and are invited into) their everyday lives, is understood as mutually exploitative. Young people appropriate, transform, and recontextualize the meanings of media texts, though always within the boundaries set by other people's interests, that is, by society at large. In other words, a holistic understanding of the communicative relations created by the dialectic processes of media production and reception demands a conceptualization in terms of both their agentive and structural dimensions (Holland et al. 1998, 5; Livingstone 1998, 248).

The theory of media-enabled social imagination, on which this study is based, pays attention to ordinary youths' unspectacular, everyday practices of media appropriation. Avoiding a narrow conceptualization of young people's interpretative agency as either subordination or resistance, it is sensitive to those forms of active viewing and consumption which are located in between these poles. Understood as a social practice which is neither purely emancipating nor entirely disciplining, but a space of contestation, the "work of the imagination," as conceptualized by Arjun Appadurai (1996), points to the cultural competences that are crucial for how and to what extent young people are able to use the media as a resource for knowledge generation, learning, and identity work.

Methodological and Epistemological Issues

Fieldwork in the three cities was conducted between February 2003 and October 2004. Except in Recife, where I did additional research in December 2005, only a single stay of three to four weeks in each location was possible. Given the specific focus of my research on the media-enabled work of the social imagination, I did not think a quantitative, survey-based research design would be useful. And given the limited duration of field research, a media-ethnographic approach, based on profound familiarization with and participant observation of a few selected individuals, was also out of the question. I therefore decided on a more conventional audience-studies approach, organized around a number of qualitative, open-ended interviews, informal conversations, and observations.

I conducted all field research in close cooperation with local assistants, who played a crucial role, not only by interpreting, but also by establishing contacts, arranging interviews, and providing me with a basic understanding of the urban scene and the sociostructural and cultural realities that I had come to investigate. In many ways, they were my primary informants, helping me to develop a more differentiated perspective on both young people's practices of media use and appropriation and the conditions under which these situated practices unfold.

Although I tried to include both lower- and middle-class youth, the prime criterion of selection was not the young people's residential area, but rather some of the media and non-media leisure activities they engaged in. In practical terms, this means that I have approached, observed, and interviewed young people not only at home, but also (even primarily) in places away from the home that offer them a space for experimentation with social identities and a stage for the enactment of lifestyles and media-facilitated imaginations. In my open-ended interviews I sought, as a starting point, to identify some of the dreams, ambitions, and future plans of the individuals I talked to through questions centered on their general conditions of living and motivations for engaging in the cultural activities in which we met and observed them.

Youth and Media in Recife

When visiting Recife, one's immediate impression is that the media are a pervasive feature of everyday life. A considerable variety of newspapers and magazines are on sale at newsstands, especially in downtown Recife and the better-off neighborhoods. The occasional Internet café and cinema contribute to this picture of a media-saturated urban environment. The latest in home entertainment products are on display in the air-conditioned shopping malls, the preferred sites for strolling, purchasing, and public entertainment for those who can afford them. In contrast, less fashionable retailers, for example in the downtown shopping area of Boa Vista, offer a choice of ordinary TV, video, and audio equipment, both new and secondhand. Street vendors, who sell music and movies of Brazilian and Western origin, are another common sight, illustrating the desire of young and old to consume a broad variety of media products. While domestic and foreign movies can be bought or rented from established video chains, the majority of video rental shops are located in the poorer neighborhoods. Likewise, the small, unpretentious video- and computer-game parlors found in Recife's *barrios* and *favelas* constitute low-budget counterparts to the upmarket city game centers frequented by middle- and upper-class youth.

A visit to private homes reinforces this impression of the ubiquity of the media in Recife. All the homes I visited in 2003 and 2005 had at least one television set. Access to television is comparable to that in the developed world, though households with a single TV still dominate the scene.[1] In the poorer parts of Recife, homes consisting of one or two small rooms are commonplace. Though poor, these homes usually have a TV, if only a small black-and-white one. These are usually visible from the central bed, which doubles as a daytime place to sit. The living room in slightly better off households is often organized around consumer electronics, which both satisfy practical demands and serve as objects of pride, allowing the family's wealth to be displayed. The widespread decoration of these assets with plastic flowers and family pictures underlines the affection with which they are invested.

While the mix of media available to young people in Recife and their patterns of media use cannot be generalized, most of the young people I spoke to acknowledged watching TV regularly. Listening to music is another essential part of young people's everyday practices of media use. Listening to music-centered radio broadcasts typically complements other activities, like doing homework, chatting with friends, working at a job, or doing housework.

The consumption of radio involves brief spans of heightened attention, or listening, and extended periods of less focused attention, or hearing. Occasionally, young people's time spent with television is structured in a comparable way, depending on the genre of program. While a substantial number of the young people we interviewed claimed to listen to music-centered radio formats frequently, talk radio was rather low on their agenda.[2] This suggests that youth in Recife tend to prefer television over radio when they spend leisure time on forms of exclusive and attentive media consumption, while music and music-centered radio seem to be their prime choice to accompany other activities. Luciana (15 years old), a single mother from the low-income residential area of Peixinhos, explained, "When I'm not listening to radio I watch TV. When I'm not watching I turn on the radio. It all depends on what I am doing."

Other forms of media communication, such as print media, computer media, and movies (in cinemas, on DVD, and on videotape), may compete with television and radio. However, most young people from low-income backgrounds have limited access to these commercially distributed media. While the Brazilian middle and upper classes are set apart by their desire for oversized flat-screen TVs, high-end stereos, portable computers, multi-function cellular phones, Playstations, MP3 players, and other fashionable hardware devices, the less privileged majority prioritize ordinary television sets and audio equipment (i.e., transistor radios, boom-boxes, and stereo systems). Poor youths' practices of media consumption are thus predetermined to a greater extent than those of their counterparts in the developed world. Patterns of access and ownership markedly define the range of possible media uses and appropriations in material terms.

Popular Television

While young people's interpretative agency deserves attention, the institutions which structure the reception of symbolic forms, and the textual characteristics of the media content these offer for consumption, are no less important. TV readings are sought and imaginations realized among the totality of televised texts which individuals have access to. They depend on the raw material the medium provides. While some TV genres and formats strongly invite identification and the work of the imagination, other popular programs aim primarily at other forms of viewer engagement, pleasures, and gratifications. Among the many national and regional TV programs young people watched in Recife, the following genres were mentioned repeatedly:

1. Talent and game shows
2. Popular entertainment and talk shows
3. Reality shows
4. Telenovelas and serial fiction
5. Feature films, both Brazilian and foreign
6. Sitcoms and humor programs
7. Sports programs
8. News and current affairs
9. Documentaries and cultural programs, mainly shown on the non-commercial channel TV Cultura
10. Music and celebrity shows
11. Cartoons
12. Crime shows

Young people often despised the sensationalist shows that report incidents of crime and violence in Recife (regional channels) and Brazil (national channels) using dramatic pictures. Not a single interviewee admitted enjoying them, though everybody seemed to know them, and several young people said they watched them on occasion, because other household members did. Young people were most clearly split in their evaluation of Denny Oliveira's and Pedro Paulo's talent shows. While not a few said they were ardent fans of these programs, others distanced themselves vehemently from what they considered commercial, vulgar, and sexist formats based on the exploitation of young people's dreams of stardom and fame.

Apart from some cartoons, music clips, and movies, the bulk of available TV programming is of Brazilian origin. However, images of a global, media-driven youth and leisure culture inspire and shape Brazilian television. That is, Western formats and narrative themes are "translated" in the productions shown on national and regional channels. The global thus becomes imagined, by both producers and consumers, primarily as a "local," particularized representation. This localization enables broadcasters to address a mass audience of (young) viewers with comprehensible tales of other lives, located in a recognizable Brazilian context. The audience confronts images of youth and contemporary lifestyles which signify late-modern, globalized identities, mainly as a phenomenon of life in the urban centers of the south. Rio de Janeiro and São Paulo are the imagined focus of lives that are different from those lived in the "traditional," less developed northeast. The discursive practice of Brazilian television reproduces this stereotyped dichotomy between the white, prosperous, modern, and rational south and the black, impoverished, archaic, and colorful northeast. Youth in Recife therefore project their desire to pursue a (future) life under different conditions above all onto metropolitan centers in Brazil.

In nourishing the imagination of a more demanding but also promising life, television plays a central role in providing the young with more or less realistic conceptions of life as it is lived elsewhere. Many TV programs are centered on the well-known narratives of success that are prevalent in Brazilian popular culture generally, that is, tales about becoming a football star or a famous actor or singer, of marrying into wealth, winning the lottery, and so on. This dream of radically improving one's life through talent and luck has its imaginative counterpoint in narratives of crime and personal disaster. Tales of success and failure are hence central to young people's "work of the imagination."

Practices of TV Viewing

Young people's TV viewing practices can be differentiated into the valued activity of watching a favorite program and the "filling in" of otherwise unstructured time (Livingstone 2002, 100). In our interviews, we encountered young people who watched, by their own estimate, four to six hours daily. Without exception, these "heavy" TV consumers were from poor backgrounds. One of them was Gilvan (23 years old), who was neither employed nor in school when we met him at the offices of Torcida Jovem, the youth fan club of Recife's football team, Sporto. Living with his sister, grandfather, and wife in Amora Branco, he spent most of his weekdays together with other Sporto fans, chatting and drinking at the downtown office of Torcida Jovem. There he watched not only most daytime football shows, but also many other TV programs. Coming home late at night, he usually watched *Jô Soares*, one of his favorite shows, before going to bed. Relations with his wife were not the best, Gilvan explained. While he did the odd job and earned "some money" selling Sporto merchandise at the Torcida office, he had no concrete plans for the future. In his own words: "I'm wondering what I'm going to do. I don't know yet. I haven't decided. [. . .] I'm thinking a little bit more . . . also my parents give me a sum of money monthly."

In addition to watching the programs which reinforced his almost obsessive identification as a football fan, Gilvan also watched TV to kill time. The closest he came to articulating a constructive imagination was when he told us about *O Rap do Pequeno Príncipe,* his favorite film: "That history about Helinho and Garnizé, their lives developed completely differently . . . they followed different destinies. That proves that appearances are deceptive. Garnizé had to struggle to become the person he is today, become successful. And Helinho had all the prerequisites, but he did the opposite, he chose to become a criminal. . . . A guy who grows up in a *favela,* he may not became an outlaw. Maybe his education is not sufficient, but he may succeed. It all depends on his personality."

Luciana was another "heavy" viewer. Living in her mother's house, she attended school in the evenings. Daytimes she claimed to spend mainly at home, taking care of her baby son and watching TV: "My mother objects because I sit in front of the TV for many hours. Hypnotized! I live in front of the TV—my mother, my sister, my grandfather, they all object." Apparently, the seven or eight terrestrial TV channels that can be received in Recife allow enough choice and diversity to hold the attention of young people like Luciana and Gilvan, whose circumstances of life entail plenty of unstructured time.

Given the narrow, highly formatted, and repetitive character of the bulk of the programs, it is tempting to lament this "waste of time" and to blame it either on the viewers themselves, on the social context of their lives, or on the seductiveness of the TV programs they seemingly fall prey to. Alternatively, we can acknowledge the fact that their leisure alternatives are limited and that television is the cultural activity most easily engaged in, given their circumstances of life. Young people like Luciana and Gilvan seek pleasures and other emotional gratifications from a diet of TV, which is characterized by the commercial imperatives of its broad audience appeal. However, in doing so, they try to obtain something "meaningful" in return for the time and energy they invest. That is, the experience of pleasure and the making of meaning do not exclude each other, but go hand in hand in the process of media-enabled imagination.

Situated Imaginations

Part of the attraction of the global media for local audiences is that their consumption often provides meanings that enable not only imagined identifications, but also "the accentuation of symbolic distancing from the spatial-temporal contexts

Figure 8.1. Participants in and teacher of a social awareness course at Nascedouro, an autonomous youth center in Peixinhos. Recife, 2003. *Photo: Norbert Wildermuth*

of everyday life" (Thompson 1995, 175). No doubt some youth are more skilled than others in accentuating this distancing. They confront the preferential mean-ings of the programs they watch with a more profound understanding of the constructed nature of television, and evaluate them against a more questioning, demanding expectation regarding the "truthfulness" of the mediated imaginations proposed to them. Watching a lot of television does not necessarily indicate less skill in active viewing. Like the attempt to label the viewing habits of the young as in bad or good taste, any evaluation of their ability to interpret the media that is based on the number of hours they watch prioritizes cultural judgments over attempts at comprehension.

Exploring the promises and offers of television, the "critical" agency of the young is expressed in the more or less informed, continuous choice they make: an unremitting series of decisions reflective of the structured space of opportu-nities and constraints that they occupy. When Luciana was asked to name her favorite character or TV personality, her reply hinted at possible identifications that the programs she used to watch had provided her with: "That one on *Espe-rança* [Hope]; she is called Maria. She loves a man who was so nice and then he had to go to Brazil [the story had begun in Italy] to earn money and afterward she was to join him. But he fell in love with another girl. And Maria traveled to conquer his heart again. [. . .] And on this ongoing soap opera . . . Laissa, she was 14 years old when she had a baby. Her mother took her daughter to educate her, because Laissa was too young to do it by herself . . . and the father didn't know he had a daughter."

Luciana was the youngest and probably least media-critical person we interviewed in Recife. Her limited capacity to reflect on her own media practices and to articulate a differentiated characterization of the programs of her choice revealed the character of a cheerful teenager, psychologically still more of a child than a woman, though already a mother herself. Our attempt to make Luciana elaborate on the characters she apparently identified with demonstrates the eclectic nature of her media-facilitated imagination. While Luciana clearly enjoyed the preferred subject position constructed by her favorite soap operas, she expressed some ambiguous distance from the responsibilities narratively constructed by these roles. However, as became obvious from her lack of understanding when questioned, Luciana's "resistance" was less an act of intentional opposition than a consequence of her lack of maturity: "*Q: Do you think is it possible to learn something watching soap operas?* Oh yes! There was a soap opera in which a girl who was very poor helped her mother to earn money. She wanted to be somebody in life, to win. She helped all her family. *Q: And do you follow her example?* What do you mean? *Q: Do you help your mother?* Ah! I say all the time, 'if I had money I would help you, mom; if I was rich I would help you to repair the house, buy a car.' And then she smiles."

The examples of Luciana and Gilvan demonstrate that although the capacity of young people to appropriate the content of media selectively is important, that does not in itself make them "critical with respect to, and literate in the ways of, mass mediation and media representations" (Silverstone 2004, 440). We frequently encountered a skeptical attitude toward television and its dominant representations. This attitude underlines the contested nature of young people's appropriation of television. Though consumed and embraced by many, the mediated tales of winners and losers, of admirable and problematic (young) people, certainly did not go unchallenged. In the words of Josemar (27 years of age), the leader of Torcida Jovem, "I think TV manipulates stereotypes. For example, TV shows a young person to be healthy and in good shape, when this guy is from A [the highest] class—with a good financial situation, healthy, who goes surfing at the weekend, you know? When TV shows a guy from the suburbs, he is usually dependent on drugs, dealing in narcotics, or fighting at a football game. TV associates only negative things with poor people—it doesn't show that the suburbs also have honest people, who are in good shape, working."

Comments like Josemar's on the poor quality of television were common and emphasized the ambiguous character of young people's experiences with what Brazilian TV offered. Discontented with the mass of programming, but rather

Figure 8.2. Members of Torcida Jovem, the youth fan club of Sporto. Recife, 2003.
Photo: Norbert Wildermuth

unspecific in their criticisms, several young people expressed their negative assessment of television (and the media in general) in terms of a broad dissatisfaction with the highly stratified, discriminating character of the social reality of
their everyday lives. However, the despised medium, which they described in the
terms of a populist discourse about "them [i.e., the institutions of the state, the
polity, private companies, the elites in general] not giving us what we deserve,"
was seldom completely rejected. Being critical and at times almost cynical about
the programming shown on television does not necessarily rule out continually
attempting to spend time on programs "worth watching" and to maximize the
pleasures and informational uses opened up by active engagement with them.

   Which cultural competence can significantly influence the outcome of this
attempt? What individual abilities guide young people's mediated imagination in
the direction of either an escapist or an empowering experience? Apart from the
intention and quality of the TV programs available to them, what are the other
factors that determine the communicative relation between particular media texts
on the one hand, and the young people who select and consume them on the
other? Put more concretely, does the Recife part of my study suggest structural
conditions and individual competences that further the "educational potential"

of popular, mass-distributed media, and what kind of knowledge generation and learning processes may be enabled?

My answers to these questions are based on circumstantial, rather than hard, evidence.[3] If I nonetheless proceed here with my attempt to point out some decisive conditions and competences, I am doing so because I consider it crucial to attempt to address the questions outlined if we are to contribute to a more differentiated understanding of the enabling or disabling character of young people's practices of media consumption.

In Recife, a substantial part of the flow of accessible terrestrial television is directed toward a young audience, though few programs address youth exclusively. The observed pervasive popularity of television goes hand in hand with a supply of programs that are highly commercialized and entertainment-oriented, rather than educational and public service–oriented. Through their interpretative engagement with television, young people probe and assess the social roles represented by television with regard to both their quality as narrative constructs and their usefulness as scripts for imagined identities. As became evident in our interviews, the ambition and ability to work through the ambiguous relationship between wishful thinking and pragmatic imaginations differed markedly from person to person. Engaged in local contexts and responsive to larger transnational processes, some of the young people we talked to demonstrated a highly selective, critical, and constructive approach. Neither entirely embracing nor altogether rejecting the offers of Brazilian TV, they seemed to engage the media in general, and television specifically, discriminatingly, with an analytical rather than referential understanding of the text.[4]

Though most of these youth are from Recife's middle and upper classes, some lower-class youth also articulated a critical-analytical perspective on the media and put forward a highly self-reflective viewpoint on their own practices of media consumption. What set them apart from their less articulate and media-skeptical peers was their active involvement in organizations for collective social and cultural action (NGOs, subcultural movements, and youth initiatives). As some of the interviews presented in Wildermuth and Dalsgaard 2006 indicate, the politicized social awareness they developed through these forms of engagement apparently also shaped their practices of media consumption.

Our theoretical understanding and empirical investigation of young people's active engagement with the media suggest that their access to other discourses and interpretative repertoires plays a crucial role. In other words, "literacy," which is acquired, trained, and developed mainly in the institutional systems of formal education but also in other contexts, is a key cultural competence for engaging with the media. The "restricted" reflective and critical character of Luciana's and Gilvan's viewing practices is therefore due to more than age, maturity, or personality alone: it indicates that young people need a broad spectrum of individually accessible reading positions in order to use the media to generate knowledge and empower themselves. While the institutionalized and systematic forms of media education encountered in Recife are promising (Wildermuth and Dalsgaard 2006), they are also very rare. Young people's use of the (available) media as a resource for knowledge generation, learning, and identity work is structurally hampered by this lack of media education.

Youth and Media in Hanoi

In contrast to Recife, with its relatively stable media landscape, Vietnam's capital city is characterized by rapid and profound transformations. Since the start of the new millennium, the range of broadcasting channels available in Hanoi has increased rapidly. While state-controlled Vietnamese Television (VTV) still dominated the scene, by spring 2004 an estimated 10–15 percent of all households either had cable or were able to receive direct-to-home services via satellite.[5] Such households now receive some dozen foreign and transnational satellite channels: the well-known Anglo-American "package" of TV channels targeting South, Southeast, and Far East Asia, with the occasional German and French service as well. In addition, Chinese CCTV and VTV4 (the satellite service of the Vietnamese state broadcaster) are also available through cable and satellite.

While satellite TV, which has been accessible since 2000, was initially more popular than cable TV, the number of subscribers to the latter is rising fast.[6] The government, which maintains tight control over cable service, has so far excluded CNN and the BBC World Service from the cable packages offered, but satellite television is unrestricted. A major factor limiting the number of households with cable or satellite TV is inadequate knowledge of European languages. At the same time, Vietnam is not yet a strong enough consumer market for local "editions" of transnational programming, funded by advertising or subscriptions, to be viable. Apart from HBO, which is subtitled in Vietnamese, all the transnational services were transmitted in foreign languages. VTV, which transmits three terrestrial channels in Hanoi, has a mixture of locally produced programs and imported ones dubbed into Vietnamese.[7] Thus the state broadcaster has selectively incorporated international program formats and "best practices," while strongly reembedding them within the local and national contexts (Becker and Salamanca 2003).

Radio in Hanoi comprises the broadcasts of state-controlled stations and entertainment-oriented private stations like FM 99 and FM 100. As the private stations are not supposed to provide journalistic content or to debate political issues, they focus on a wide spectrum of music, traditional, modern Vietnamese, and foreign. Young people are the prime audience for these commercial services.

The newspaper and magazine sector is characterized by a less direct but, in terms of its impact, comparable degree of "state control" (Hoang-Giang Dang 2002). All publications aspiring to political journalism are subject to it. In addition, a number of commercial, entertainment-oriented magazines published in Vietnamese target a primarily young and urban market segment. A number of weekly and monthly publications in English have recently appeared, including *Outlook, New Fashion,* and *Time Out.*

This brief outline of the Hanoi media landscape in 2004 reveals an evolving, but far from fully realized, multi-channel radio and television environment. Compared with that in other Asian countries, such as India, Thailand, the Philippines, and South Korea, the deregulation of broadcasting in Vietnam has just begun and so far is confining itself primarily to entertainment.

Appropriating Journalistic Accounts of the World

In April 2004, I interviewed twelve students at the German Goethe Institute in Hanoi who were participating in the institute's intensive language program and planning to study in Germany. A majority of them claimed to watch the VTV news, daily or occasionally. As might be expected given their plans to study and live for several years in Germany, these young people, aged between 19 and 28, expressed a great interest in images and accounts of life abroad. Without exception, they felt that VTV's in-house news and current affairs did an insufficient job of providing them with a useful picture of everyday life and of social, political, or cultural events unfolding outside Vietnam, for example, in Europe.

In the words of Ming (26 years old), "Watching the BBC and CNN allows one to receive information directly from abroad. Not so with VTV, which seldom has its own correspondents on location." Asked to rate the journalistic credibility of the BBC on a range from zero to ten (with ten as the maximum), he answered "eight to nine." To VTV, in comparison, he gave a mediocre five. Not surprisingly, Ming—who has already spent a year in Germany and gone on short trips to India, China, and Thailand—regretted the fact that he was not able to receive the BBC World Service, CNN, or German DW TV in his current home.

Until a few years ago, Vietnam was remarkably closed off, isolated from global cultural and economic flows. Ming's generation has not grown up being exposed to the mediated representations of Western (popular) culture on a scale experienced by middle-class youth in other, non-socialist countries in Asia, nor did his generation have much of an opportunity to meet or to observe foreigners in Hanoi before the mid-1990s.[8] Finally, opportunities to travel abroad have been, and still are, rare for the young in Hanoi.

Though this isolation has been challenged by Vietnam's ongoing economic liberalization (*doi moi*) and the accompanying commercialization and interna-tionalization of its cultural sector (Hoang-Giang Dang 2002), many of the young people we talked to seemed to have only limited knowledge about and experience with people, lifeworlds, and cultures originating from outside Vietnam. Yet most of the students I interviewed seemed highly motivated to learn about the world outside Vietnam. Their example suggests that young middle-class Vietnamese are seeking to enhance their knowledge of a global modernity by actively consum-ing mass media images and textual representations from and about abroad. That is, they are seeking to understand their own existence, identities, and actions in the context of a global frame of reference, to paraphrase John Tomlinson (1999, 11).

As in Recife, access plays a decisive role in both their (and their families') economic ability to consume the vehicles of this mediated experience of global modernity, and the politically regulated and market-determined availability of these "windows onto the world." But watching television, whether of local, na-tional, or foreign origin, is just one of many ways through which youth seek to make meaningful accounts of their social existence. Journalistic, factual accounts, such as those offered by TV news, are neither the only nor the most privileged source of the kind of heightened individual reflectivity signified by the imagina-tion of meaningful other lives. In Hanoi, other media and other forms of medi-ated cultural consumption play an important role in the everyday practices of existentially significant meaning construction in which the young are engaged.

The Lure of the New Media

The young people we met and talked to in Hanoi were more involved in appro-priating new, computer-based media in their daily lives than our interviewees in Recife or Lusaka.[9] Computer media not only reach a broad segment of young people in Hanoi, but they do so in a very public and very visible way, as is suggested by the ratio of PC owners to Internet users.[10] More importantly, young people appear to be coming to view computer-based media as more promising and more useful than broadcast media. One likely reason is the widespread dissatisfaction with radio and (terrestrial) television that we encountered in Hanoi. In contrast to the young people we spoke to in Recife, in Hanoi many of our interviewees claimed to prefer other forms of media communication.

All the students we interviewed at the Goethe Institute said that they had very busy lives and little leisure time. As most of them were taking the institute's Ger-man language course, which met three times a week, in addition to their studies at university, this sounded credible. They also claimed to spend between half an hour and three hours a day using a computer to chat, e-mail, surf the Internet, play games, and so on. By their own estimate, that was more time than they spent on all other media together. This suggests that their shortage of unstructured time was not the only reason they considered computer-based media the most promising form of media appropriation.

What are the expectations that motivate this preference? What uses and gratifications can computer-based media provide to young Vietnamese, in perceived contrast to the press and broadcast media? My interviews suggest that computer-based media are used by young people in Hanoi to undermine, circumvent, and challenge forms of social control and demarcations of legitimate knowledge. As I seek to show, using the examples below, they do not necessarily do this in direct confrontation with the norms and values of Vietnamese society as defined by their parents' generation. Rather, their media-centered contestation of the dominant value system unfolds as a pragmatic and creative way to explore the boundaries of what is acceptable and possible under the present and future structural conditions of their lives as adults in the making.

The Private Spaces of Computer-Mediated Communication

Cha (22 years old) is a student of foreign languages, who lives with her parents in a middle-class neighborhood. She has her own room with a television and a personal computer. Since summer 2003 she has had access to the Internet at home. By her own estimate, Cha uses the Internet and e-mail two to three hours a day on average. As she has plans to study in Frankfurt, she recently searched the Internet to learn more about Western Europe, and she regularly reads German and French newspapers online.

Huang (22 years old), also a student of foreign languages, was Cha's classmate at the Goethe Institute. Like Cha, she admitted to spending a considerable part of her leisure time surfing the Net, searching for music and reading Web editions of German newspapers and magazines at home. She told us that she regularly visits an Internet café, especially if she wants to chat or to surf the Internet "in private" (in public, but without her family members around). In this way, Huang delineates two different spaces of mediated communication and consumption, both of which allow knowledge appropriation, entertainment, emotional engagement, and social interaction, yet each with a different, specific communicative purpose and potential.

No less interesting is another dimension of the situated use of computer-based media, which Huang pointed out when she told us that she often chats online for hours in her room at night. Several other young people confirmed that they did as well. Once or twice a week Li (20 years old) spends much of the night sending e-mails and chatting, mostly between midnight and 5 AM, "when Internet rates

Figure 8.3. Motorbikes everywhere. Hanoi, 2004. *Photo: Karen Tranberg Hansen*

are lowest," she adds. While her Goethe Institute classmate Hua (20 years old) prefers to chat on public forums, especially those discussing Korean TV serials and movies, or to shop online, Li's communications are more private: at night, she is mostly communicating with her boyfriend.

With few exceptions, the young women we interviewed lived with their parents and were not allowed to be out with friends after 10 PM. Adults try to monitor and regulate the sexual activity of girls and young women by setting rules for appropriate behavior, which are markedly different from the rules that young people in the developed world are nowadays subjected to. In our interviews, young women and men in Hanoi often emphasized the degree of surveillance they were subject to, by society in public and by their parents at home. As Sa (24 years old) explained, "If we talk to a girl in our neighborhood, there will always be somebody who takes notice of it . . . and then they will soon ask you about your intentions to get engaged."

Because living space in Hanoi is limited, most young people lack a private space that they control themselves. Meeting and being together with the other sex is an activity almost exclusively relegated to public spaces, such as those provided by educational institutions, roadside teashops, Internet cafés, and parks. One way to avoid parental, institutional, and neighborhood control is to seek out the anonymity of Hanoi's urban spaces, by spending leisure time and time between obligations (such as classes or work) at a distance from home. The motorbike, which today is one of the foremost status symbols and most desired objects among the young, enhances mobility and signifies more than a means of physical transport. For young people who are able to afford one, a motorbike is a way of escaping social or family surveillance, at least temporarily. The explosive increase in cellular phone ownership, not least among the younger generation, points in the same direction, as do some of the social uses of computer media, as we learned from our interviews.

Chat and e-mail are attractive to many young people in Hanoi because they enable them to stay in touch, even when physically confined in their parental homes. Moreover, they seem to qualitatively improve young people's communicative interactions as well. As Dung (28 years old) told us, e-mail, instant messaging, and chat allow young people to bring up issues of an intimate or sexual character, which might be too embarrassing to articulate in face-to-face conversation. Though there are many normative and repressive attempts to monitor and control the sexual activity of the young, Vietnamese society has seen a diversification of public knowledge regarding sex, love, and affection. Clearly, one of the promises that the new media in Hanoi hold out is the opportunity to learn more about sexual relations and the realm of love and passion. The new media hold out the promise of an emotionally and cognitively gratifying appropriation of other social and narrative constructs of gendered relations than those offered by the dominant mass media. The young are at the center of this development, because of their interest in exploring the mediated imaginations made possible by Vietnam's increasingly globalized mediascape. In the words of Hoa (15 years old), "We are psychologically curious enough to go to 'prohibited' Websites, which are very impressive. [. . .] I think young people want to try what they are told to keep away from. Many youngsters just try to get to know the taste."

Hoa, like other young people we interviewed, was aware of this change, whether by intuition or reflection. When we asked her about relations between young women and men in the past and the present, she indicated that she was concerned about the media's role: "Before, it used to take a long time for a boy and a girl who fell in love to decide to get married. Now there are a lot of marriages based on 'love at first sight,' which results in the fragility of marriages. [. . .] In the past, parents used to decide children's marriages. The fiancé and fiancée didn't go out together until they had become husband and wife. The mystery of each other attracted them to each other for a long time, while nowadays they know so much about each other that there is nothing to discover after the marriage."

Although somewhat inconsistent in its arguments, Hoa's reflection on the role of media points to an ongoing process of meaning negotiation. Admitting

Figure 8.4. A group of Vietnamese breakdancers at the Cultural Palace. Hanoi, 2004. *Photo: Norbert Wildermuth*

to the pleasures and gratifications of her own, media-enabled imagination, she reproduces society's dominant conceptions of the dangers of young people's un-controlled media consumption: "We want to know about the world. However, we have to pay for that. Teenagers are most sensitive to being negatively affected. It is inevitable for us to spend time on the Net because we don't want to be scorned for 'knowing nothing from the Net, like a peasant.' You may be considered back-ward by society. [. . .] Our teacher forbids us to go to the Internet shop. But how can she do that? The stricter her actions, the greater becomes our thirst for the Internet. In my opinion, it is more effective when adults advise us without prohibiting us. Violent measures are the worst."

Here Hoa comes to the heart of the conflict, the contradiction between parents' desires to see their children capitalize on the skills and knowledge enabled by the new media and their deep concerns about the apparently uncontrollable nature and potentially negative effects of information and communication technology. Interpreted optimistically, Hoa's discussion of this contradiction exemplifies the struggle of young people in Hanoi to challenge society's simplified image of the (new) media. However, while commenting on their own and other young people's

Figure 8.5. Young men and women eager to learn hip hop style. Hanoi, 2004.
Photo: Norbert Wildermuth

practices of media consumption and appropriation from a non-adult perspective, youth are neither fully independent in their evaluations nor unaware of society's dominant discourses and perceptions of the media.

Judging from our interviews, quite a few of the young in Hanoi seem unsure of how to evaluate their own rapidly changing practices of media consumption. If this dilemma remains unresolved, it will be difficult for them to develop a more differentiated view of the electronic and computer media, and with it a highly selective and discriminatory practice of media appropriation. Some of the older and more self-reliant young people we interviewed had worked through the ambiguity of personal experience and contradictory public evaluations of the new forms of communication. They were able to evaluate the potential uses and meanings of the new globalizing media in relation to their own identity projects.

The vehement rejection by many youth, including Hoa, of adult attempts to maintain strict control signifies a more differentiated understanding of young people's practices of media appropriation than is found within public discourse. Screen-based media offer significantly new forms of knowledge representation, which in turn require new forms of literacy. Media regulation, as understood by the state and its educational institutions in Vietnam, tends to be restrictive, enforcing rules intended to limit young people's mediated exposure to the world. An alternative conception of regulation, centered on social norms and framed in the positive terms of guiding and expanding youth's experience of the world, so far seems absent from the educational philosophy of the Vietnamese schooling system and the Youth Union. Arguably, their efforts would be better spent regulating the boundary between public and commercial content, encouraging participatory as well as receptive engagement, and permitting discussion of topics that challenge rather than underestimate the intelligence of young people.

Youth and Media in Lusaka

Lusaka's media landscape displays both differences from and parallels to the situation in Recife and Hanoi. Government-controlled ZNBC (Zambia National Broadcasting Corporation) has neither the editorial nor the economic autonomy of a public-service broadcaster. Institutionally it can be compared to Vietnamese VTV, rather than to the privately organized Brazilian TV channels.

The Zambian national press (published in English) is characterized by political pluralism, expressed in both oppositional and pro-government party journalism. Privately owned newspapers contribute to political and public debate in Zambia and have gained a certain editorial independence since the one-party system was abolished in 1991.[11] Still, as the Media Institute of Southern Africa states, judicial, verbal, and sometimes even physical attacks with the aim of silencing media and journalists critical of the government are common (MISA 2005, 20). Today, press freedom and diversity face harsh conditions, even in multi-party Zambia.[12]

The domestic television landscape is directly controlled and less pluralistic than the Zambian press. Besides ZNBC, there is only one terrestrially transmitted TV channel, Pentecostal Trinity TV. There was still no private Zambian TV broadcaster in December 2004. All the cable and satellite channels available were of foreign origin. Besides transnational news, sports, music, and other niche channels, several South African stations had a high profile. As Zambia is neither big enough nor attractive enough as a TV market, Zambian versions of transnational programming are so far not economically viable. Thus, none of the cable and satellite programs accessible in Lusaka are dubbed or subtitled into Bemba, Tonga, Njanja, Lozi, or other Zambian languages, nor are they localized in other ways. While a very few television programs in these languages are broadcast by ZNBC, providing the only shows for those who do not speak English, vernacular radio broadcasts are common.

A number of private, entertainment-oriented radio channels, formally independent of the ruling party, the state, and the government, are transmitted locally.

They mainly broadcast music-centered programs, complemented by journalism that concentrates more on private and social issues than on the state or politics. The fact that they depend on a government license that has to be renewed periodically may explain a certain editorial cautiousness.

Media Uses and Appropriations by the Young

In October 2004, we conducted lengthy interviews at the YWCA (Young Women's Christian Association) in Lusaka. Lulu (21 years old) was taking a course in business administration, conducted on the YWCA's premises. She had completed a B.A. in science in June 2003 and then worked for a software company. She now had strong intentions to go into business computing, and the course was a first step in realizing this ambition. Telling us how she had come to this decision, she explained, "I wanted to study natural science when I finished my A-levels . . . so I chose to combine science and business. . . . Then usually I watch Business News on BBC, then there is this lady who did just about the same thing that I did. . . . She was working for the World Bank and she did just about the same thing. She got a bachelor's in science and business computing. . . . So I think that came at the right time, my watching this, the Business News and everything."

Angela (18 years old), a classmate of Lulu's, stressed that reading papers and magazines at her parents' house was useful and important. Like many other young people we talked to, Angela got little pleasure or useful information from locally produced ZNBC programs. Complaining about the state broadcaster's focus on educational and development-oriented formats, she claimed to prefer radio broadcasts. These, Angela pointed out, hold the promise of interesting but less didactically formatted programs on "education, HIV, AIDS, gender, defilement, women." Listening to the radio provides the young with practical information not offered by television, Angela argued: "If there is going to be a party somewhere, they tell you about it."

Several young people we interviewed emphasized ZNBC's paternalistic, unprofessional, and unattractive approach to communicating with them. A majority wished for more topics specifically interesting to youth. Some claimed to watch the national news more or less regularly, while others acknowledged interest in ZNBC's rebroadcasts of imported programs like the daily *Oprah Winfrey Show* and reality shows (*Big Brother Africa, Project Fame,* and *Survivor*). The only two types of program that were notably popular with young people were international football and *Isidingo,* a TV serial from South Africa retransmitted by ZNBC.

The failure of domestically produced television to live up to the expectations of the young is creating a divide between those who have no access to TV at all, those with terrestrial TV only, and those few whose families can afford a cable or satellite connection. The media-rich group may have abandoned the state broadcaster, apart from the 7 o'clock news and the occasional popular serial, sports event, or reality show. This group generally prefers to use media in certain ways, as exemplified by Barbara (21 years old), who studies journalism and works part-time at Youth Media, an internationally funded media NGO. Commenting on the poor performance of ZNBC, she explained, from a perspective implicitly indicating her upper-class background,

> They [ZNBC] had a couple of serials, I mean, which everybody was so in tune with . . . in the early 1990s, everybody was watching these serials and cartoons; they were quite developed. Now . . . when you hit the year 2000, everybody was getting into satellite . . . because it was more entertaining. ZNBC lacked the entertainment that everybody wanted because there was a repetition of old shows, yet things were moving much faster in the rest of the world. You knew that there were new serials, new shows, and new entertainment stuff that were going on and ZNBC was still stuck in the eighties.

Julia, a first-year student in social work at the University of Zambia, volunteered for work at Youth Media, where we met and talked to her. Though born in Lusaka, she had grown up in Sweden, France, and China, because her father was a diplomat. Julia had returned to Lusaka in 1997 with her parents, with whom she lived in Rhodes Park, a high-income residential area. Her view of the uses and gratifications of ZNBC was as disapproving as Barbara's, though her emphasis differed:

> [ZNBC] is very bad. There is not much there. [. . .] There is not much that you can learn from [them], whether this is regular learning, school stuff, or learning about international stuff. There are maybe too many religious shows, especially on Saturdays and days when it is not really relevant. It is there, every day. Also very old shows, which don't help. And I don't think, just watching ZNBC, you can get a good picture of even Zambia, let alone the world.

Julia's and Barbara's characterizations of domestic television as unsatisfying, in terms of both entertainment and information, echo the critique of terrestrially distributed television by middle- and upper-class youth in Recife and Hanoi, but with a difference. In Recife, the highly commercialized, sensationalist, and populist entertainment-oriented character of privately organized Brazilian TV production was at the heart of young people's criticisms. Their main demand was not for more youth-centered and entertaining TV productions, but for more "truthful" representations and less cheap, irrelevant entertainment. In Lusaka, where terrestrial broadcasts offer few youth-oriented programs, the unprofessional, politically controlled, paternalistic, and proselytizing character of ZNBC and Trinity TV was at the center of young people's criticisms.

Ignoring Youth

Young people in Lusaka are not dissatisfied only with the content of domestic television. They also believe they are not properly served by either television or the press in Zambia. In the view of Anna Phiri, co-founder of Youth Media and since 1994 involved in publishing the NGO's *Trendsetters,* a monthly newsletter by and for the young,[13] young people were and still are marginalized in the national and local mainstream media: "There is no presence of young people, of young people's concerns in the media—things that we want to read about, or that we're talking about, our aspirations and all the rest of it."

Anna Phiri also stated that, on the few occasions when the media do focus on young people, they are primarily portrayed in negative terms. They are mostly represented as a category, such as students who are rioting or not attending class, rather than as individuals. Many other young people made a similar point to us.

Mass media forms of communication that neither take youth seriously nor represent them realistically are not likely to involve the young in meaningful ways. In Lusaka, where the choice of domestic TV content and daily newspapers is felt to be unsatisfactory and where access to more attractive programs and print media is the privilege of a few, young people have good reason not to expect that they will gain useful knowledge or skills from watching television or reading the papers, though they may choose to hang on as TV viewers for the sake of entertainment or just to kill time. Our interviews indicate that they often prefer non-media leisure activities, such as playing football, hanging out with friends, participating in church activities, drinking beer, and becoming involved in sexual affairs. Also, if young people have the opportunity, they may turn to other, more personalized practices of media consumption, such as watching films on video and DVD, or accessing computer-based media.

Alternatives to Mass-Distributed Media

Attempts to popularize more meaningful, youth-centered media products do exist, as the examples of *Trendsetters* and *Speak Out,* a magazine published by the Catholic Church, show. Does dissatisfaction with the existing mass media create a commercially viable demand for such initiatives? It seems not. Neither magazine has been able to support itself financially. The purchasing power of the young in Zambia and their willingness to spend money on such products is limited.[14] *Trendsetters* has depended on funding from foreign donor organizations throughout its existence.[15] Only a few young people in Lusaka are both able and willing to spend money on these kinds of magazines. Most of those

Figure 8.6. Visitors to Mtendere's youth center, Africa Directions. Lusaka, 2004.
Photo: Norbert Wildermuth

we talked to preferred to consume highly valued entertainment products, that is, to rent videos and DVDs, buy music cassettes and CDs, visit the cinema, or spend some time in an Internet café. Educational and development-oriented forms of media communication that seek to increase young people's knowledge of HIV/AIDS, such as *Trendsetters,* compete with the commercial media for young people's attention.

The Promise of Information Technology

While many young people found the Internet attractive because of its potential as a research tool, they remained skeptical that it was worth the money. Lulu, for example, said, "To tell you the truth, the money that you spend on the Internet is too much. . . . You want to get a lot of information, you know, with very little money, so like for me, the maximum I get on the computer is like two hours a week." Donald (25 years old), a fourth-year student of social economics at university, agreed with this: "I have an email address and I rarely use it. By the time

Figure 8.7. Young women relaxing outside Mtendere's youth center, Africa Directions. Lusaka, 2004. *Photo: Norbert Wildermuth*

you send it, it costs you 5,000 kwacha [approximately US$0.85]. So I rarely use it. Besides . . . I don't have a lot of friends who use e-mail."

Young people we talked to in the low-income compounds of Mtendere and Kalingalinga were even more skeptical and constrained in their use of the Internet. In fact, most had never used a computer. Among those who had were Tom (15 years old) and William (19 years old). Tom, a peer educator at Mtendere's youth center, Africa Directions, claimed to go to an Internet café every second month, mainly to send e-mails and to access information:

> We don't have newspapers, which can tell you the news that is happening abroad. . . . The Internet is fast, you can get the information fast. Like hearing about the celebrities from Hollywood. I'll get their views and their lives, how they live there and about musicians. [. . .] Like me. I usually browse a Website about film and I get the information about acting, how they make their film, because I want to be an actor. [. . .] So I usually get the information, what's all about acting and what you can do if you want to be an actor and what kind of acting they do in other countries, and I compare it to Zambian acting.

Figure 8.8. Spectators in front of an HIV/AIDS prevention billboard at Africa Directions. Lusaka, 2004. *Photo: Norbert Wildermuth*

More than other media, the Internet, with its promise of information and knowledge, has caught the imagination of many young people in Lusaka. William, conversely, was not an Internet user. Referring to Tom's statement, he sought to accommodate his own skeptical approach with an acknowledgment of the "usefulness" of the Internet to his friend:

> There are very few Zambian institutions which have a Website, there are very few, of which some maybe talk about music, Zambian music . . . there is a lot of craze about music, soap opera. Young people are very into that. They try to find the most entertaining on the Net. Usually you find them looking at the Website of *Isidingo.* [. . .] He [Tom] wants to be an actor, so he will be able to get something from there.

Widespread proficiency in English allows young people in Lusaka to use many foreign Websites. Yet young people are less enthusiastic about, and less likely to appropriate, computer media than their counterparts in Recife and especially Hanoi because of material constraints on their access, rather than because of "cultural screens"[16] or a failure on their part to fully appreciate the potential uses of the Internet, e-mail, and so on. Given the limitations of television, print, and computer media that have been outlined, what alternative media do youth in Lusaka turn to?

Radio: Popularity and Potential

According to Anna Phiri, a 2003 British Council survey showed that young people in Zambia prefer radio to TV or print media. This finding corresponds to the patterns of media consumption described by the majority of our interviewees. Radio broadcasts seem to be widely listened to, especially by the majority of lower- and middle-class youth, who have limited access to more personalized media products and computers. One reason, though not the only one, for this preference is the popularity of music. Music dominates the private channels.[17] Their informal way of addressing listeners, compared to that of ZNBC or the press, identifies young people as their intended audience. While television and the press are perceived as addressing mainly adults, with few exceptions the private Zambian radio stations that have been established over the last decade project a youthful channel identity. Natasha Phiri (21 years old), sister of the three co-founders of Youth Media, described the difference she perceived from both personal and professional points of view:

> I think media in general in Zambia are still not very encouraging, like . . . bring-ing out young people's issues, especially the government media; . . . you rarely see anything about young people, and even then young people don't really have the space to talk or to express their opinions. . . . On some of the private radio stations you find that, because a lot of them are targeted at young people, they are more youth-friendly. So you find [that] they have certain programs, like talking about sex or relationships . . . there people can call in, they can say how they feel.

While acknowledging the youth-centered character of radio in general, Barbara (21 years old) made another critical point. She mentioned phone-in shows on Radio Phoenix, Q FM, and other popular stations, and suggested that radio should try to reach out to youth and encourage them to participate in programming in other ways too. She regarded the Zambian radio stations as very limited and studio-based in their format. She also complained that journalistic approaches which seek out youth "on the streets" in order to tell stories about their lives and raise questions about the circumstances under which they unfold are still the exception.

According to Barbara, Anna Phiri, and others, Zambian radio programs do not give much coverage to youth-related issues, except for the programs sponsored by development agencies, NGOs, and state institutions. And these are one-off programs, apart from Club NTG, a regular broadcast by the Society for Family Health. Radio in Lusaka is thus a mass medium that has opened up a communicative space not only to talk to young people, but also in which young people can express themselves. However, its potential does not yet seem to have been fully utilized (Panos Institute 2005).

Conclusion

As I have sought to demonstrate, the media provide frames of orientation and reference that widen the cognitive horizons of young people in Recife, Lusaka, and Hanoi. They are a central resource in young people's understanding of the particular spheres of modern, urbanized lifeworlds and of the relations between these spheres, something that they are not able to come to terms with through direct experience alone. From the perspective of the adolescent generation, the nature of modern, urbanized lives implies that they can no longer acquire the skills and knowledge they need to become adults by participating in the world of production. More than ever, the young are involved in a plurality of everyday lives, living simultaneously in a family reality, in a peer-group reality, in a school or employment reality, in an enlarged social reality, and in a reality of symbolic significance, which includes the world of media representations. As a result, the lifeworlds of children and young people are divided into distinct spheres of school, leisure, home, and work, their symbolic reality shaped by projects of identity, images, and imaginations of the world. The media play a central role in this transformation of everyday knowledge. Young people not only have the chance to appropriate this knowledge, they are in a sense also obliged to orient themselves in new ways, because "traditional" trajectories of adult lives have lost most of their value as normative models for possible social roles.

Young people from poor backgrounds are more familiar with, and prefer, the symbolic realities and knowledge provided by the media, which are less diversified than those accessed by more privileged young people living in the same city. In addition, many of these poor young people do not have the personal resources to see easily through the ideological practices and crude manipulations of the local media landscape, nor are they especially well prepared to scrutinize the knowledge of "other" lives that local, national, and transnational media provide. They do not always evaluate these media representations, their meaning, and their relevance to their own lives critically or analytically enough. In consequence, the work of the imagination that they realize tends to become more of an escape than the basis for personal and collective empowerment. However, the example of some of the young people we interviewed showed that the growth in everyday knowledge enabled by the media may serve other purposes than merely entertainment and wishful but unrealistic identification. In effect, the media can be more than a window on a desirable but unattainable world and can create more than impossible dreams and subsequent frustrations.

Young women and men consume media under conditions that are not of their own choosing. However, while orientations toward and expectations of mediated texts are socially shared, an individual's ability to engage the media critically and constructively is not a priori decided by the social position he or she occupies, nor does it remain the same over time. That is, young people's capacity to use media highly selectively, by either rejecting the media's textual offers or critically negotiating them, can be improved. Their practices of appropriation and imagination, which rely on established strategies for identification and meaning making, can be encouraged.

The findings I have presented indicate that the state and its educational institutions leave young people more or less alone in their attempt to utilize old and new media, as they struggle to create for themselves future lives and empowered personal identities. This is something that all three cities have in common. The new forms of critical (media) literacy,[18] which the progress and ever-growing presence of the media in Recife, Hanoi, and Lusaka demand, ideally provide the socially constituted and situated young media user with new cultural repertoires. The creation and mobilization of social alliances that reach beyond the interpretative communities that (underprivileged) youth are normally a part of play a central role in this process, as is demonstrated by the positive example of (media) NGOs and certain other organizations focusing on the political and cultural self-expression of youth. Systematic attempts at media education—a subject unfortunately more or less absent from the policies and curricula of public education in Vietnam, Zambia, and Brazil—have the potential to further youth empowerment. That is, it is policies intended to foster young people's media literacy that are needed, rather than attempts to control their media consumption through censorship and other forms of regulation.

The potential role of the state, civil society, and the private economy in furthering young people's media-empowered literacy depends on the broader context. Attempts which make sense in Recife, Hanoi, and Lusaka are comparable, but necessarily also different. Concrete measures and policies demand a better understanding of the situated practices of media consumption through which youth engage with the globalizing urban space they confront. Enormous socioeconomic disparities and uneven development characterize Recife, Lusaka, and Hanoi, though each manifests these in its own particular way. A study based on short-term, interview-centered research trips such as those that have informed the present study may provide preliminary insights and suggestions. Further research efforts might focus on the relationship between the empowering practices of media imagination and systematic efforts by the state and civil society to enable young men and women to make optimum use of the media available to them.

Acknowledgments

My sincere thanks to all the people who made this study possible and in particular to my local assistants, André Telles in Recife, Joseph Silavwe in Lusaka, and Chi and Sa in Hanoi. Without them, I would have achieved much less in this study.

Notes

1. In 2003, the overall number of TV sets in Brazil was estimated at 36.5 million, or 0.196 sets per inhabitant (CIA 2003). Machado-Borges reports that 87 per cent of Brazilian households contain a television (2003, 6).

2. The major exception was sports reports and radio programs on football by Rádio Clube, Jovem Cap, and Rádio Jornal, which were popular with several of the young men we interviewed.

3. Their validation demands more than the roughly thirty interviews that inform my analysis. Moreover, I lack the space here to present parts of my empirical data which might strengthen my argument. However, some of these interviews have been discussed as examples of the critical and empowering work of young people's imagination in Recife (Wildermuth and Dalsgaard 2006).

4. For a description and comparison of both modes, see Liebes and Katz 1990.

5. In late 2003, the overall number of TV sets in Vietnam was estimated at 3.57 million, or 0.043 sets per inhabitant (CIA 2003). However, Vietnam's rates of television ownership vary markedly between urban and rural areas. According to other sources, terrestrial TV sets are quite common in Saigon and Hanoi households (Le Thanh Binh 2002). Also, televisions are multiplying in Vietnam at a pace that suggests that the above figures may have been outdated by the time they were published. Current estimates (December 2005), report 6.9 million TV sets in the country (Vietnam Research by Veterans n.d.).

6. The set-top box required for satellite TV is available for about US$180, so that transnational services have become affordable for Hanoi's growing middle class. Cable TV requires a subscription, but it is available at a lower initial cost: a cable TV connection can be set up for around US$25, while the full program package costs less than US$2 per month. However, as not all parts of Hanoi are wired up yet, cable TV is mainly available in those parts of the city which have been built recently or are mainly inhabited by middle- and upper-class households.

7. The VTV national evening news in English and French is one of the few exceptions.

8. Young Vietnamese growing up in Ho Chi Minh City, the urban center of Vietnam's south, may have had more exposure to such representations. Ming may nonetheless adequately represent young people of his age from the Hanoi region.

9. This may be partly due to the fact that we interviewed relatively fewer middle-class youths in Recife and Lusaka than in Hanoi. Many of the middle- and upper-class young people we interviewed in Brazil engaged in computer-based forms of mediated communication, for

purposes of both knowledge generation and leisure. This was also the case in Zambia, though apparently on a lesser scale. Defined in quantitative terms, Brazil has the most Internet users per inhabitant, namely 0.118, followed by Vietnam with 0.070 and Zambia with 0.021 (CIA 2005). Since Hanoi and Lusaka are both national capitals and are inhabited by a substantial part of the political and economic elite, while Recife is only a regional capital, the difference between these cities may be less pronounced.

10. Judging from the estimated number of PCs in those countries in 2005, Brazil has 2.6 Internet users per computer, Zambia 3.3, and Vietnam 10.1 (these figures were compiled from http://www.nationmaster.com/countries, which cited its source for them as the International Telecommunications Union). This difference underlines the abundance of Internet cafés and other sites of shared access to Internet and computer media in Hanoi, in comparison to the more privatized culture of access in Recife and Lusaka.

11. The once noted independence of the press was compromised by government and party control: ownership of the *Times* of Zambia passed to the party in 1982, while the *Zambia Daily Mail* has been in government hands since 1965. The church-owned weekly, the *National Mirror,* founded in 1970, was able to take a more independent line, as has the *Weekly Post,* which first appeared in 1991 in the wake of moves toward a more pluralist political system.

12. Recent examples of the ruling party's attempts to curtail media freedom in Zambia, directed not only against the press but also against private radio stations, have been documented by MISA Zambia (see http://www.misazambia.org.zm).

13. *Trendsetters* was founded as a result of NGO interest in HIV/AIDS prevention. Initially Youth Media focused exclusively on reproductive health and abstinence. This focus has been enlarged over the last years, with *Trendsetters* and other media products of Youth Media taking up youth-related issues in general. I interviewed Anna Phiri on November 1, 2004.

14. Anna Phiri estimated young people in Zambia to be willing and able to pay about 5,000 kwacha for a youth magazine like *Trendsetters* or *Speak Out.* Whether it is possible to produce such magazines at this price depends on the number of copies printed. Given the number of copies sold at the time of my research (2004), production was barely viable.

15. The commercial edition of *Trendsetters,* which lost its funding in February 2004, had in fact not appeared in the past eight months, Anna Phiri told us in November. By 2006, the magazine had returned to the newsstands with new funding.

16. Dallas Smythe introduced the concept of the "cultural screen" in his discussion of language and other natural barriers to the global dominance of Hollywood suggested by media imperialism theory (Pendakur 2004).

17. This includes the Christian radio broadcasts, which also rely heavily on music, though mainly on gospel.

18. The concept of "critical literacy" has been explored in relation to practices of media consumption by Silverstone (2004), Livingstone (2002), and others. Two recent issues of *American Behavioral Scientist* (vol. 48, nos. 1–2 [September–October 2004]) focus on media literacy in the twenty-first century and provide an in-depth summary of the contemporary discussion.

References

Ang, Ien. 1989. Wanted: Audiences. In *Remote Control: Television, Audiences and Cultural Power*, ed. Ellen Seiter, Hans Borchers, Gabriele Kreutzner, and Eva-Marie Worth, 96–115. London: Routledge.

Appadurai, Arjun. 1996. *Modernity at Large: Cultural Dimensions of Globalization.* Delhi: Oxford University Press.

Becker, Jörg, and Daniel Salamanca. 2003. Massenmedien und Informationstechnologien in Vietnam. http://www.interasia.org/vietnam/becker-salamanca2.html. Accessed February 2006.

CIA (Central Intelligence Agency). 2003. *The World Factbook 2003.* Washington, D.C.: Central Intelligence Agency. The current edition of the *World Factbook* is available at https://www .cia.gov/library/publications/the-world-factbook/index.html; older editions can be downloaded from https://www.cia.gov/library/publications/download/.

———. 2005. *The World Factbook 2005.* Washington, D.C.: Central Intelligence Agency.

Drotner, Kirsten. 1991. *At skabe sig selv: Ungdom, aestetik, paedagogik.* Copenhagen: Gyldendal.

———. 1996. Unge og medier: Problemstillinger og perspektiver. In *Øjenåbnere: Unge, medier og modernitet,* ed. Kirsten Drotner and Anne Scott Sørensen, 9–37. Copenhagen: Dansklærerforening.

Hoang-Giang Dang. 2002. Einheit der Gegensätze: Fernsehen in Vietnam. In *Flimmerndes Asien: Die Fernsehentwicklung eines Kontinents im Aufbruch,* ed. Jörg Becker and Kurt Luger, 174–83. Vienna: Österreichischer Kunst- und Kulturverlag.

Holland, Dorothy, William Lachicotte, Jr., Debra Skinner, and Carole Cain. 1998. *Identity and Agency in Cultural Worlds.* Cambridge, Mass.: Harvard University Press.

Le Thanh Binh. 2002. Vietnamese Television and the Market Economy. In *Wege des Wasserbüffels: Kunst, Kultur und Medien in Vietnam,* ed. Jörg Becker, 39–46. Iserlohn: Evangelische Akademie Iserlohn.

Liebes, Tamara, and Elihu Katz. 1990. *The Export of Meaning: Cross-Cultural Readings of "Dallas."* New York: Oxford University Press.

Livingstone, Sonia. 1998. Relations between Media and Audiences: Prospects for the Future. In *Media, Ritual, Identity,* ed. Tamar Liebes and Janet Curran, 237–55. London: Routledge.

———. 2002. *Young People and New Media.* London: Sage.

Machado-Borges, Thaïs. 2003. *Only for You! Brazilians and the Telenovela Flow.* Stockholm, Sweden: Dept. of Social Anthropology, Stockholm University. Distributed by Almqvist & Wiksell International.

Miles, Steven. 2000. *Youth Lifestyles in a Changing World.* Buckingham, England: Open University Press.

MISA (Media Institute of Southern Africa). 2005. *MISA Annual Report, April 2004–March 2005.* http://www.misa.org/documents/annualreport2005.pdf. Accessed September 25, 2007.

Panos Institute. 2005. *Reporting AIDS: An Analysis of Media Environments in Southern Africa.* London: Panos Institute.

Pendakur, Manjunath. 2004. Global versus Local Tensions in Cultural Policy: Canada and India. Paper presented at Canadian Cultural Research Network Colloquium, Ottawa, June.

Silverstone, Roger. 2004. Regulation, Media Literacy and Media Civics. *Media, Culture & Society* 26(3):440–49.

Thompson, John B. 1995. *The Media and Modernity.* Cambridge: Polity.

Tomlinson, John. 1999. *Globalisation and Culture.* Cambridge: Polity.

Vietnam Research by Veterans. n.d. Vietnam Television Station History. http://vietnamresearch .com/media/vn-tv.html. Accessed February 2006.

Wildermuth, Norbert, and Anne Line Dalsgaard. 2006. Imagined Futures, Present Lives: Youth, Media and Modernity in the Changing Economy of Northeast Brazil. *Young: Nordic Journal of Youth Research* 14(1):9–31.

9

Conclusion: Urban Youth in a Global World

Karen Tranberg Hansen

Recent headlines about a rapidly urbanizing world whose growth is most marked in the large cities of the Global South pay little attention either to the place of young people or to the implications of the youth bulge for such cities tomorrow (Davis 2006). Diverging from much recent work, this book's focus on the combination of youth and the city has enabled us to reveal several important dynamics that are crucial to understanding the unique situation of young people. What is more, by linking the urban and the global, we have developed a perspective informed by interdisciplinary research into several overlapping areas of young people's everyday lives in three different cities on three different continents. Taken together, our work showcases Recife, Hanoi, and Lusaka as spaces for both agency and reaction on the part of the young, depending on who they are in age, gender, and class terms, and on their sociospatial positions. Our ability to capture the complexity of globalization through young people's agency in urban space is the result of the interdisciplinary research collaboration on which this volume is based. When geography, media research, education studies, and anthropology together address the urban youth problematic in the development context, rich interpretive potentials arise. This conclusion briefly identifies what is unique about this work and why our observations matter.

Recife, Hanoi, and Lusaka are cities of the young in many different ways. Youth and cities are both global categories that command our attention because both are growing rapidly. Young people today comprise a major part of the populations of rapidly growing cities in developing countries and, judging by demographic projections, they will continue to do so in the future. Highly visible in public, they invigorate the urban scene, investing space with meanings that help to organize social life. Yet social science scholarship and development intervention have by and large viewed youth and the city as separate topics: youth as a globally circulating category that has become part of development policy, and cities as settings that are playing an increasing role in the global human experience. In recent years, each of these topics has witnessed a spurt in both interdisciplinary scholarship and development-oriented reports, which we alluded to in the introduction, invoked to different degrees throughout our discussions, and will return to shortly in an effort to bring these two topics, youth and the city, together.

The chapters in this volume depart from widespread representations of big-city youth in developing countries, both in the social sciences and in the popular media that foreground socioeconomic crises, violence, and marginalization. Our inclusion of young people from diverse class backgrounds provides a deeper understanding of some of the forces and institutions that shape young people's livelihoods than would an exclusive focus on poor youth who are marginalized at the formal institutional level. Our contribution here is intended to fill a knowledge gap in urban scholarship on developing countries by examining urban young people's relations with both their peers and the older generation. Our qualitative and cross-sectional research approach to youth has explored everyday urban life across an encompassing range of settings and sites in order to draw connections between and across home and household; streets and markets; schools and work; politics, associations, and churches; media and popular culture; and relationships and sexuality, among others. Focusing on a variety of places and situations, from the built environment to singing in a church choir, each chapter provides observations that overlap with those of the others. These many angles enable us to view, for example, young people's sexual experiences from a broader context than the narrow optic of HIV/AIDS prevention, which has held back the development of scholarship on love and affection because of its exclusive focus on reproductive health.

The world in which the young people we have studied seek to get on with their lives is very different from that of twenty years ago, as a result of, among many other things, changes in the capitalist world economy, local political and economic transformations, rapid globalization, the growth in information and communication technology, and the spread of HIV/AIDS (United Nations 2005a, 2). Unlike their parents, the young people we have come to know did not grow up in a time of political repression. Global ideological polarizations have declined. The authoritarian state apparatuses of past decades have given way to multi-party political systems in Brazil and Zambia, opening up the possibility for greater participation in institutions across society, including the new open markets. Even Vietnam's communist state has allowed some degree of market liberalization to take place. Still, almost everywhere, young people are part of generational hierarchies and institutional structures that subordinate them to the powers of others in many domains of everyday life. Young people in Recife, Hanoi, and Lusaka live not only in different social and political worlds: because of economic circumstances they also, as Wildermuth points out, live in different media worlds. Recife is a setting for television viewing, Hanoi connected to the Internet, while in Lusaka young people are more engaged with the radio. No doubt, such media practices change rapidly as cell phones and the Internet daily find more young users, also in Lusaka.

The comparative perspective driving this book's observations about young people demonstrates the social and cultural construction of the category of youth in ways that differ, not only in gender and class terms within and across the three cities, but also from definitions of youth as a distinct stage in the life course. We join recent scholarship on youth in questioning the model of youth as a distinct life stage that determined much of the comparative research agenda throughout the 1970s. New research from across Europe, the United States, and Australia has documented a lack of continuity between the generations and shown that a grow-ing proportion of young people are not experiencing the transition the previous generation took for granted when leaving school and going straight into jobs. In some places, the transition between home and work has become discontinu-ous. The developmental teleology inherent in the life-stage youth model derived from the West never squared well with youth experiences in many parts of the developing world. If, as we noted in the introduction, the experiences of global youth are converging today, this is in part a result of the adverse effects of recent global economic conjunctures on youth employment prospects everywhere.

The generational dynamics shaping the shift from youth to adulthood take vastly different forms in the three urban settings of our study, and not only because individual authors have given differential methodological weight to this process. How the trajectory from youth to adulthood develops and, along with it, how youth assumes specific meanings varies across class in the three research sites. Dalsgaard and her collaborators demonstrate how young people from poor family backgrounds in Recife negotiate their own life course around vital events that delineate not one but many trajectories toward the future. Their middle-class age-mates and the members of the Youth Union in Hanoi on whom Valentin focused enjoy different prospects for economic mobility than did their parents. In Lusaka, the imprint of economic decline shows up in many household biographies through the markedly different experiences of first- and last-born family members, as opportunities to pursue education and find jobs have shrunk over the last twenty years. Although generational succession, about which Karl Mannheim wrote so incisively half a century ago, works itself out differently in these three urban settings, it is everywhere experienced as new and different, though not always positively.

The meanings of youth in the three cities are elastic and characterized by a good deal of ambiguity that hinges on where young people are and with whom they interact. Many young people's lives are uncertain because of economic changes and shifting household fortunes. Changes in living arrangements, socioeconomic status, schooling, and personal relationships complicate many other difficulties that young people may face. As Gough illustrates in her work on the significance of home, many young people experience home as a cramped place where physical crowding has implications for daily life and social relations. Although the home is a safe and secure place for some youth, it is a place full of conflict and contradictions for others. Most young people experience changes in their home, either physically or socially, and not necessarily for the better. For many low-income youth the prospect of becoming a homeowner is remote, and even renting the cheapest accommodation can be beyond their means. Therefore, young people may during the life course set up their own home once, more than once, or not at all. The relationship between youth and the home is complex and transitions between youth and adulthood are neither one-way nor one-time events. Far from being static, the meanings of youth shift situationally, depending above all on context, as we discuss below in highlighting some of our findings.

Context Matters

The young people we have studied live in worlds of marked contrasts and striking inequalities within Recife, Hanoi, and Lusaka, regionally in their own countries, and between them and the world at large. The numerical ranking of the three countries on the UNDP Development Index (referred to in the introduction) provides one measure of these contrasts, with Zambia near the bottom of the least-developed countries, while Vietnam and Brazil are ascending the ranks of the middle-income countries. Yet such measures do not correlate with urban space in any straightforward way. The same is true of class, as Dalsgaard and Valentin note in the methodology chapter when reflecting on the uneasy fit between socioeconomic groups and urban location in the three cities. Although poverty is widespread in all three cities, it manifests itself very differently across urban space. In fact, we found poverty to be far less visible in Hanoi than in Recife and Lusaka, perhaps for historical and cultural reasons specific to Hanoi.

Hanoi stands out as a highly politicized urban space where the communist state, through the Youth Union, maintains a definition of young people that subordinates them to elders and the family in the face of rapid socioeconomic changes. In this case, the state seeks to remain involved in organizing social relations in the reproduction of society. Even though Hanoi, like Recife and Lusaka, has population segments that are very poor, many of the young Youth Union members on whom Valentin focused had prospects for upward mobility. Although Recife is often described as a city of stark contrasts, with gated communities cheek-by-jowl with *favelas*, Dalsgaard and her colleagues reveal a range of socioeconomic situations. In Lusaka, the twin reality of low-density (meaning high-income) walled or fenced residential areas and high-density (meaning low-income) compounds is superimposed upon a garden city of colonial design. The highly visible contrasts between livelihoods in Recife and Lusaka bear witness to a gulf of inequality between means and wants that is the key to many young people's imagination. They do not belong to tightly knit organizations like Vietnam's Youth Union, with its subset of structures and guidelines for advancement, but are left pretty much to their own devices in the here and now.

The young people we have come to know through this work, and many others like them, dominate the landscapes of Recife, Hanoi, and Lusaka. Their dispro-portionately large number in relation to the overall population in these rapidly growing cities means that young people are more likely to experience poverty than other age groups, and more likely to be unemployed or have only precari-ous employment (United Nations 2005a, 7). In sub-Saharan Africa in 2003, 63 percent of the total unemployed were youth even though they comprised only 33 percent of the labor force. Young women's unemployment is widely underes-timated, disguised by their unpaid domestic work and self-employment in the informal economy (Economic Commission for Africa 2005, 10–11). Falling into poverty, becoming stuck in the compound, in the phrase I use from Lusaka, or escaping from it depends on a conjunction of several factors, structural as well as idiosyncratic, ranging from socioeconomic background and institutional re-sources to individual abilities and desires and global inspirations. This volume casts comparative light on the double dynamic of simultaneous exclusion and inclusion that is a result of many young people's experience of exclusion from the institutions of the wider society at the same time as the cities they live in function as gateways to a wider world of opportunities that they are keen to tap into. The contrast between many young people's limited ability to consume global goods and appropriate new media and their fervent desire to do so, as in Lusaka, vividly demonstrates the ambiguity that arises from this dynamic.

Since globalization helps change economies, restructure markets, and trans-form urban space, it affects young people's opportunities, as we have demonstrated in this volume. Globalization is not a matter of these processes alone, but also involves political and cultural issues. Senior politicians' hold on power leaves young people relatively uninvolved in formal party politics in the three cities in which we conducted this research. This does not mean that they are uninterested in politics: in Vietnam some young people follow the party line through the Youth Union, and young people in Recife and Lusaka belong to networks of various sorts and alliances arising around NGO-facilitated activity. While at first sight such interaction revolves around individual abilities and personal interests, it is played out in the longer term with reference to the social relations in which these young actors are embedded. In Hanoi, ideally, these relations center on the extended family, while in Lusaka and Recife they are increasingly structured around fluid social organizational arrangements that challenge long-held gerontocratic norms concerning the composition of households, household headship, and marriage. We have suggested that it is in such contexts that long-held conceptions of youth as dependent change and take on new meanings. It is not surprising that some of the young people we introduce in Recife, for example, whose freedom is constrained by entrenched norms defining proper ways of progressing to adulthood, wish to be considered as individuals, as young persons who can make a difference, rather than as adults-in-waiting who must abide their turn.

A celebration of individualism, as in issue-oriented politics, faith-based activity directed at salvation, or popular culture involving music and media, does not necessarily separate young actors from broader social relations: whether it does so depends on context, on the structural openings available to young people. Ambrosius Madsen captures the importance of context pointedly when she argues that site matters to the study of the global flow of influential ideas and concepts. Each of the three cities has accepted the global ideas of schooling that she discusses in her chapter, but has reacted to them in different ways. Resistance to new curricula is diffuse in Recife, where many low-income people consider school to have lost its significance. In Lusaka, resistance to global ideas of education is fueled by widespread poverty that means such ideas will not be realized for many. Resistance in Hanoi is expressed in settings away from school, where young people are not supervised by teachers or guardians, for example when they use the Internet in their quest for knowledge.

Quite clearly, as this volume demonstrates, globalization has raised hopes and expectations of improved well-being in many areas. Young people's consciousness of a world of opportunity, consumption, and popular culture affects how they see their local lifeworlds and the meanings and uses they assign to global goods. Young people in Recife, Hanoi, and Lusaka know about what is out there. In this regard there is no linear continuity between the exposure and experiences of the generations. Some young people are impatient with society's construction of them as minors, like the male secondary-school students whom Ambrosius Madsen met in Lusaka, who saw no fit between their curriculum and life. Although their pathway toward adulthood has become treacherous because of a sluggish economy, it is not just one-way. As Dalsgaard and her colleagues show from Recife, there is not one dominant youth trajectory but many.

Definitions Matter

How scholars and planners delineate age categories to designate youth makes a difference when it comes to policy. Many international development organizations and NGOs extend their efforts to both children and young people, thus implying a continuum of experiences. For example, in its policy document, *Partnership 2000,* the Danish International Development Agency (DANIDA) made children and youth a development focus, that is, a target group to be prioritized in relevant programs and projects (Denmark, Ministry of Foreign Affairs 2005, 3). The portfolio of the relevant ministry in Zambia covers sport, young people, and children. Yet "everyone knows" in Zambia that the ministry mainly deals with sport. This blurring of boundaries and merging of categories masks the specific needs and concerns of children on the one hand and young people on the other. These categories must be differentiated if policy measures and intervention programs are to be developed that respond to the specific, and distinct, needs of children and young people. Not covered by the UN Convention on the Rights of the Child (for which children are those in the age range from 0 through 18), young people tend to fall between the cracks of other categories, for example, women, refugees, or the disabled, who are identified in very specific terms for purposes of very targeted policy interventions. In effect, for policy purposes young people are surprisingly easy to overlook.

Whether we understand youth as an inherently problematic phase of life or one that is endowed with potential has policy implications for how the situation of young people is recognized. Despite international development advocacy for young persons' rights and abilities, many governments, including that of Zambia, continue to depict young people in ways that leave little scope to acknowledge their agency. One way is the welfare angle that treats young people as dependent and immature, and therefore in need of "improvement." Another is problem-oriented and characterizes young people as troublesome and therefore prone to problematic behavior that needs controlling and curtailing, as through the institutionalized example of Vietnam's Youth Union. What is more, these attributions of trouble are often highly gendered and, in Recife and Lusaka, tend to be rendered in male terms. When such understandings inform policy planning, top-down measures are likely to follow.

How we understand youth, as a stage or an experience, also makes a difference. Advocacy stylings of youth as the "leaders of tomorrow" call out for qualifications. Such appellations imply waiting and deferring decisions to the authority of elders. But when we view youth as an experience, we recognize young people's agency in the present. And in that present, there are situational, gender, and class-related distinctions that turn youth into a heterogeneous category. By questioning the unilinear unfolding of the life-stage youth-transition model, the chapters in this volume cast light on the diverse trajectories that the young people in our three cities follow. In Recife and Lusaka, the school system and the labor market no longer deliver what they did to the parental generation. Today, young people play different roles in families and households, the economy, and leisure. Involved in a range of social relationships, many young people are embedded in new ways: for example, they head households, are in relationships, earn incomes to support their elders, siblings, and household dependents, and work as church intercessors and lay evangelists. Far from being dependent and subordinate, they help redefine youth, by their actions, into a category of social achievement (Maira and Soep 2005, xviii). Rather than waiting for adulthood, young people act out their lives in the here and now under circumstances that are not of their own making but which they sometimes contribute to changing. The results are both positive, such as the use young Zambians make of popular music in political mobilization, and negative, such as the violence that poor young men in Recife easily fall into because of economic frustration. Both types of outcome must be taken into account when we address young people's futures.

Making Youth Count

The type of knowledge, largely based on ethnographic research, that the Youth and the City research project has produced is aimed less at policy formulation than at providing background understanding and context, as well as offering perspectives, drawn from primary observations on the ground, on youth policy as a development priority. In the remainder of this conclusion, we identify what we consider to be some of the most striking policy-relevant observations that flow from our work.

When addressing young people's futures, scholars and policy-makers must take into account the new meanings of youth that the last two decades of political and economic transformations, with their changes in household arrangements, employment, and markets, have helped create. Key concerns in our research were how and where young people acquire the abilities and resources that are critical to their future. Skills and knowledge obtained through formal schooling, technical or vocational training, and higher education have different relevance for youth today than they had for their parents, some of whom went straight from school into jobs. The social and cultural production of the educated person is affected by globalization and, along with it, economic reforms, and the spread of the market means that many of the young people we spoke with in this study have found that exams and certificates are not sufficient to land them jobs. In the process, the meaning and significance of education changes. For as long as they participate in education, they feel connected to the processes of modernization, with the expectations of better lives that globalization entails. Away from schools and classrooms, today's youth also acquire interpersonal skills and knowledge of the home and the world beyond it by interacting with others, both peers and adults, as well as from their rapidly growing exposure to the mass media. The proliferation of social groups, associations, and networks, and the emergence of new sites of interaction around media use and the globalization of consumption and popular culture, permit new forms of sociability. These processes have shifted many responsibilities for urban social reproduction away from families or households and states or governments and onto individuals and variously constituted groups.

In spite of young people's individual achievements, their capacities are not adequately recognized. While advocacy rhetoric praises youth agency and potentials, the opinions of the young are rarely sought.[1] Young people's perspective on their own situation needs to be taken seriously. Because young people today are living in a different world than did any previous youth generation, policy interventions must be relevant to the current generation and go beyond merely replicating what worked in the past. Brazil has an active youth policy in place, ProJovem, passed into law in 2005 and directed toward young people between 18 and 25 years of age who have not completed grade 8 and do not hold formal jobs. Its focus is on accelerated formal education and subsidized vocational training. A new youth law has been under consideration in Vietnam since 1983, with a draft policy presented to the National Assembly in 2005. After two years of deliberations, the Zambian parliament in 2006 accepted a new youth policy, replacing one instituted in 1994. Yet although some countries, including Zambia, have youth policies or youth development programs in place, few of these policies and programs have been fully implemented. The low priority that many governments give to youth reflects not only inadequate funds to support programmatic action but above all, as we have stressed throughout, wide-ranging local and global changes that are affecting young people's circumstances everywhere. As a result, youth easily becomes a politically contested category.

Much current writing on development leaves out of consideration what we regard as some of the most crucial observations about the contemporary youth situation, which have to do with urban growth, the youth bulge, and sexuality. The World Program of Action for Youth, adopted by the United Nations General Assembly in 1995, identified ten priority areas for policy: education, employment, hunger and poverty, health, environment, drug abuse, juvenile delinquency, leisure activities, girls and young women, and young people's participation in decision-making. In 2003, the General Assembly identified five additional priority areas: intergenerational relations, youth and armed conflict, globalization, information and communications technology, and HIV/AIDS (United Nations 2005a, 2–3). However, neither the 1995 nor the 2005 report referred to cities as the main stage for young lives either at present or in the future, nor do they disaggregate the dramatic figures that form the youth bulge in urban and rural terms. And although HIV/AIDS is now a priority area, the 2005 report barely analyzes the pandemic, and above all it does not treat sexuality as a concern that reaches to the heart of youth experiences.

When it comes to country-specific development strategies—for example, the World Bank's most recently advocated policy approach toward poverty reduction—we note that Vietnam, Zambia, and many countries in Africa have put together so-called Poverty Reduction Strategy Papers (PRSPs) that the Bank has approved. The policy interventions are remarkably similar, hinging on freeing up the market and developing good governance based on participation, which itself encompasses local NGOs, associations, and social and faith-based groups. It is individuals and organizations like these, not governments, that PRSPs envisage as being pro-active. Zambia's PRSP pays lip service to gender by briefly discussing the empowerment of women and improvements in their participation in decision-making. Much like that of Vietnam (Vietnam 2003), Zambia's PRSP makes no reference to young people, even though, for the purposes of strategy development, they constitute an extraordinarily relevant category because their livelihoods cut across the specific sectors on which Zambia's PRSP focuses: agriculture, tourism, and health and education. Zambia's PRSP provides no evidence of any engagement with the issues of rapid urban growth or the future of urban livelihoods. Therefore it does not recognize housing as an urgent urban development issue and, most strikingly, it does not single out unemployment as a problem in its own right.[2] The PRSP introduces matters related to earnings and income by way of investment, trade promotion, and the development of small and medium-size enterprises in both rural and urban settings (Zambia 2002).

A development focus on enterprise and entrepreneurship shifts responsibility for initiatives from the state to the individual. It is increasingly young people themselves, families, and households that have to pick up the costs of housing, education, social services, and health. Above all, this focus draws attention away from the vulnerable position of young people in the labor market. In World Bank and international donor-supported programs for technical and vocational training in Africa that are specifically oriented toward micro-enterprises, current development policy seeks to link training with demand, which today is overwhelmingly held to arise from within the informal economy. While this policy shift is a reaction to the lack of fit between the skills taught in formal institutions and the needs of the labor market, it does not reckon with the workings and organization of the informal economy, nor does it engage with the structural barriers of the labor market in the era of late capitalism. The technical and vocational training approach does not sufficiently acknowledge that today's increasingly competitive and technological job market is likely to leave growing numbers of young trainees without formal jobs or at best underemployed and performing casual labor.

Time will tell if young people will benefit from this reinvigorated emphasis on technical and vocational training. Certainly in Recife and Lusaka currently, such policies easily end up creating make-work schemes because the informal economy is already producing competence and business skills through apprenticeships and learning on the job. In short, entrepreneurship and micro-enterprises in the informal economy cannot be considered grassroots solutions to unemployment. A focus on such activities implies that the informal economy can absorb ever-increasing numbers of newcomers. This view is flawed for many reasons, one of which is its tendency to lump all workers together. In the case of Lusaka, age- and gender-based employment hierarchies of the informal economy restrict access for young people, propelling them into casual work and low-grade jobs that curtail upward mobility and acquisition of the skills and qualifications required for job promotion.

The shifting of initiative from the state onto the individual is evident across many of the areas we have examined in this volume. As Ambrosius Madsen explains in her chapter on schooling, the focus on the individual in educational policy celebrates a structure of social relations that has little relevance to the needs and requirements of everyday life in either Brazil or Zambia. An individualistic response is also central to Pentecostal church messages, mediascapes, and much popular culture, through which young people, at least for a moment, believe that they are the authors of their own lives. Do such processes of self-promotion help reduce long-entrenched gender differences and generational hierarchies? Are there more opportunities in this new youth moment for women than for men? Are young women subject to more challenges than men because of their vulnerability, as Hansen suggests is the case in Lusaka? Class is one relevant factor in clarifying this question, one that is likely to work itself out very differently than it did in the past because of ongoing economic changes (Wyn and White 2000). Because our observations do not provide an unequivocal answer, we conclude that, in the process of taking on new and different roles, although young people may transform widely entrenched stereotypes about gender and youth, they may also help to reproduce them.

Global Cities of Youth

In recent years, major international development agencies and research organizations have issued reports and programmatic statements about young people, at times including children, on the one hand (National Research Council and Institute of Medicine 2005; UN-Habitat 2005; United Nations 2005a; UNICEF 2005; World Bank 2005b), and about global urban expansion on the other (National Research Council 2003; World Bank 2005a, 2005c). Even then, international development agencies and local governments have by and large refrained from intervening actively in matters related to either youth or urban growth, leaving the field open to small-scale initiatives by foreign and local NGOs, some of which are faith-based organizations with limited practical development experience. For example, since the focus on the school-leaver problem in Zambia and many other African countries in the 1970s (soon after independence), very little has occurred to improve young urban people's place in society. The World Bank has not involved itself actively in overarching urban projects since its engagement in the 1970s with squatter upgrading in many cities in developing countries, among them Zambia (Arku and Harris 2005). In short, perhaps for different reasons but with the same result, major international agencies and national governments have until very recently approached the reality of urban growth in developing countries with neglect, hostility, and a downright anti-urban attitude (World Bank 2005a, 101).

There is no doubt that limited local and international engagement and dialogue over critical issues concerning the short- and long-term livelihoods of urban youth in many parts of the developing world help exacerbate "urban wounds" (Susser and Schneider 2003), to evoke a notion capturing the enormous social and economic issues facing city-dwellers which we referred to in the introduction and took up in some of the chapters. The idea that cities have wounds puts into focus both the destructive and restorative dimensions of urban living that characterize the distinct experiences and expectations of young people in Recife, Hanoi, and Lusaka at the beginning of the twenty-first century. The destructive aspects of urban life are evident in the structural violence we noted everywhere, as expressed through widespread and growing socioeconomic inequality and the difficulties of access to many basic services. While Recife, for example, has a disproportionate share of teenage pregnancies and one of the world's highest violent death rates for young men, Lusaka has an HIV/AIDS pandemic that is wreaking havoc in the conventional fabric of social life.

While the metaphor of wounds evokes a warning, it also points to possibilities for healing. We suggest that a regeneration of youth must be driven by both global and local equity-enhancing and distributional politics that incorporate young people beyond the here and now as invested actors and members of collectivities in the economic, political, and cultural work of urban social reproduction. While it emphasizes the very severe constraints on the lives of many of the young people we have studied, due to entrenched poverty and inequality, this volume also demonstrates how central these young urban people already are to urban social reproduction. By recognizing that a growing proportion of the world's population is both urban and young and by acting in collaboration with young people, both national governments and international development agencies can transcend their long-held reluctance to intervene in youth and urban issues by launching initiatives that invest in young people's urban futures across the board, from education through culture to the urban environment and health. Such efforts to effect change on a wider scale will create fresh stakes for young people in the urban futures of their countries and in turn help build new forms of participation and democracy. In that sense, youth and the city are becoming a shorthand for the increasingly urban future on which the new meanings of youth that we have identified in this volume are making participatory claims.

Acknowledgments

I thank the members of the research team for their valuable input in pointing out issues in need of clarification. I alone accept all shortcomings of this conclusion.

Notes

1. Although the UN's 2005 World Youth Report reiterates the desirability of including young people in consultations (e.g., United Nations 2005a, 170, 171, 172), the expert group meeting set up in its wake to consider formulating youth development indicators did not include any youth representatives (United Nations 2005b).

2. In its 2005 report, the Economic Commission for Africa tersely observes that "the employment content of PRSPs in Africa remains weak" (Economic Commission for Africa 2005, 14).

References

Arku, Godwin, and Richard Harris. 2005. Housing as a Tool of Economic Development since 1929. *International Journal of Urban and Regional Research* 29(4):895–915.

Davis, Mike. 2006. *Planet of Slums.* London and New York: Verso.

Denmark. Ministry of Foreign Affairs. 2005. Children and Young People in Danish Development Cooperation: Guidelines. Danish International Development Agency. http://amg .um.dk/en/menu/policiesandstrategies/prioritythemes/childrenyouth. Accessed January 19, 2006.

Economic Commission for Africa. 2005. Meeting the Challenges of Unemployment and Poverty in Africa: Economic Report on Africa 2005. Addis Ababa, Ethiopia: Economic Commission for Africa.

Maira, Sunaina, and Elisabeth Soep. 2005. Introduction to *Youthscapes: The Popular, the National, the Global,* xv–xxxv. Philadelphia: University of Pennsylvania Press.

National Research Council. 2003. *Cities Transformed: Demographic Change and Its Implications in the Developing World.* Washington, D.C.: National Academies Press.

National Research Council and Institute of Medicine. 2005. Executive summary of *Growing Up Global: The Changing Transitions to Adulthood in Developing Countries,* 1–14. Washington, D.C.: National Academies Press.

Susser, Ida, and Jane Schneider. 2003. Wounded Cities: Destruction and Reconstruction in a Globalized World. In *Wounded Cities: Destruction and Reconstruction in a Globalized World,* ed. Jane Schneider and Ida Susser, 1–23. Oxford: Berg.

United Nations. 2005a. World Youth Report 2005: Young People Today, and in 2015. New York: United Nations.

———. 2005b. Report of the Expert Group Meeting on Youth Development Indicators. http:// www.un.org/esa/socdev/unyin/youthindicators.htm. Accessed January 18, 2006.

UN-Habitat (United Nations Human Settlements Programme). 2005. *The State of the World's Cities 2004/2005: Globalization and Urban Culture.* UN-Habitat and Earthscan.

UNICEF. 2005. *Childhood under Threat: The State of the World's Children 2005*. http://www
.unicef.org/sowc05/english/. Accessed November 10, 2005.

Vietnam. 2003. *The Comprehensive Poverty Reduction and Growth Strategy*. Hanoi: Government of Vietnam.

World Bank. 2005a. *The Dynamics of Global Urban Expansion*. Transport and Urban Development Department. Washington, D.C.: World Bank. http://www.citiesalliance.org/
publications/homepage-features/feb-06/urban-expansion.html. Accessed February 13,
2006.

———. 2005b. Introduction to *The Provisional Outline of the 2007 World Development Report:
Development and the Next Generation,* i–ii. Washington, D.C.: World Bank. http://econ.
worldbank.org/. Accessed January 24, 2006.

———. 2005c. *The Urban Transition in Sub-Saharan Africa: Implications for Economic Growth
and Poverty Reduction*. October 2005. Washington, D.C.: World Bank.

Wyn, Johanna, and Rob White. 2000. Negotiating Social Change: The Paradox of Youth. *Youth
& Society* 32(2):165–83.

Zambia. 2002. Poverty Reduction Strategy Paper. Lusaka: Ministry of Finance and National
Planning.

Contributors

Anne Line Dalsgaard, Associate Professor, Department of Anthropology and Ethnography, Aarhus University, Denmark, is a medical anthropologist who has conducted research in Brazil since 1997 in close collaboration with Brazilian researchers. Her work focuses on reproductive health, gender, youth, urban poverty, and citizenship. She has published several articles on these issues and is the author of *Matters of Life and Longing: Female Sterilisation in Northeast Brazil* (Museum Tusculanum Press, 2004).

Mónica Franch, Assistant Professor of Anthropology, Federal University of Paraiba, Brazil, and researcher at the Center of Studies on Gender, Family and Sexuality (FAGES), Federal University of Pernambuco, Brazil, is an urban anthropologist who has been engaged in several academic and applied research projects in Brazil. Her research on youth, poverty, leisure time, and gender issues has been published in a range of journals and books both within Brazil and internationally.

Katherine V. Gough, Associate Professor, Department of Geography, University of Copenhagen, Denmark, is a human geographer whose research focus is urbanization in developing countries, with a special interest in West Africa and Latin America. Her research on low-income housing, home-based enterprises, the peri-urban interface, and urban governance has been published in a range of international journals, including *International Planning Studies, Cities, Urban Studies,* and *Children's Geographies.*

Karen Tranberg Hansen, the Principal Investigator of the Youth and the City project and Professor of Anthropology, Northwestern University, United States, is an urban and economic anthropologist whose long-term research in Zambia deals with urban livelihoods, gender issues, the informal economy, and housing, consumption, and dress. She is the author of several articles, chapters, and books on these issues. Her most recent book is *Salaula: The World of Secondhand*

Clothing and Zambia (University of Chicago Press, 2000). With Mariken Vaa, she co-edited *Reconsidering Informality: Perspectives from Urban Africa* (Nordic Africa Institute, 2004).

Ulla Ambrosius Madsen, Associate Professor, Center for Educational Research, Roskilde University Center, Denmark, works within the field of youth, education, and schooling in developing countries. She edited *Pædagogisk antropologi: Reflektioner over feltbaseret viden* [Educational Anthropology: Reflections on Field-Based Knowledge] (Hans Reitzels, 2004) and several books and articles on education and schooling in Denmark and the South.

Russell Parry Scott, Professor of Anthropology, Graduate Programs in Anthropology and Sociology, Federal University of Pernambuco, Brazil, has worked on relations between family, household and gender, and wider power structures, as well as comparative ethnographic and demographic studies of peasants, rural laborers, the urban poor, and the middle class. He has edited journals and published numerous articles and books, including *Sistemas de cura: As alternativas do povo* [Healing Systems: People's Choices] (MAC-UFPE, 1986), *Saúde e pobreza no Recife: Gênero, poder e representações de saúde* [Health and Poverty in Recife: Gender, Power and Representations of Illness] (NUSP–Editora Universitária, UFPE, 1996), and, with Roberto Mota, *Sobrevivência e fontes de renda: Estratégias das famílias de baixa renda no Recife* [Survival and Income Sources: Strategies of Low-Income Families in Recife] (Massangana, 1983).

Karen Valentin, Associate Professor, Institute of Educational Anthropology, Danish School of Education, Aarhus University, Denmark, is an educational anthropologist with regional interests in South and Southeast Asia, working within the fields of childhood and youth, schooling, urban development, policy, planned development, and migration. The Danish editor of *Young: Nordic Journal of Youth Research,* she is also the author of *Schooled for the Future? Educational Policy and Everyday Life among Urban Squatters in Nepal* (Information Age Publishing, 2005) and co-editor, with Laura Gilliam and Karen Fog Olwig, of *Lokale liv, fjerne forbindelser: Studier af børn, unge og migration* [Local Lives, Distant Connections: Studies of Children, Youth and Migration] (Hans Reitzels, 2005).

Norbert Wildermuth, Associate Professor, Center of Media Studies, Institute of Literature, Culture and Media, University of Southern Denmark, is a scholar whose research focuses on media globalization and development communication in South Asia and on news and current affairs on television, especially international events coverage. His recent publications include "Negotiating a Globalised

Modernity: Images of the 'New' Indian Woman on Satellite Television," in *Global Encounters: Media and Cultural Transformation,* ed. Gitte Staid and Thomas Tufte (University of Luton Press, 2001); and "Miss World Going 'Deshi': Addressing an Indian Television Audience with a Global Media Product," in *Media in a Globalized Society,* ed. Stig Hjarvard (Museum Tusculanum Press, 2003).

Index

Page numbers in italics refer to illustrations.

Tracking Globalization